HOSTELLING
NORTH AMERICA

**THE OFFICIAL GUIDE TO HOSTELS
IN CANADA AND THE UNITED STATES**

**LE GUIDE OFFICIEL DES AUBERGES
DU CANADA ET DES ÉTATS UNIS**

**EIN WEGWEISER FÜR JUGENDHERBERGEN
IN KANADA UND DEN VEREINIGTEN STAATEN**

ホステルの案内書
カナダ・アメリカ合衆国

HOSTELLING ®
INTERNATIONAL

HOSTELLING INTERNATIONAL–
UNITED STATES OF AMERICA
American Youth Hostels
733 15th Street, N.W., Suite 840
Washington, D.C. 20005
USA
202-783-6161

HOSTELLING INTERNATIONAL–
CANADA

1600 James Naismith Drive
Gloucester, Ontario
Canada K1B 5N4
613-748-5638

Trade Distribution: Key Porter Books Ltd.
70 The Esplanade, Toronto, Ontario, Canada M5E 1R2.
ISBN: 1-55013-455-8

HOSTELLING NORTH AMERICA 1993

Executive Editors: Nina Chung, Heather Grate, Gayle Maurin
Managing Editors: Paul Crooks, Marlene Trossman,
   Brett Watkins
Contributing Editors: Laura Borsecnik, Keith Ivey, Tom Keen,
   Sheila McArtis, Toby Pyle, Aitken Thompson
Advertising: Justin J. Cline, Paul Crooks
Photographers: Torsten Blackwood, Jamie Coppola,
   William Douglas, Richard George, Tom Keen,
   Jim Marquardt, Eric Minugh, Toby Pyle, Greg Siple
Maps: Rob Dorival
Cover Design: Scott Richardson
Map on cover © Rand McNally & Company

Special thanks to the hostel managers, AYH councils, and
HI-Canada regional offices and advertisers for their assistance
and support in compiling this publication.

Hostelling International–American Youth Hostels
President: Lew Litsky
Executive Director: Richard Martyr

Hostelling International–Canada
President: Paul S. Magowan
Executive Director: Richard McCarron

HOSTELLING NORTH AMERICA is published annually by
Hostelling International–American Youth Hostels,
733 15th Street N.W., 8th Floor,
Washington, D.C. 20005, and
Hostelling International–Canada,
1600 James Naismith Drive, Suite 608,
Gloucester, Ontario K1B 5N4.

Contents

About the Organization

The International Youth Hostel Federation— Hostelling International

American Youth Hostels and Hostelling International–Canada are nonprofit membership organizations founded in 1933–34 as national members of the International Youth Hostel Federation (IYHF).

The Federation comprises 60 national member associations and 26 associate organizations. The mission of the organization is "To promote the education of all young people of all nations, but especially young people of limited means, by encouraging in them a greater knowledge, love, and care of the countryside and an appreciation of the cultural values of towns and cities in all parts of the world, and as ancillary thereto to provide hostels or other accommodation in which there shall be no distinctions of race, nationality, color, religion, sex, class, or political opinions and thereby to develop a better understanding of their fellow men, both at home and abroad."

HOSTELLING INTERNATIONAL® is the new seal of approval of the IYHF which maintains a worldwide network of 6,000 hostels in 70 countries.

Introduction

Welcome to Hostelling International!

The 260 hostels in Canada and the United States offer more than a place to stay for $5 to $22 a night. North American hostels are comfortable, environmentally sensitive places for budget-minded travelers—like you—to lodge for the night. Hostels are friendly people-oriented places filled with others who are looking for the same things you are—adventure, excitement and an opportunity to discover this marvelous world.

In addition to the lowest prices anywhere, many hostels provide do-it-yourself kitchens, lockers, laundries, and more. You may get the very best travel information, not only from the hostels' diverse travel libraries, but also from the people you'll meet who have already been where you're going and can give you valuable information on the best places to eat, shop, and sightsee.

Hostels also offer vast opportunities for programs and activities such as architectural and historic walking tours, interpretive environmental walks and programs, cultural events, theater outings, and uniquely North American pastimes, such as baseball games and barbecues. Mountain biking, trekking, horseback riding, skiing, and nature walks are just another part of the hostelling experience. All across North America, youll find hostels in cities and towns, national parks and cultural centers—just about anywhere you want to visit. From lighthouses and historic homes to ranch bunkhouses—even a former jail—each hostel has a personality of its own. All hostels have dormitory-style gender-separate accommodations. Many hostels have private rooms for families and individuals travelling together.

Hostelling International membership

Your passport to a world of 6,000 hostels, discounts, and other benefits!

Your Hostelling International membership card entitles you to use the global hostel network. In addition to the phenomenally low overnight rates, your membership entitles you to hundreds of discounts on air fares, railway tickets, ferry tickets, car rentals, restaurants, museum admissions, festivals, ski lifts, environmental classes, and much more. Look in each province/state section for the discounts that interest you.

Memberships can be purchased at any hostel listed in this book as an MSA (membership selling agent) or at any of the offices throughout North America (they're listed by province/state or the national offices).

International visitors may purchase a Hostelling International Guest Card. This card allows use of hostels around the world—just like a Hostelling International membership.

How to find us

Look for the blue triangle Hostelling International sign for hostels that are regularly evaluated and meet the quality standards of Hostelling International.

Note: The information in this guide was correct at the time of publication. Ask for updates and new developments at each Hostelling International facility that you visit or contact.

Making the most of this guide

This guide highlights information on the province/state tourist offices and hostels, and provides maps illustrating locations. Alphabetically arranged, by province/state and city, the guide also has an index in the back of the book...just in case you aren't sure what city or state a hostel is in.

Be sure to use the discounts listed in the province/state and membership sections of the book. Check for more discounts at each hostel when you arrive.

Reservations

You're welcome on a walk-in basis, but during peak travel times advance reservations are recommended. You can make a reservation yourself by mail, telephone, or fax. A new International Booking Network has been established, making international reservations easier than ever before.

By mail: send a letter or postcard to the hostel with the date and estimated time of your arrival, number of nights, and number of male and female beds or private rooms desired. Include a one-night deposit in the form of a check, money order, or bank draft in U.S. (for U.S. hostels) or Canadian currency (for Canadian hostels), and a self-addressed, stamped reply envelope. Please allow at least two weeks for confirmation, four weeks if writing from abroad.

By telephone: many hostels accept phone reservations, using a credit card to guarantee the first night's fee. Call the hostel during open hours and have your credit card number and expiration date on hand. At busier hostels you'll need to reserve a least 48 hours in advance.

By fax: hostels with fax machines will accept fax reservations with a credit card to guarantee the first night's fee. Your fax should include the same information as for reservations by mail plus your credit card number, expiration date, and cardholder's name. A booking fee of $1 U.S. or CDN may be added to your credit card for the cost of confirmation by fax. You should reserve at least 48 hours in advance.

Reservations for North American hostels from abroad

Two additional services are available for international visitors wishing to book hostels prior to arrival in North America:

IBN: a new computerized international advanced booking network, developed specifically for Hostelling International, allows instant reservations to major gateway hostels in North America, with payment in your own currency. Contact your local Hostelling International office for details on the latest in availability.

FAX-A-BED: allows Australian, New Zealand, and Japanese travellers with a credit card to book major North American gateway hostels. This service is available from all Hostelling International offices, gateway locations in Australia and New Zealand, and in some Japanese offices and hostels. In most cases the booking is instantaneous as long as 48 hours' to seven days' notice is given.

International hostel reservations from North America

The IBN and FAX-A-BED reservation systems allow members to book hostels internationally. These services are available from many Hostelling International offices and gateway hostels in North America. Contact your local office or hostel for details.

Families and individuals travelling together

Many hostels have private rooms for families or individuals travelling together. A surcharge may apply. They're popular, and reservations are advisable.

Children under 12 traveling with parents may receive a discounted rate. Call the hostel for details. In the U.S., family memberships allow parents or guardians and their children under 18 to use hostels together with one membership card. Children covered by a Family membership may receive a discounted rate when travelling with a parent or guardian who holds a Family or Life membership card. In Canada, children under 18 travelling with parents receive a free membership. Children under 10 should be accompanied by a parent or guardian of the same sex. Call the hostel for further information.

Group travel

Many hostels provide group accommodations. Specialized and interpretive programs and catered meals can often be arranged. Meeting rooms and audio-visual equipment are available at many hostels for meetings, workshops, and seminars.

Planning a trip for your nonprofit organization? A group membership for 5 or more in the U.S. and 10 or more in Canada and internationally, is available. Return the membership application in the back of this book or call the office nearest you. Reservations are essential.

Accessibility

More and more hostels are adapting their facilities to provide accessibility for the disabled. Check individual hostel listings and call the hostel in advance for your special needs.

Hostel customs

In Canada, most hostels have full-day access. In the U.S., most hostels are closed between 9:30 a.m. and 4:30 p.m., but many have expanded hours or a common room set aside for day use or luggage storage. Quiet hours are generally 11 p.m. to 7 a.m.

Blankets and pillows are provided. Guests may bring their own sheets or rent them at the hostel. Sleeping bags are usually not permitted except where noted in the hostel listing.

To help keep prices as low as possible and foster the community spirit of hostelling, we ask you to clean up after yourself. You may also be asked to help with a simple task such as sweeping or emptying the trash.

To accommodate as many travellers as possible, hostels may limit the length of stay beyond three nights. Check with individual hostels to be sure they can accommodate you for the entire length of your visit.

Each hostel in the North American network asks guests to follow a set of guidelines to ensure a safe, pleasant, comfortable experience, and an enjoyable stay.

- At check-in hostels may require identification such as a passport or driver's license in addition to a Hostelling International membership card.
- The only pets allowed at hostels are guide dogs for the disabled or those belonging to the hostel manager.
- Neither the hostel nor the hostel managers assume responsibility for theft or loss of personal property on hostel premises.
- Hostels primarily serve educational and recreational travellers and may choose not to accept guests who live in the immediate area.
- To ensure the safety and comfort of guests, the hostel staff may refuse service to anyone.
- Alcohol is prohibited on hostel premises, but some hostels have separate cafés or cafeterias where beer and wine may be available.
- HI-Canada/HI-AYH may revoke a membership card at the hostel manager's request.
- Hostels provide a smoke-free environment; a designated smoking area may be provided.
- Individuals under 18 years of age may be asked to provide parental permission.

We value your opinion

We would appreciate your comments. Please feel free to use the "comment cards" at each hostel or write the hostel or national office with your ideas or complaints. We want your input to continue making hostelling as much fun as possible, and the best travel experience you can have.

If you have questions

There are over 50 regional offices throughout North America with information on hostels, Hostelling International memberships, and volunteer programs. Many offices have travel stores with guidebooks, backpacks—even Eurail passes—all available at members discount prices! Check the beginning of each province/state section for the Hostelling International office nearest you.

How to read a hostel listing page

There are three types of facilities: full-service hostels, home hostels, and supplemental accommodations. Full-service hostels have a full-page listing and a map showing the hostel location. The shaded box on each page provides details on the hostel using the following symbols and headings:

Mail (✉): the street and postal address appears at the top of each box. If there is a different address for information during off-season it is listed under **Reservations** at the bottom of the fact box.

Phone (☎): the telephone number for the hostel.

Price (●): price per person per night is listed in either U.S. dollars or Canadian (CDN) dollars. Prices are guaranteed through January 1, 1994.

Closed (X): the dates the hostel is **not** open.

Grade: indicates level of services available at each hostel. Grades are **not** necessarily a standard of quality.

Note: the U.S. hostels are undergoing a grading change; therefore, all U.S. full-service hostels are simply listed as "Hostel". Other distinctions in the U.S. include Home Hostel and Supplemental Accommodation.

Home Hostel (🏠): hostellers are guests in a private home and share their host's kitchen and common area. Advance reservations are required.

Supplemental Accommodation (SA) : a college dormitory, hotel, inn, B&B, YM/YWCA, or other facility shared by hostellers and others. SAs often lack kitchens, charge a higher overnight rate, and are usually located in areas where hostels are not available.

Hostelling International–Canada uses the following additional grades:

Superior (🏠): large hostels with 40 beds or more, full-service kitchen, hot and cold showers, dining area, and a common area. Families/couples rooms, laundry facilities, bicycle storage, activity programs, and other special features are usually available.

Standard (🏠): hostels with 24 or more beds, full-service kitchen, hot showers, dining area, and a common room. Rooms for families or couples, laundry facilities, and other special features may be available.

Simple (🏠): smaller hostels with full-service kitchen, combination dining/common area, running water, and indoor toilets.

Basic (🏠): rustic lodging. Beds may be cots or pads on the floor, and sleeping bags are necessary. Rooms might be shared by men and women, with separate dressing areas. Cold running water is available for bathing and there may be outdoor toilets. Heating is provided.

Beds (🛏): indicates the total number of beds at the hostel.

Facilities: lists special features at the hostel including luggage/equipment storage, kitchen, laundry facilities, linen rental, lockers, parking arrangements, recreational and tourist programs available, and special notes or requirements; also indicates if the hostel is **wheelchair accessible (♿)** and if it sells Hostelling International membership cards (**MSA**).

Meals (🍴): indicates availability and type of meals.

Family rooms (🏠): available indicates the hostel has family/double rooms available.

Groups (🏨): welcome indicates accommodations available for groups.

Reservations: dates or seasons when reservations are **advisable (📞a)** or **essential (📞e)** are noted, along with the address and phone **(By phone)** if different from the hostel address at the top of the fact box. If a fax number **(By FAX)** for reservations is available you'll find it here; if applicable the off-season **(Off-season)** address and phone number are listed.

Credit cards: indicates which credit cards are accepted (e.g., Visa, MasterCard, JCB).

Managers: name of manager(s) of the hostel.

Directions: provides basic instructions on how to arrive at the hostel. The map located below this will also help to locate the hostel.

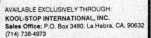

Don't forget to write.

Now that you've said, "Let's go,"
it's time to say, "Let's get
American Express® Travelers Cheques."
Because when you want your travel money
to go a long way, it's a good idea
to protect it. So before you leave,
be sure and write.

Dans la partie qui suit vous trouverez les explications en français, allemand et japonais des renseignements contenus dans ce guide.

Le format du guide nous empêche de le traduire en entier mais nous espérons que ces explications aideront nos lecteurs non anglophones d'en tirer tout le profit possible.

Der hier folgende Abschnitt bringt die Erklärungen in französisch, deutsch und japanisch zu den Informationen in diesem Herbergsführer.

Sein Format macht es uns unmöglich, ihn ganz zu übersetzen. Wir hoffen aber, daß die folgenden Erklärungen unseren nicht englischsprachigen Lesern helfen, den Herbergsführer sehr nützlich zu finden.

次章にはこの案内書の使い方がフランス語、ドイツ語、日本語で書いてあります。

場所が限られている関係上、全部を訳すわけにはいきませんでしたが、この章が英語以外の国の読者に少しでもお役にたてばと、願っております。

Services

Réservations

Il vous suffit de vous présenter dans une auberge pour vous inscrire, mais nous vous conseillons de réserver votre hébergement à l'avance pendant la haute saison touristique. Pour effectuer vos réservations, vous pouvez utiliser la poste, le téléphone, le télécopieur ou encore le nouveau réseau informatisé de réservations de Hostelling International. Vous trouverez les détails particuliers à chaque auberge dans les informations la concernant.

Par la poste. Il vous suffit d'envoyer une lettre ou une carte postale à l'(aux) auberge(s) en question, en y indiquant la date et l'heure approximative de votre arrivée, la durée de votre séjour et le nombre de lits pour hommes ou pour femmes, ou de chambres familiales que vous souhaitez réserver. Incluez, à titre de dépôt, un chèque, un mandat-poste ou une traite bancaire, d'un montant équivalent au prix d'un séjour d'une nuit, en dollars canadiens ou américains, et une enveloppe-réponse affranchie. Veuillez prévoir au moins deux semaines pour la réception de votre confirmation, et quatre semaines si vous écrivez de l'étranger.

Par téléphone. De nombreuses auberges acceptent les réservations par téléphone, à condition que le client donne un numéro de carte de crédit pour garantir le paiement de la première nuitée. Il vous suffit d'appeler l'(les) auberge(s) pendant ses heures d'ouverture, en ayant soin d'avoir sous la main le numéro de votre carte de crédit et sa date d'expiration. Dans le cas des auberges les plus fréquentées, vous êtes priés d'effectuer vos réservations au moins 48 heures à l'avance.

Par télécopieur. Des auberges équipées de télécopieurs acceptent les réservations par ce moyen, à condition que le client donne un numéro de carte de crédit pour garantir le paiement de la première nuitée. Votre message télécopié doit contenir les mêmes renseignements que ceux exigés pour les réservations par écrit, ainsi que votre numéro de carte de crédit, sa date d'expiration et le nom du(de la) détenteur(rice) de la carte. Il se peut qu'on ajoute à la facture figurant sur votre carte de crédit des frais de confirmation par télécopieur d'un montant d'un dollar canadien ou américain. Vous êtes priés d'effectuer vos réservations au moins 48 heures à l'avance.

Réservations dans les auberges d'Amérique du Nord depuis l'étranger

Les visiteurs étrangers qui souhaitent effectuer des réservations dans des auberges avant d'arriver en Amérique du Nord peuvent

Services

utiliser deux services supplémentaires :

IBN : ce nouveau réseau international informatisé et avancé de réservations a été élaboré spécialement pour Hostelling International et permet aux clients d'effectuer leurs réservations instantanément dans les principales auberges portes d'entrées d'Amérique du Nord, en effectuant le paiement dans leur propre devise. Communiquez avec le bureau local de Hostelling International pour obtenir des détails au sujet de la prestation de ce service, et

FAX-A-BED : les voyageurs australiens, néo-zélandais et japonais détenteurs d'une carte de crédit peuvent effectuer leurs réservations dans les principales auberges portes d'entrées d'Amérique du Nord. Ce service est offert dans tous les bureaux de Hostelling International et dans toutes les auberges portes d'entrées d'Australie et de Nouvelle-Zélande, ainsi que dans certains bureaux et certaines auberges du Japon. Dans la plupart des cas, la réservation est instantanée à condition qu'elle soit effectuée de deux à sept jours à l'avance.

Réservations dans les auberges de l'étranger à partir de l'Amérique du Nord

Les services de réservations IBN et FAX-A-BED qui permettent aux membres de réserver des nuitées à l'étranger sont également offerts dans de nombreux bureaux de Hostelling International et de nombreuses auberges portes d'entrées en Amérique du Nord. Communiquez avec le bureau ou l'auberge de votre localité pour obtenir des détails concernant la prestation de ces services.

Familles et personnes voyageant ensemble

De nombreuses auberges disposent de chambres à l'intention des familles ou des personnes qui voyagent ensemble et qui souhaitent préserver leur intimité, parfois moyennant des frais supplémentaires. Ces chambres étant très en demande, il est préférable de les réserver. Il se peut que les enfants de moins de 12 ans bénéficient d'un tarif réduit par rapport à celui de la nuitée, mais ils doivent être accompagnés par un adulte. Communiquez par téléphone avec les responsables de l'auberge pour connaître les détails. L'adhésion est gratuite pour les jeunes de moins de 18 ans qui voyagent avec leurs parents.

Groupes

De nombreuses auberges accueillent les groupes. On peut souvent organiser des visites guidées ou prévoir un service de

Services

traiteur. Nombre d'auberges disposent de salles de réunion et d'équipement audiovisuel, ce qui permet l'organisation de réunions, d'ateliers et de colloques. Les groupes de plus de dix personnes voyageant ensemble peuvent se procurer une adhésion dans la catégorie des organisations. Il leur suffit de remplir le formulaire de demande d'adhésion qui se trouve au dos du présent Répertoire ou de communiquer avec le bureau régional le plus proche. Il est essentiel de réserver.

Accès en fauteuil roulant

Un nombre de plus en plus grand d'auberges adaptent leurs installations dans le but de les rendre accessibles aux personnes en fauteuil roulant. Vérifiez les caractéristiques de chaque auberge sur la liste et communiquez au préalable avec ses responsables au sujet des besoins spéciaux que vous pourriez avoir.

Règles des auberges

Certaines auberges ferment leurs portes de 9 h 30 à 16 h 30, mais la plupart d'entre elles ont des heures d'ouverture élargies et une salle commune réservée à l'usage des ajistes pendant la journée ou à l'entreposage des bagages. Il faut généralement respecter le silence des lieux entre 23 h et 7 h.

Les couvertures et les oreillers sont fournis. Les clients peuvent apporter leurs propres draps ou les louer à l'auberge. Les sacs de couchage sont généralement interdits, sauf si l'inverse est précisé sur la liste d'informations sur l'auberge.

Nous vous prions de bien vouloir nettoyer votre chambre avant votre départ afin de contribuer à maintenir les tarifs le meilleur marché possible et de répandre l'esprit communautaire de l'ajisme. On pourra aussi éventuellement vous demander d'apporter votre contribution en effectuant de simples tâches comme de balayer les lieux ou de vider la poubelle.

La durée du séjour pourra aussi être limitée à trois nuits en pleine saison dans certaines auberges de manière à pouvoir accueillir le plus possible de voyageurs. Vérifiez auprès de chaque auberge si vous pourrez être hébergé pendant la totalité de votre séjour.

Chaque auberge du réseau nord-américain demande à ses clients de respecter une série de lignes directrices afin de garantir à tous un séjour agréable, confortable et sans danger.

Services

- De nombreuses auberges exigent, au moment de l'inscription, la présentation d'une pièce d'identité comme un passeport ou un permis de conduire, en plus de la carte de membre de Hostelling International.
- Les seuls animaux domestiques acceptés dans les auberges sont les chiens d'aveugle ou ceux qui appartiennent au(x) gérant(e)(s) de l'auberge.
- Ni les auberges ni leur(s) gérant(e)(s) n'acceptent de responsabilité en matière de vol ou de pertes de propriétés personnelles dans les installations de l'auberge.
- Les auberges sont principalement au service des personnes en voyage éducatif ou de loisir, par conséquent elles peuvent élire de ne pas accepter de clients vivant à proximité.
- Les membres du personnel des auberges peuvent refuser de servir certaines personnes afin de garantir la sécurité et le confort de leurs clients.
- L'alcool est interdit dans l'enceinte des auberges, mais certaines d'entre elles disposent de cafés ou de cafétérias séparés où on sert de la bière et du vin.
- HI-Canada et HI-AYH peuvent révoquer une carte de membre à la demande du(de la) gérant(e) d'une auberge.
- Il est interdit de fumer dans les auberges. Toutefois, celles-ci peuvent avoir une zone réservée aux fumeurs.
- On peut demander aux jeunes de moins de 18 ans une autorisation de leurs parents.

Vos commentaires sont les bienvenus

À titre de client(e) d'une auberge, vous êtes le(la) meilleur(e) «contrôleur(euse)» dont nous puissions rêver. Vous pouvez donc vous procurer des cartes de commentaires dans toutes les auberges. Nous vous prions d'en remplir une pour nous faire part de vos observations sur l'auberge et pour nous communiquer vos suggestions afin que l'auberge où vous venez de séjourner devienne encore plus agréable.

Si vous avez des questions à poser...

Vous pouvez trouver dans 51 bureaux régionaux répartis dans toute l'Amérique du Nord des informations au sujet des auberges, de l'adhésion à Hostelling International et des programmes de bénévoles. Beaucoup de ces bureaux ont également une boutique de voyages dans laquelle vous pouvez trouver des guides, des sacs à dos... et même des laissez-passer Eurail! Vérifiez l'adresse du bureau de Hostelling International le plus proche. Elle se trouve au début de chaque partie du Répertoire consacré à une province canadienne ou à un état américain.

Comment lire la fiche d'une auberge

Le présent Répertoire présente la liste de trois types d'installations : les auberges offrant un service complet, les auberges privées et les hébergements d'appoint. Une page entière est consacrée aux renseignements sur les auberges offrant un service complet, ainsi qu'à une carte indiquant son emplacement. La boîte ombrée figurant sur chaque page fournit des détails relatifs à l'auberge à l'aide des symboles et des titres suivants :

Mail (✉): La rue et l'adresse postale sont indiquées en haut de chaque boîte ombrée. Au cas où il faudrait s'adresser ailleurs hors-saison pour obtenir des informations, l'autre adresse est donnée en regard du titre **Reservations** en bas de la boîte d'information.

Phone (☎): Il s'agit du numéro de téléphone de l'auberge.

Price (●): Le tarif par nuitée et par personne est indiqué soit en dollars canadiens (CAN), soit en dollars américains (U.S.). Ces tarifs sont garantis jusqu'au 1er janvier 1994.

Closed (X): Il s'agit des périodes pendant lesquelles l'auberge n'est **pas** ouverte.

Grade   : Indique le niveau de service offert par chaque auberge. Le type ne correspond pas nécessairement à une norme de qualité.

Nota : On effectue actuellement un remaniement des procédures relatives aux normes des auberges aux États-Unis, par conséquent toutes les auberges américaines qui offrent un service complet ne figurent sur la liste qu'à titre de **Hostel**. En ce qui concerne les auberges américaines, il est en outre indiqué s'il s'agit d'un **Home Hostel** ou d'un **Supplemental accommodation (SA)**.

Home Hostel (🏠): Les ajistes sont invités dans une maison privée et ils partagent la cuisine et les salles communes avec leurs hôtes. Vous devez absolument réserver d'avance.

Supplemental accommodation (SA): Il peut s'agir du dortoir d'un collège, d'un hôtel, d'une auberge, de chambres d'hôtes, d'un YM/YWCA ou de toute autre installation partagée par les ajistes et d'autres personnes. Souvent, les SA n'ont pas de cuisine, ont un tarif de nuitée plus élevé et sont situés dans des lieux où il n'y a pas d'auberge.

Hostelling International - Canada emploie les types supplémentaires d'auberges suivants :

Superior (🏘): Il s'agit de grandes auberges de 40 lits ou plus, munies d'un service complet de cuisine, de douches chaudes et froides, d'une salle à manger et d'une zone commune. Généralement, elles offrent aussi des chambres familiales ou pour les couples, des machines à laver, un endroit pour ranger les bicyclettes, des programmes d'activités et d'autres caractéristiques spéciales.

Comment lire la fiche d'une auberge

Standard (♠): Il s'agit d'auberges de 24 lits ou plus, munies d'un service complet de cuisine, de douches chaudes, d'une salle à manger et d'une pièce commune. Elles offrent aussi dans certains cas des chambres familiales ou pour les couples, des machines à laver et d'autres caractéristiques spéciales.

Simple (♠): Il s'agit d'auberges plus petites, munies d'un service complet de cuisine, d'une salle commune qui sert aussi pour les repas, d'eau courante et de toilettes intérieures.

Basic (♠): Il s'agit de logements rustiques dont les lits peuvent être des lits de camp ou des matelas à même le sol, et pour lesquels il faut des sacs de couchage. Les hommes et les femmes peuvent avoir à partager les chambres, mais les zones d'habillage sont séparées. Il y a l'eau courante, froide, pour se laver et il se peut qu'il y ait des toilettes extérieures. Le logement est chauffé.

Beds (⊨): Ce chiffre indique le nombre total de lits de l'auberge.

Facilities: (Traits caractéristiques, services, programmes) Il s'agit de la liste des caractéristiques spéciales de l'auberge, notamment les zones d'entreposage, la cuisine, les installations de lavage, la location de draps, les casiers, les modalités de stationnement, les programmes touristiques et de loisirs offerts, ainsi que des remarques ou exigences spéciales. Il est également indiqué si l'auberge est accessible aux personnes ayant un handicap (♿) et si on y vend des cartes de membre **(MSA)**.

Meals (⚒): Ce signe indique que des repas sont offerts et, le cas échéant, quel genre de repas.

Family rooms (⚘): available Ce signe indique que l'auberge dispose de chambres familiales ou pour les couples.

Reservations: Les dates ou les saisons auxquelles il est préférable (⚑a) ou obligatoire (⚑e) de faire des réservations sont indiquées, ainsi que l'adresse et le numéro de téléphone **(By phone)** au cas où ceux-ci seraient différents de l'adresse de l'auberge indiqué en haut de la boîte d'information. Si vous pouvez effectuer vos réservations par télécopieur, cela est également indiqué à cet endroit **(By FAX)**. Le cas échéant, l'adresse postale et le numéro de téléphone à utiliser hors-saison sont aussi indiqués **(Off-season)**.

Credit Cards: Indique si l'auberge accepte les cartes de crédit (par exemple, Visa, MasterCard, JCB).

Managers: Le(s) nom(s) du(de la)(des) gérant(e)(s) de l'auberge sont indiqués.

Directions: On y donne les instructions de base expliquant comment se rendre à l'auberge. La carte qui figure juste en-dessous vous aidera aussi à localiser l'auberge.

Reisedienst

Reservierungen

Im Prinzip sind Sie zu jeder Zeit unangemeldet in einer Herberge willkommen; in der Hochsaison ist es jedoch ratsam, Ihren Platz zu reservieren. Sie können per Post, Fax oder über das neue Komputernetz von Hostelling International reservieren. Einzelheiten darüber finden Sie in der Beschreibung der einzelnen Herbergen.

Per Post: Schicken Sie einen Brief oder eine Karte an die Herberge(n) und geben Sie das Datum und die ungefähre Zeit Ihrer Ankunft an, die Zahl der Nächte, die Zahl der Betten nach männlichen und weiblichen Gästen getrennt bzw. die Zahl der Familienzimmer, die sie brauchen. Legen Sie die Anzahlung in Form eines Schecks, einer Anweisung oder eines Bankschecks in Höhe des Preises für eine Übernachtung in amerikanischer bzw. kanadischer Währung und einen selbstadressierten, frankierten Briefumschlag bei. Rechnen Sie bitte mit zwei Wochen Wartezeit für die Bestätigung, bzw. mit vier Wochen, wenn Sie von Übersee schreiben.

Per Telefon: Viele Herbergen nehmen telefonische Reservierungen entgegen, wobei der Preis für die erste Nacht mit Kreditkarte vorausbezahlt werden muß. Rufen Sie Ihre Herberge während der Arbeitszeiten an und halten Sie die Nummer und das Auslaufdatum ihrer Kreditkarte bereit. Bei sehr gefragten Herbergen sollten Sie mindestens 48 Stunden im voraus reservieren.

Per Fax: Herbergen mit Faxanschluß nehmen Reservierungen per Fax entgegen, bei denen die Bezahlung der ersten Nacht durch Kreditkarte gesichert wird. Diese Reservierung sollte die gleichen Informationen enthalten wie die mit der Post und darüberhinaus die Nummer und das Auslaufdatum der Kreditkarte sowie den Namen, auf den sie ausgestellt ist. Eine Buchungsgebühr von $1.- in amerikanischer bzw. kanadischer Währung muß eventuell auf den durch Kreditkarte zu bezahlenden Betrag aufgeschlagen werden für die Faxkosten der Bestätigung. Auch hier sollten Sie mindestens 48 Stunden im voraus reservieren.

Reservierung bei nordamerikanischen Herbergen von Übersee aus

Zwei weitere Möglichkeiten gibt es für Hostelling International Besucher, die von Übersee aus Unterkunft in

Reisedienst

Herbergen Nordamerikas reservieren wollen:

> **IBN :** Ein neues, speziell für Hostelling International entwickeltes, internationales Komputernetzwerk für Reservierungen erlaubt Ihnen, unverzüglich Platz in den wichtigsten Herbergen Nordamerikas zu reservieren und dafür in Ihrer eigenen Währung zu bezahlen. Setzen Sie sich mit Ihrem örtlichen Hostelling International Büro in Verbindung, um Genaueres darüber zu erfahren.

> **FAX-A-BED :** Dies erlaubt Anreisenden aus Australien, Neuseeland und Japan mit einer Kreditkarte Platz in den wichtigsten nordamerikanischen Herbergen zu reservieren. Das kann von einem der Hostelling International Büros oder jeder größeren Stadt in Australien und Neuseeland aus geschehen, wie auch in einigen Büros und Herbergen in Japan. In den meisten Fällen tritt die Reservierung direkt in Kraft, sofern sie sieben Tage bis 48 Stunden im voraus erfolgt.

Internationale Reservierung innerhalb Nordamerikas

Unsere Mitglieder können auch internationale Reservierungen über IBN und FAX-A-BED von vielen Hostelling International Büros und von größeren Herbergen Nordamerikas aus vornehmen. Setzen Sie sich mit Ihrem örtlichen Büro oder der Herberge an Ihrem Ort in Verbindung, um Näheres darüber zu erfahren.

Familien und Einzelreisende in Gruppen

Viele Herbergen haben Zimmer für Familien und für Gruppen, die unter sich bleiben möchten; dabei kann ein Zuschlag erhoben werden. Da solche Zimmer besonders beliebt sind, empfiehlt es sich, früh genug zu reservieren. Kinder unter 12 bezahlen eventuell weniger pro Nacht und müssen von einem Erwachsenen begleitet sein. Erfragen Sie Näheres dazu in Ihrer Herberge (Ihren Herbergen). Die Mitgliedschaft für Jugendliche unter 18 in Begleitung ihrer Eltern ist frei.

Gesellschaftsreisen

Viele Herbergen bieten Übernachtung für Reisegruppen an. Führungen und Bestellungen von Mahlzeiten können oft organisiert werden. Gesellschaftsräume mit audio-visueller Einrichtung stehen in vielen Herbergen für Tagungen, Arbeitskreise und Seminare zur Verfügung. Für Gruppen von mindestens 10 Reisenden gibt es eine

Reisedienst

Organisations-Mitgliedschaft. Füllen Sie einfach den Antrag auf Mitgliedschaft aus, den Sie auf der Rückseite dieses Führers finden, oder wenden Sie sich an Ihr nächstes, regionales Büro. Reservierung ist wichtig in diesem Fall.

Einstellung auf Rollstühle

Immer mehr Herbergen machen ihre Gebäude rollstuhlgerecht. Sehen Sie die Liste der Herbergen danach durch, und fragen Sie bei Ihrer Herberge (Ihren Herbergen) früh genug an, ob diese Ihren speziellen Bedürfnissen entgegenkommen kann (können).

Die Hausordnung in Herbergen

Einige Herbergen bleiben zwischen 9:30 und 16:30 geschlossen, aber die meisten sind länger offen oder aber stellen tagsüber einen Gemeinschaftsraum zur Benutzung oder zum Abstellen des Gepäcks zur Verfügung. Die Nachtruhe geht im allgemeinen von 23:00 bis 7:00.

Bettlaken und Kopfkissen werden im allgemeinen gegen Gebühr gestellt. Die Gäste können ihre eigenen Decken bringen oder welche in der Herberge ausleihen. Schlafsäcke sind im allgemeinen nicht erlaubt, sofern sie in der Beschreibung der Herberge nicht ausdrücklich vorgesehen sind.

Um die Preise so niedrig wie möglich zu halten und den Gemeinschaftsgeist der Herbergen zu fördern, wird vom Gast erwartet, daß er den Platz aufgeräumt und sauber verläßt. Die Herbergen können von ihren Gästen auch leichte Mitarbeit verlangen wie Fegen oder Hinaustragen des Mülleimers.

Um so vielen Reisenden wie möglich weiterzuhelfen, kann es auch vorkommen, daß Herbergen die Aufenthaltszeit in der Hochsaison auf drei Nächte beschränken. Versichern Sie sich bei jeder Ihrer Herbergen, ob Sie für die Zeit ihres geplanten Aufenthalts dort bleiben können.

Alle dem nordamerikanischen Netz angeschlossenen Herbergen erwarten von ihren Gästen die Befolgung einer Reihe von Vorschriften, um Ihren Aufenthalt so sicher und angenehm wie möglich zu machen.

- Bei der Ankunft verlangen viele Herbergen einen Ausweis zur Person in Form eines Reisepasses oder eines Führerscheins neben der Mitgliedskarte von Hostelling International.

Reisedienst

- Die einzigen Haustiere, die in Herbergen erlaubt sind, sind die Blindenhunde von Reisenden und der Herbergsleitung, wenn Sie darauf angewiesen sind.

- Weder die Herberge noch ihre Leitung übernehmen irgendeine Verantwortung für Verlust von Eigentum in der Herberge oder auf dem Herbergsgelände durch Diebstahl oder sonstwie.

- Herbergen dienen in erster Linie der Bildung und Erholung von Reisenden; Herbergen können es ablehnen, Gäste aus der nächsten Umgebung aufzunehmen.

- Im Interesse der Sicherheit und Erholung seiner Gäste kann das Personal einer Herberge nach eigenem Gutdünken jedwede Person abweisen.

- Alkohol darf nicht in die Herberge gebracht werden; einige Herbergen haben aber Cafés oder Imbißstuben dabei, in denen Bier und Wein ausgeschenkt wird.

- HI-Kanada/HI-AYH können jede Mitgliedschaft annullieren, wenn die Leitung einer Herberge es beantragt.

- Herbergen bieten ihren Gästen eine nikotinfreie Umgebung; ein besonderer Raum für Raucher steht aber eventuell zur Verfügung.

- Dabei können Jugendliche unter 18 Jahren aufgefordert werden, eine diesbezügliche elterliche Erlaubnis vorzuweisen.

Sagen Sie uns Ihre Meinung

Ihre Meinung als Gast unserer Herbergen gilt uns als die fachlich wertvollste. Jede Herberge legt darum vorgedruckte Karten aus, auf denen Sie Ihre Bemerkungen eintragen können. Bitte, machen Sie davon Gebrauch und lassen Sie uns wissen, was sie von der Herberge halten und welche Vorschläge sie eventuell machen können, um den Aufenthalt dort angenehmer zu gestalten.

Erklärung der Angaben zu den einzelnen Herbergen

Das Verzeichnis führt drei Arten von Unterkünften auf: Vollherberge, Privatherberge und Ersatzunterkunft.

Vollherbergen sind jeweils auf einer ganzen Seite beschrieben und ihre Lage ist auf einem Landkartenausschnitt angegeben. In dem dunkleren Viereck finden Sie die näheren Angaben zu der Herberge, wobei die folgenden Zeichen und Stichwörter benutzt werden:

Mail (✉): Die Straßen- und Postadresse steht ganz oben in dem Viereck. Falls für die Zeit außerhalb der Saison eine andere Adresse für Auskünfte gilt, ist diese unter **Reservations** unten in dem Viereck angegeben.

Phone (☎): Die Telefonnummer der Herberge.

Price (💰): Das ist der Preis pro Nacht und pro Person in U.S. oder kanadischem Dollar. Die Preise gelten bis zum 1. Januar 1994.

Closed (X): Die Tage, an denen die Herberge geschlossen bleibt.

Grade   : Hier werden die Einrichtungen aufgezählt, die in der Herberge vorhanden sind. Die Kategorie sagt nicht unbedingt etwas über die Güte der Herberge aus.

Anmerkung: Die U.S. Herbergen sind z.Zt. im Begriff, neu in Kategorien eingeteilt zu werden; darum sind hier alle U.S. Vollherbergen einfach als "Herbergen" eingetragen. Zu den weiteren in den U.S.A. unterschiedenen Übernachtungsmöglichkeiten gehören die Privatherberge und die Ersatzunterkunft.

Home Hostel (🏠): Mitglieder von Hostelling International sind zu Gast in einem Privathaushalt und teilen die Küche und andere Gemeinschaftsräume mit ihren Gastgebern. Reservierung ist hier unabdingbar.

Supplemental Accomodation (SA): Es kann sich da um Schlafräume von "Colleges", um Hotelzimmer, Gasthäuser oder Privatpensionen mit Frühstück handeln, um YMCA/YWCA Hotels oder noch andere Unterkünfte handeln, in denen unsere Mitglieder neben anderen Gästen bleiben können. In diesen Fällen gibt es oft keine Küchen und der Preis pro Nacht ist höher. Eine derartige Unterbringung wird im allgemeinen da angeboten, wo es weit und breit keine Herberge gibt.

Hostelling International - Canada unterscheidet außerdem zwischen den Bezeichnungen

Superior (🏨): Große Herberge mit 40 oder mehr Betten, voll eingerichteter Küche, warmen und kalten Duschen, Speisesaal und Aufenthaltsraum. Auch findet man hier im allgemeinen Zimmer für Familien/Paare, eine Waschküche mit Maschinen, einen Abstellraum für Fahrräder,

Erklärung der Angaben zu den einzelnen Herbergen

Betätigungsprogramme und andere besondere Vorzüge.

Standard (♠): Herberge mit 24 oder mehr Betten, voll eingerichteter Küche, warmen Duschen, Speisesaal und Aufenthaltsraum. Zimmer für Familien oder Paare, Waschmaschinen und andere Annehmlichkeiten können auch vorhanden sein.

Simple (⌂): Kleinere Herberge mit voll eingerichteter Küche, einem Eß- und Aufenthaltsraum, fließend Wasser und Toilette im Haus.

Basic (⌂): Unterkunft vom Typ einer Hütte. Das Nachtlager kann aus Feldbetten bestehen oder aus Matratzen auf dem Boden. Schlafsäcke sind vorgeschrieben. Männliche und weibliche Gäste teilen eventuell einen Schlafraum, haben nur getrennte Umkleideräume. Fließend Wasser zum Waschen ist vorhanden; die Toiletten sind eventuell außerhalb vom Haus. Das Haus ist beheizt.

Beds (🛏): Zahl der Betten in der Herberge.

Facilities : Hier geht es um Einrichtungen wie Abstellräume, Küche, eingerichtete Waschküche, Ausleihmöglichkeit von Bettwäsche, Schließfächer, Parkplatz, Erholungs- und Besichtigungsprogramme und hier werden gegebenenfalls auch besondere Anmerkungen oder Bedingungen aufgeführt; dazu gehört auch die Angabe, ob die Herberge rollstuhlgerecht (♿) ist und ob man dort Mitgliedskarten kaufen kann **(MSA)**.

Meals (🍴): Angabe ob und welche Mahlzeiten angeboten werden.

Family rooms (👪): "Available" bedeutet, daß die Herberge Zimmer für Familien/Doppelzimmer hat.

Groups (🏠): "Welcome" heißt, daß Schlafräume für geschlossene Gruppen vorhanden sind.

Reservations: Die Tage oder die Jahreszeiten zu denen es ratsam (📅a) oder notwendig (📅e) ist Platz zu reservieren. Dazu werden Adresse und Telefonnummer (By Phone) angegeben, falls sie verschieden von der oben im Viereck angegebenen Adresse der Herberge sind. Falls eine Faxnummer (By Fax) für Reservierungen vorgesehen ist, finden Sie sie an dieser Stelle. Auch hier finden Sie, wenn nötig, die außerhalb der Saison (Off-season) gültige Adresse und Telefonnummer.

Credit Cards: Aufzählung der Kreditkarten, die angenommen werden (z.B. Visa, MasterCard, JCB).

Managers: Name (Namen) der Herbergsleitung.

Directions: Beschreibung des Zufahrtwegs zur Herberge mit darunterstehender Skizze, die die Lage deutlich macht.

サービス

予約

　ホステルは予約なしのお客様も歓迎いたしますが、旅行シーズンには前以て予約をいれておかれることをおすすめいたします。　予約は郵便、電話、ファックスでも承りますが、コンピュータによるホステリング・インターナショナルの予約ネットワークもお使いになることができます。　詳しくはホステルのリストの箇所をご参照ください。

郵便：　手紙で、ご利用日、だいたいのご到着時刻、ご宿泊日数、男女別の場合はそれぞれの人数、ご家族づれの場合は個室のご希望の有無などをお知らせください。　一泊分の料金を前金として、USドル、カナダドルで個人小切手か銀行、郵便局発行のマネーオーダーでお支払いください。　また、返信用の封筒をご用意いただき、お客様のご住所を書き、切手を貼って一緒にお送りください。　予約の確認には国内で二週間、国外からの場合は四週間ぐらいかかりますのでご了承ください。

電話：　大抵のところでは電話でのご予約を受け付けます。　クレジット・カードで一泊分の前金の保証ができますから、ホステルの営業時間内にお電話いただき、クレジット・カードの番号、有効期限をお知らせください。　込んでいるホステルでは、少なくとも48時間前の予約が必要です。

ファックス：　ファックスのあるホステルではファックスで予約を受け付けます。　その際はクレジット・カードによる前金の保証をお願いいたします。郵便によるお申込みと同じ要領でお書きいただいた上、カードの番号、カードの有効期限、カード保持者のご氏名をお書き添えください。　ファックスによる予約の確認の場合は、手数料としてUS，カナダドル共に1＄加算させていただきます。48時間前にお願いいたします。

海外からの北米のホステルの予約

　北米到着前にホステルの予約をご希望の海外からのお客様には、ほかにふたつの予約の方法があります。

IBN：　コンピュータを使っての新しい国際的なネットワークによる予約システムで、ホステル・インターナショナルのために特別に開発されたものです。　これを使うと北米の主なホステルの予約はすぐできます。　しかもその国の貨幣（日本円）でのお支払いが可能です。　詳細はお近くのホステリング・インターナショナルの事務所にお問い合わせください。

FAX-A-BED：　オーストラリア、ニュージーランド、日本からは北米の主なホステルの予約はクレジット・カードを使ってできます。　このサービスはオーストラリア、ニュージーランド、日本各地のホステリング・インターナショナルの事務所、ホステルで扱っています。　48時間から一週間の余裕をとっていただければ大抵の場合、予約はその場でできます。

サービス

北米国内からの国内、国外のホステルの予約

IBN、FAX-A-BED の予約サービスによって、会員はホステリング・インターナショナルの事務所、北米各地のホステルから世界中どこのホステルの予約も可能となりました。詳しくはお近くの事務所、ホステルにご連絡ください。

家族、グループ旅行

多くのホステルには多少料金が高くなりますが、家族用、またはプライバシーをご希望のグループ旅行の方々のための個室があります。最近個室をご希望の方が増えてきましたので早目にご予約ください。大人と一緒の12才未満のお子さまには割り引きがあります。詳しくは各ホステルにお問い合わせください。会費については、両親と一緒の18才未満のお子様には不要です。

団体旅行

大抵のホステルは団体旅行を取り扱っています。説明会、特別のお食事のサービスなどもいたします。集会、ワークショップ、セミナーのための集会室、視聴覚室などの用意もあります。10名以上のメンバーのためには法人会員が適用できます。この案内書の終わりにある申込書にお書き込みの上、近くの事務所までお届けください。また、電話でも受け付けます。予約は必ずお願いいたします。

身障者用の設備

車椅子をご使用の方々にご不便のないように設備を整えたホステルが近年ふえてきました。ホステルのリストをチェックし、ご希望がある場合には予めお電話ください。

ホステルのきまり

9:30a.m.から 4:30p.m.まで閉まるホステルもありますが、大抵は営業時間を延長し、日中だけのご使用や荷物のお預かりなどもしています。通常11p.m.から 7a.m.は就寝時間となっていますからお静かにねがいます。

毛布、枕は用意してあります。シーツはお客様がご持参になるか、ホステルで借りてください。寝袋はホステルのリストに使用可の記載がないかぎりご遠慮ください。

コストをできるだけ押さえるために、またホステルの精神を育むためにも、後片付けは各自でお願いいたします。また、掃除、ごみ捨てなどの軽い仕事をお願いすることもあります。

できるだけ沢山の方々にご利用いただくため、シーズン中は3泊までとしているホステルもあります。各ホステルにご希望だけの宿泊が可能かどうかご確認ください。

皆様が安全で快適な旅行を楽しむことができるために次の注意事項をお守りいただくよう、北米ホステル関係者一同お願いいたします。

- チェック・インのとき、ホステリング・インターナショナルの会員証のほか、パスポート、運転免許証などの身分証明書の提示が義務付けられています。
- 盲導犬、ホステルの経営者のペット以外は、ペットは禁止されています。
- ホステルはお客様の私有物の盗難、紛失については責任はもちません。
- ホステルは原則として研修旅行のグループ、旅行者を対象としたもので、地域の方々のご利用はお断わりすることがあります。

サービス

- お客様の安全とサービスに専念するため、個々のサービスはお断わりすることがあります。
- アルコール類はホステルでは禁止になっていますが、別棟にビールやワインのサービスのできるカフェやカフェテリアのついているホステルもあります。
- HI-Canada/HI-AYHはホステルからの要請により会員証を無効にすることができます。
- ホステルは原則として禁煙ですが、喫煙コーナーが整えられていることもあります。
- 18才以下の方が保護者の付き添いなしでご利用になるときは、保護者の了承を示す書類の提示が求められることがあります。

皆様のご意見、歓迎

日頃ホステルをご利用の皆様は、ホステルについてのいろいろなご意見を伺うのに最適な方々かと思われます。 各ホステルにはそのための用紙がおいてありますので、ご利用いただいたホステルについてのご意見をお聞かせください。 さらに皆様のご期待に添うよう参考にさせていただきます。

お問い合わせは・・・

北米各地には合わせて51の事務所があり、北米のホステル事情、ホステリングインターナショナルの会員、特別行事などのお問い合わせにお答えしております。 売店ではガイドブックや日用品、またユーレイルパスの販売まで扱っています。 本書の各州のはじめに記されている近くのホステリング・インターナショナルの事務所をご確認しておいてください。

ホステルのリストの読み方

この案内には、フルサービスのホステル、ホームホステル、そのたの宿泊設備の3つのタイプが紹介されています。 フルサービスのホステルには1ページをとり、ホステルの位置を示す地図もつけました。 各ページの影つきの枠内にはつぎの項目を設け、ホステルについての詳しい情報を乗せました。

Mail 所在地 (⊡) : まず初めは住所。 オフシーズン中の連絡先がこの住所と異なるときは一番下にある予約のところに連絡先の住所が書いてあります。

Phone 電話 (☎) : ホステルの電話番号

Price 宿泊料 (⊖) : お一人さま一泊の料金、USドル、カナダドル(CDN)。 この料金は1994年1月1日まで有効。

Closed 休業中 (X) : この期間ホステルは休業。

Grade 等級 : ホステルでできるサービスをあらわすもので、かならずしもホステルの質をあらわしたものではありません。

ホステルのリストの読み方

註： USのホステルはホステルの基準が変ってきているので、USのフルサービスのホステルを単にホステルとし、他はホームホステル、その他の宿泊施設とします。

Home Hostel ホームホステル (⌂) ： 皆様々個人の家のお客様で、台所、洗面所等はホストファミリーと同じものを使います。予約が必要です。

Supplemental Accommodation その他の宿泊設備（ＳＡ）： 大学の寮、ホテル、旅館、B & B（ベッド & 朝食）、YM/YWCAその他の宿泊施設では諸設備は共同で使用します。 SAには台所はついていないことが多く、宿泊料は割り高です。 普通ホステルなどがない地域に所在しています。

ホステリング・インターナショナル—カナダは次の等級別を使っています。

Superior (⌂) ： ベッド数40以上、台所完備、温水シャワー、食堂、居間などの共同で使える場所があります。 家族／夫婦用の個室、洗濯設備、自転車置場、行事など特別のプログラムが用意されています。

Standard (⌂) ： ベッド数24以上、台所完備、温水シャワー、食堂、居間などの共同で使える場所があります。 家族／夫婦用の寝室、洗濯設備などがあります。

Simple (⌂) ： 台所完備の小ホステルで、食堂など共同で使用できる場所、水、屋内の洗面所があります。

Basic (☆) ： 簡易宿泊施設。簡易ベッドまたは床にマット。寝袋が必要。 部屋は男女共用のこともありますが、その際は男女別更衣室付き。水はあります。 洗面所は屋外の場合もあります。 暖房付き。

Beds ベッド (🛏) ： ベッド数

Facilities 設備： 物置、台所、洗濯設備、貸シーツ等の有無、ロッカー、駐車場、レクリエーション等のプログラムなど。 また、**wheelchair accessible 車椅子用の設備 (♿)、MSA 会員証の発行**

Meals 食事 (🍴) ： どのような食事が可能か。

Family rooms 家族用個室 (👪) ： available とあれば、家族／夫婦用個室可能。

Groups グループ (👥) ： welcome と書いてあればグループの宿泊可能。

Reservations 予約： advisable (⌂) は予約をしたほうがいい季節、月で、essential (⌂)は必ず予約をしなければならない季節、月です。 予約の連絡先が初めに書いてあるホステルの住所とちがう場合には、**(By phone)** のところに必要な住所、電話番号が書いてあります。 ファックスによる予約は**（By FAX）**のファックス番号でどうぞ。 オフシーズンの住所は**（Off-season）**のところにあります。

Credit Cards クレジットカード ： ご使用になれるクレジットカード（ たとえば、Visa, MasterCard, JCB）

Managers マネージャー ： ホステルのマネージャーの氏名。

Direction 道順： ホステルまでの簡単な行き方。地図もご参照下さい。

Visiting Canada?

Call Home Direct!

Simply dial the *Home Direct* access number for your country. When you dial this number, you will reach an operator from your own country — an operator who speaks your language! This operator will then complete your call.

You can call collect, or charge your call to your telephone company calling card. Either way, *Home Direct* lets you call home more easily.

North America Map

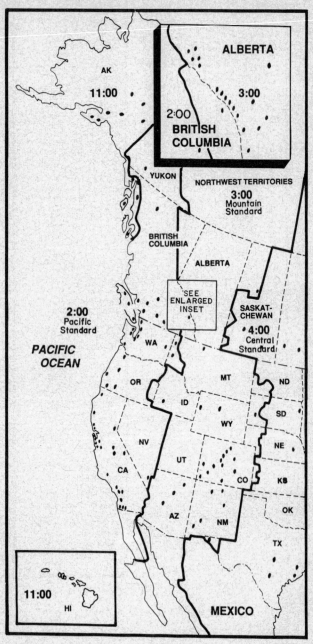

ALBERTA

AK

11:00

3:00

2:00

BRITISH
COLUMBIA

YUKON

NORTHWEST TERRITORIES

3:00
Mountain
Standard

BRITISH
COLUMBIA

ALBERTA

SEE
ENLARGED
INSET

SASKAT-
CHEWAN

2:00
Pacific
Standard

4:00
Central
Standard

*PACIFIC
OCEAN*

WA

OR

MT

ND

ID

SD

WY

NV

NE

UT

CO

KS

CA

AZ

OK

NM

TX

11:00

HI

MEXICO

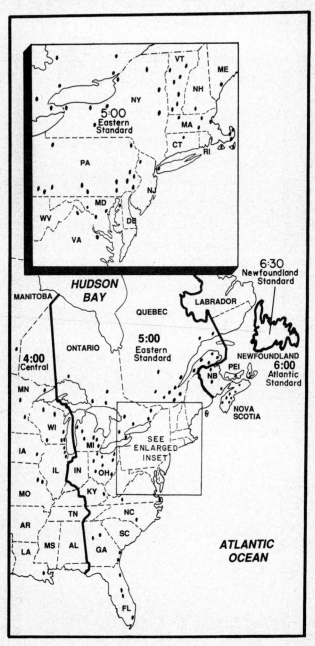

Canada

Population:	27 million
Area:	3.9 million sq. mi., 10 million km^2
Capital:	Ottawa
Languages:	English and French
Currency:	Canadian dollar ($) = 100 cents
Total hostels:	80

Canada offers an incredible variety of landscapes, cultures, urban centres, and rural settings. The weather, which varies from crisp snowy winters to hot summers, and the wide open spaces combine for an endless list of recreational possibilities. Some of the world's best downhill skiing is found here, as well as great cross-country skiing, mountain biking, wind surfing, hiking, canoeing, white water rafting, and hang gliding.

HOSTELLING ®
INTERNATIONAL

Hostelling International–Canada
National Office
1600 James Naismith Drive
Gloucester (Ottawa), Ontario K1B 5N4
Canada
Telephone: 613-748-5638

In the pages that follow, you will find detailed information on Hostelling International hostels throughout Canada. Each listing includes a brief paragraph on local features and activities. The provincial tourism office is given at the beginning of each province section. Further tourism information is available at the hostels or through local tourism information centres.

Alberta

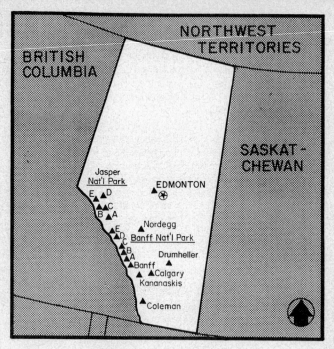

Helpful Organizations

Hostelling International—Canada Regional Offices

Northern Alberta
10926 88th Avenue
Edmonton, Alberta T6G 0Z1
Phone (☎): 403-432-7798
FAX: 403-433-7781

Southern Alberta
1414 Kensington Road NW, #203
Calgary, Alberta T2N 3P9
Phone (☎): 403-283-5551
FAX: 403-283-6503

Provincial Tourism Office

Alberta Tourism
3rd Floor, City Centre Building
10155 - 102 Street
Edmonton, Alberta T5J 4L6
Phone (☎): 403-427-4321,
800-222-6501 (in province),
800-661-8888

Alberta hostels offer all day access

Alberta is Canada's showcase for the splendour of the Rocky Mountains with their massive glaciers and amazing turquoise-blue lakes. Jasper, Lake Louise, and Banff are all attractions that draw visitors from around the world. This is the province with real western flair and hospitality!

Discounts

Present a valid hostel membership card at the time of purchase to receive the following discounts:

Banff

Aardvark Pizza and Sub - 304a Caribou Street, 762-5500. 10% off all food items.
Abominable Ski and Sports - 115 & 229 Banff Avenue, 762-2905. 10% off regularly priced items.
Avis Rent-A-Car - 209 Bear Street, 762-3222. Extra 50 kms on standard daily rates.
Bactrax Bike Snowtips - Located at Douglas Fir Resort, 762-0436. Discounts on bike and ski rentals.
The Banff Centre - Julien Road, 762-6100. Discounts off selected arts and entertainment features.
Banff Music Plus - Sundance Mall, 762-8582. 5% off selected musical lower accessories and instruments.
Banff Park Sports - 222 Lynx Street, 762-5425. 15% off all clothing and ski/bike rentals.
Banff Recreation Centre - Mt. Norquay Road, 762-1235. Free ice skate rental with the purchase of skating admission.
Barbary Coast Restaurant - 119 Banff Avenue, 762-4616. 10% off food orders.
Bow Valley Office Supplies - 229 Bear Street, 762-4228. 10% off non-sale merchandise.
Brewster Transportation & Tours - 100 Gopher Street, 762-6700. 15% off all transportation and tours, excluding Banff involving 2nd operators and the Galgary Airporter.
Film Lab - Banff/Canmore/Lake Louise, 762-2126. 15% off film and developing.
Guido's - 116 Banff Avenue, 762-4002. Free spumone ice cream with dinner.
Hydra River Guides - 762-4554. Discount on white water rafting.
Luxton Museum - 1 Birch Avenue, 762-2388. Student admission rate for hostel members.
Melissa's Restaurant - 218 Lynx Street, 762-5511. 10% off food orders.
Minnewanka Tours - Minnewanka Boat House, 762-3473. 10% off tours in May, June, September. 10% off 5 p.m. to 7 p.m. tours in July, August adult fares only.
Mountain Magic Equipment - 224 Bear Street, 762-2591. 10% off all rentals.
Nexus Sound - 229 Bear Street (lower level), 762-3858. 10% off regularly priced merchandise.
Performance Ski & Sports - 208 Bear Street, 762-8222. 15% off all rentals.
Pop's Bakery - 111 Banff Avenue, 762-2259. 10% off baked goods.
Rose and Crown Restaurant - 202 Banff Avenue, 762-2121. 10% off food orders.
Smitty's Restaurant - 227 Banff Avenue, 762-2533. 10% off all meals.
Somova Kindova Pasta and Pizza - 137 Banff Avenue, 762-5742. 10% off any food item.
Spence Brothers Sportwear - 210 Bear Street, 762-2811. 15% off all regularly priced merchandise.
The Turning Point - Upper Harmony Mall, 762-2878. 10% discount off health food and juice bar.
Velbella's Deli Corner - Lower Level Sundance Mall, 762-4819. 10% off all food items.
Visions Hair Design - 222 Lynx Street, 762-5655. Discount on hair services up to 20%.
Warner Guiding and Outfitting "Holiday on Horseback" - 132 Banff Avenue, 762-4551. 10% off all in-town rides.
The Yard Restaurant - 137 Banff Avenue (3rd floor), 762-5678. 10% off all purchases.

Calgary

A Creative Image - 1609C Kensington Road N.W., 270-7515. 10% off passport, reunion, anniversary, sports, and location photography. 10% off all framing.

Discounts

Calgary(continued)

Abominable Ski & Sportswear - three Calgary locations, 245-2812. 10% off regular rental items including skis, bikes and rollerblades. 10% off ski tune-ups.

Cactus Coulee Float Tours - 283-8379. 10% off rafting, hiking, and biking tours in the badlands surrounding Drumheller.

Calgary Tower - 266-6171. $1.25 off the regular member rate for elevation passes.

Calgary Canoe Club - 6449 Crowchild Trail South, 246-5757. $6.00 off daily rental rate of $16.00 per day for canoes on Glenmore reservoir.

Campus Recreation - University of Calgary (University of Calgary Campus, 220-5038). 10% off all rental equipment.

Explore Magazine - 270-8890. $2.00 off the regular subcription rate of $19.95.

The Glenbow Museum - 130-9 Avenue S.E., 264-8300. Two admissions for the price of one.

Mountain Bike City - 2707-17 Avenue S.W., 686-2453. 10% off all parts and accessories.

Rent-A-Wreck - 112-5th Avenue S.E., 237-6880. $5 off per rental or $25 off for a week or more.

Rent-A-Wreck - 4804 Edmonton Trail N.E., 273-6800. $5 off per rental or $25 off for a week or more.

Rent-A-Wreck - 3911 MacLeod Trail S., 287-9703. $5 off per rental or $25 off for a week or more.

Rent-A-Wreck - 5010 MacLeod Trail S.W., 287-9703. $5 off the regular daily rental rate of $29.95.

Ridley's Cycle - two Calgary locations, 283-1421. 10% off all regularly priced clothing and accessories.

Sports Rent - 4424-16 Avenue N.W., 292-0077. 20% off all ski, skate, boat, sailboard, bike, mountaineering, tent camping, and hiking equipment.

Totem Outdoor (1983) Ltd. - 341-10 Avenue S.W., 264-6363. 10% discount on all regularly priced merchandise excluding canoes and kayaks.

Westcan Treks - 336-14 Street N.W., 283-6115 - $150 off return airfare on any Air New Zealand flight, or a 5% discount on any KLM airfares.

Canmore

Assiniboine Heli Tours - PO Box 2430, 678-5459. 7% - 10% off heli-activities depending on method of payment.

Hunter Valley Recreative Centre - Box 1620, 678-2000. 15% off rafting trips.

Rocky Mountain Cycle - Box 1978, 678-6770. 20% off "mountain coasters" cycle tour.

Edmonton

Campus Outdoor Centre (University of Alberta) - 492-2767. 10% off all equipment rentals.

Chi-Chi's Mexican Restaurante - 650-3803 Calgary Trail, 434-7441. 15% off food items only.

City of Edmonton - $1.00 off regular admission at Fort Edmonton Park, Muttart Conservatory, Kinsmen Sport Centre, the Valley Zoo, and all 12 indoor pool/leisure centres.

Edmonton International Hostel - 25% off mountain bike rentals.

Edmonton Space Sciences Centre - 11211-142 Street, 452-9100. 50% off general admission (excluding Imax Theatre).

Edmonton Trappers Baseball - 50% off general admission to all regular season home games.

McBain Camera Ltd. - (all Edmonton locations) 10% off all photo finishing and "industrial prices" on film and selected accessories.

Northern Lights Theatre - 11516-103 Street, 471-1586. 20% off general admission to all regular season performances.

Old Spaghetti Factory - 10220-103 Street, 422-6088. 20% off food items only.

Discounts

Edmonton(continued)

Red Arrow Coach Line - 10% off regular adult fares - all routes (Direct booking available through the hostel shop 439-3089).
Rent-A-Wreck - 5811-104 Street, 434-3468. $5 off per rental or $25 off for a week or more.
Rent-A-Wreck - 11225-107 Avenue, 423-1755. $5 off per rental or $25 off for a week or more.
Revolution Cycle - 15109 Stony Plain Road, 486-3634. 15% off all accessories, parts and labour.
Sherlock Holmes Pubs - 10012-101A Avenue, 426-7784. 1650 West Edmonton Mall, 444-1752. 25% off all menu and beverage items.
Skier's Sport Shop - 8605-109 Street, 433-7227. 10% of all regularly priced items.
Toasters Submarine/Sandwich Shop - 9440 Jasper Avenue, 426-6481. 30% off all regular menu items.

Jasper National Park

Exposures Photography Inc. - 612 Connaught Drive, 852-5325. 10% off all photo finishing.
Freewheel Cycle Ltd. - 600-b Patricia Street, 852-5380. 15% off all accessories, parts, and labour.
Heritage Taxi-Cab Service - 611 Patricia Street, 852-5558. 30% off all regular fares.
Jasper Aquatic Centre - 401 Pyramid Avenue, 852-3663. 10% off general admission.
Jasper Bakery - 601 Patricia Street, 852-4881. 10% off all items.
Marmot Basin Ski Resort - 15% off all regular ski lift tickets (when purchased through the Hostel Shop or Whistler's Mountain Hostel). Discounts on equipment rental.
Skis Please - Rentals & Service - 616 Connaught Drive, 852-5595. Deluxe rental package for the same price as regular package.
Whistler's Mountain Hostel - 852-3215. 25% off mountain bike rentals.

Kananaskis

Boundary Stables - East Side Hwy. 40, 591-7171. 10% off all guided trail rides.

Lake Louise

Lake Louise Taxi & Tours - 522-2020. Local's rate for hostel members.
Pipestone Photo - Samson Mall, 522-3617. 15% off film and developing.
Sweets and Treats - Samson Mall, 522-3967. 5% off all sweets and treats.
Timberline Tours - St. Prian Road, 522-3743. $3.00 off all horseback rides.
Wild Water Adventure - 522-2211. Discount off white water rafting.

Alberta

Banff

Banff International Hostel

Banff is an internationally renowned destination which offers cultural, shopping, sporting, and outdoor recreational opportunities. While in Banff be sure to relax in the Cave and Basin Hot Springs, the discovery of which first put Banff on the map in 1883. Travellers should also be sure to take advantage of extensive hiking, biking, and skiing trails surrounding the town.

The Banff International Hostel is one of the most exciting hostels in Alberta, offering activities ranging from the monthly coffee house (evening performances from local musicians, comedians, and actors) to mountain biking and white water rafting.

Tunnel Mountain Road.
Mail (✉): Box 1358, Banff, Alberta T0L 0C0.
Phone (☎): 403-762-4122.
Price (☻): $14 CDN (Sept.–June) $16 (July & August).
Closed (X): never.
Check-in (🕐): 24 hours.
Grade: superior (👫).
Beds (🛏): 154.
Facilities: equipment storage area, kitchen, laundry facilities, linen rental, lockers, on-site parking with plug-ins, wheelchair accessible (♿), game room, cafeteria, meeting rooms, ski and cycle workshop, bicycle shed, firepit, **MSA**, open all day.
Meals (🍴): breakfast, lunch, pack lunch, dinner.
Family rooms (👶): available.
Groups (⊞): welcome.

Reservations essential (⊞o): groups.
Reservations advisable (⊞a): always. **By phone:** 403-762-4122 or 237-8282 (within Calgary calling area). **By FAX:** 403-762-3441.
Credit cards: MasterCard, Visa.
Directions: 3 kilometres from downtown on Tunnel Mountain Road. From Banff Avenue, continue to Wolf and turn left on Otter.

Alberta

Banff National Park A

Castle Mountain Hostel

The Castle Mountain Hostel offers a wide range of adventures to travellers. Hikers and skiers will enjoy trails that pass waterfalls, alpine meadows, cold springs, wildlife habitats, and historic sites. Downhill skiers are within a 30-minute drive from the Sunshine Village, Lake Louise, and Mount Norquay Ski Resorts.

The hostel features a cozy common room with wood-burning fireplace and large bay windows. Guests are welcome to take advantage of the fully equipped kitchen, outdoor barbecue, and fire pit. In the summer, the hostel often hosts games of pick-up volleyball.

Highway 1A, Bow Valley Parkway.
Mail (✉): Box 1358,
Banff, Alberta
T0L 0C0.
Phone (☎): 403-762-2367.
Price (●): $9 CDN.
Closed (X): never.
Check-in (🕐): 4–10 p.m.
Grade: simple (🏠).
Beds (🛏): 36.
Facilities: kitchen, linen rental, on-site parking, fireplace, **MSA**, open all day.
Groups (🍴): welcome.
Reservations essential (📞): groups.
Reservations advisable (📞): always. **By phone:** 403-762-4122 or 237-8282 (within Calgary calling area). **By FAX:** 403-762-3441.

Credit cards: MasterCard, Visa for reservations only.
Directions: on Highway 1A, 1.5 kilometres east of the junction with Highway 1 and Highway 93 South.

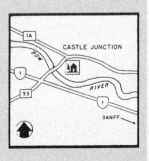

Alberta

Banff National Park B

Lake Louise International Hostel

Lake Louise is a designated World Heritage Site and all-season resort area. Visitors can hike to teahouses first opened by CP Rail to accommodate turn-of-the-century tourists, and enjoy fascinating sites such as Moraine Lake and the Plain of Six Glaciers. In winter, Lake Louise offers excellent cross-country skiing and is only a five-minute drive from Alberta's largest downhill ski resort.

The Hostel and Canadian Alpine Centre is a modern 100-bed facility with a licensed cafe, reading lounge with open-beamed ceilings and a stone fireplace, reference library, and rooms with ensuite washrooms. The hostel is jointly operated by Hostelling International and the Alpine Club of Canada, and offers guests unique recreational opportunities in the heart of the Canadian Rockies.

Village Road, Lake Louise.
Mail (✉): Box 115,
Lake Louise, Alberta, T0L 1E0.
Phone (☎): 403-522-2200.
Price (●): $15 CDN (Sept.–June)
$17 CDN (July & August).
Closed (X): never.
Check-in (◖): 24 hours.
Grade: superior (👥).
Beds (🛏): 100.
Facilities: equipment storage area, kitchen, laundry facilities, linen rental, lockers, on-site parking, wheelchair accessible (♿), cafe, mountaineering resource library, programs, tours and events, games room, ski/cycle workshop, **MSA**, open all day.
Meals (🍴): breakfast, lunch, pack lunch, dinner.
Family rooms (👪): available.
Groups (🏠): welcome.

Reservations essential (📞●): groups.
Reservations advisable (📞a): always. **by FAX:** 403-522-2253.
Credit cards: MasterCard, Visa.
Directions: turn off Highway 1 (Trans-Canada) into Lake Louise, turn right, continue 750 metres to hostel.

Alberta

Banff National Park C

Mosquito Creek Hostel

The Mosquito Creek Hostel is located just north of Lake Louise. A 20-minute drive on the beautiful Icefields Parkway brings you to the peaceful, rustic cabins of the hostel. The first complete journey from Lake Louise to Jasper along this route was accomplished in 1904 and was later dubbed "The Wonder Trail." Construction of the highway was a "make-work" project for 625 men during the Great Depression. The first automobile drove its course in 1940.

Mosquito Creek Hostel offers access to excellent high-elevation cross-country ski trails and an extensive network of hiking trails. After a busy day of activities, warm up in front of the hostel's cozy fireplace or unwind in the sauna. The rustic cabins compliment the natural setting. More information on the surrounding area can be obtained from the hostel's manager.

Highway 93.
Mail (✉): Box 1358, Banff, Alberta T0L 0C0.
Phone (☎): none.
Price (☺): $8 CDN.
Closed (X): never.
Check-in (⌂): 4–10 p.m.
Grade: basic (⌂). **Beds (🛏):** 38.
Facilities: wood stoves, fireplace, outdoor sauna, food store, **MSA**, open all day.
Family rooms (🛏): available.
Groups (𝍪): welcome.
Reservations essential (·🛏e): groups.
Reservations advisable (·🛏a): always. **By phone:** 403-762-4122 or 237-8282 (within Calgary calling area). **By FAX:** 403-762-3441.

Credit cards: MasterCard, Visa for reservations only.
Directions: 26 kilometres north of Lake Louise on Highway 93, next to Mosquito Creek campground.

Alberta

Banff National Park D

Rampart Creek Hostel

Located just 11 kilometres north of the Saskatchewan River Crossing, Rampart Creek is a popular resting spot with cyclists on the Icefields Parkway (Highway 93). World-class rock and ice climbing make the hostel a mecca for adventurers from around the world. You can also enjoy hiking and exploring nearby areas such as Rampart Creek Canyon, the Weeping Wall, and Murchison Falls. There are rock climbing and mountaineering programs available through the Alpine Club of Canada and other local organizations.

Highway 93.
Mail (✉): Box 1358, Banff, Alberta T0L 0C0.
Phone (☎): none.
Price (◓): $8 CDN.
Closed (X): Monday–Thursday (November 1–March 31 only).
Check-in (🕐): 4–10 p.m.
Grade: basic (⌂).
Beds (🛏): 30.
Facilities: kitchen, wood stoves, on-site parking, outdoor sauna, **MSA**, open all day.
Groups (🍽): welcome, reservations required.
Reservations advisable (📞a): always. **By phone:** 403-762-4122 or 237-8282 (within Calgary calling area). **By FAX:** 403-762-3441.

Credit cards: MasterCard, Visa for reservations only.
Directions: 95 kilometres north of Lake Louise and 34 kilometres south of the Columbia Icefields Centre on Highway 93.

Alberta

Banff National Park E

Hilda Creek Hostel

Located eight kilometres south of the Columbia Icefield, the Hilda Creek Hostel is a comfortable refuge for eager outdoor types seeking spectacular hiking, mountaineering, cross-country skiing, and telemarking. The Columbia Icefield is the largest sheet of subpolar glacial ice in North America, covering over 300 kilometres of mountain terrain, with meltwaters feeding three oceans. Local groups offer a variety of seasonal activities such as glacial hikes, crevasse rescue courses, and nature studies.

Highway 93.
Mail (✉): Box 1358, Banff, Alberta T0L 0C0.
Phone (☎): none.
Price (●): $8 CDN.
Closed (X): never.
Check-in (⌂): 4–10 p.m.
Grade: basic (⌂).
Beds (🛏): 21.
Facilities: kitchen, wood stove, outdoor sauna, **MSA**, open all day.
Groups (🏠): welcome, reservations required.
Reservations advisable (🏠): always. **By phone:** 403-762-4122 or 237-8282 (within Calgary calling area). **By FAX:** 403-762-3441.
Credit cards: MasterCard, Visa for reservations only.

Directions: 8 kilometres south of the Columbia Icefields Centre and 120 kilometres north of Lake Louise on Highway 93.

Calgary

Calgary International Hostel

The Calgary International Hostel is located near the site of Fort Calgary in the heart of the city. Enjoy the warm western hospitality and easy access to some of Calgary's best cultural, recreational, and shopping facilities.

The hostel offers a variety of activities throughout the year including mountain biking, behind-the-scenes tours of Canada's second largest zoo, live entertainment in nearby parks, rollerblading, and mountain hikes and has arranged discounts on entrance fees to activities such as skating at Olympic Plaza.

520 Seventh Avenue S.E., Calgary, Alberta T2G 0J6.
Mail (⊙): same.
Phone (☎): 403-269-8239.
Price (●): $12 CDN.
Closed (X): never.
Check-in (⌂): 24 hours.
Grade: superior (👤).
Beds (⊨): 114.
Facilities: equipment storage area, kitchen, laundry facilities, linen rental, lockers, limited street parking, wheelchair accessible (♿), snack bar, bicycle shed, meeting room, game room, hostel-based programs, **MSA**, open all day.
Family rooms (🏠): available.
Groups (⫿⫿⫿): welcome.
Reservations essential (⌂e): groups.
Reservations advisable (⌂a): July. **FAX:** 403-266-6227.

Credit cards: MasterCard, Visa.
Directions: Bus: take free shuttle bus to Seventh Avenue, transfer to C-train to city hall, walk 1 block to hostel; C-train is free in city centre. **Airport (✈):** take Airporter bus to Delta Bow Valley Hotel and walk to hostel.

Alberta

Coleman

Grand Union International Hostel

Located in the town of Coleman, in the Crows Nest Pass, the Grand Union International Hostel is an ideal stopover for travellers between Calgary and the Montana border. While at the hostel, guests can sample from a variety of cultural and recreational opportunities. Enjoy hiking and skiing, or visit one of Alberta's premiere museums. Nearby attractions include Head Smashed in Buffalo Jump, the Frank Slide Interpretation Centre, Bellevue Mine, and the North West Mounted Police post at Fort McLeod. The hostel is located in an old hotel that has been extensively renovated to offer private rooms with ensuite washrooms. Guests can even have meals catered to their rooms on request.

7719 17th Avenue,
Coleman, Alberta T0K 0M0.
Mail (⌂): same.
Phone (☎): 403-563-3433.
Price (◔): $10 CDN.
Closed (X): never.
Check-in (Ⅱ): 8 a.m.–11 p.m.
Grade: standard (♠).
Beds (⊨): 62.
Facilities: kitchen, laundry facilities, linen rental, lounge, on-site parking, **MSA**, open all day.
Meals (✎): available upon request.
Family rooms (♔): available.
Groups (⫯): welcome.
Reservations advisable (⫞a): always.
Credit cards: MasterCard, Visa.

Directions: 269 kilometres south-west of Calgary. Take Highway 2 south, take Highway 3 to Coleman and follow 17th Avenue to the west end of town.

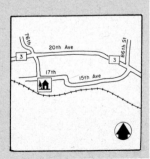

Alberta

Drumheller

Alexandra International Hostel

Drumheller is one of the most unique destinations in Alberta. The city has been made famous by dinosaur discoveries in the area. The Royal Tyrrell Museum of Paleontology, located in Drumheller, boasts one of the largest collections of dinosaur skeletons in the world. Visitors can sample from activities including local dinner theatre, hiking, and cycling in the moonscape-like scenery of the badlands, golfing, and exploring ghost towns that have been abandoned for almost 50 years.

The Alexandra Hostel is located in a refurbished hotel built toward the end of the 1930s coal boom. Situated in downtown Drumheller, it is within walking distance of restaurants, indoor and outdoor swimming pools, a fitness club, and shopping. Local tour operators offer rafting and bicycling tours for guests at the hostel.

30 Railway Avenue North
Drumheller, Alberta T0J 0Y0.
Mail (✉): same.
Phone (☎): 403-823-6337.
Price (◓): $10 CDN.
Closed (X): never.
Check-in (🛏): 24 hours.
Grade: standard (♠).
Beds (🛏): 55.
Facilities: equipment storage area, kitchen, cafeteria, laundry facilities, linen rental, lockers, on-site parking, wheelchair accessible (♿), snack bar, bicycle shed, meeting room, game room, hostel-based programs, **MSA**, open all day.
Family rooms (♔): available.
Groups (🎪): welcome.

Reservations advisable (☎a): groups (July 1–August 31).
Credit Cards: Visa, MasterCard
Directions: Three blocks east of the Greyhound bus station on Railway Avenue.

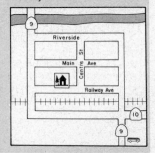

Alberta

Edmonton

Edmonton International Hostel

Edmonton began as Fort Edmonton, a fur trading post of the Hudson's Bay Company. Today it is known as Canada's Festival City and for its many parks. The Edmonton International Hostel is well-suited to take advantage of the network of parks, bicycle paths, walking trails, and recreational facilities that weave their way through the river valley. The hostel is within walking distance of the impressive provincial Legislative Buildings. Along with a major centre for the performing arts, Edmonton offers an ongoing array of summer festivals. Klondike Days rekindle the spirit of western Canada's gold rush. And don't miss West Edmonton Mall, the world's largest shopping centre with over 800 shops, 11 major department stores, 110 restaurants, 19 cinemas, an enormous wave pool and water park, and the world's largest indoor amusement park with indoor bungee jumping.

10422 91st Street,
Edmonton, Alberta T5H 1S6.
Mail (✉): same.
Phone (☎): 403-429-0140.
Price (❂): $10 CDN.
Closed (X): never.
Check-in (⏰): 5 p.m.–midnight.
Grade: standard (♠).
Beds (🛏): 50.
Facilities: equipment storage area, kitchen, laundry facilities, linen rental, on-site parking, wheelchair accessible (♿), patio deck, snack bar, fireplace, hostel-based programs, barbecue, mountain bike rentals, **MSA**, open all day.
Family rooms (👪): available.
Groups (🏨): welcome.
Reservations advisable (📠a): always. **By phone:** 403-439-3139.
By FAX: 403-433-7781.

Credit cards: MasterCard, Visa, JCB.
Directions: walk east along Jasper Avenue, south of train and bus station, to 91st Street, hostel is on north side. **Bus:** eastbound bus #1 (Stadium) or bus #2 (Highlands) both stop in front of the hostel.

Alberta

Jasper National Park A

Beauty Creek Hostel

For centuries, natives and explorers alike camped alongside the placid waters of Beauty Creek where it flows into the Sunwapta River. Descending 1,680 metres through a limestone gorge into the Parkway Valley, the creek feeds a series of eight picturesque waterfalls, each becoming more splendid than the last. The eighth, Stanley Falls, is the most spectacular.

Only 20 kilometres from the Columbia Icefield Centre, the hostel provides access to excellent hiking trails, including one beside Beauty Creek offering views of all eight falls. Follow the Pobokatan Creek trail to Jonas or Pobokatan Pass, or go north through the Maligne Pass. Choose from hikes of one hour or up to several days.

Highway 93.
Mail (✉): 10926 88th Avenue, Edmonton, Alberta T6G 0Z1.
Phone (☎): none.
Price (●): $8 CDN.
Closed (X): October–April; key system for group use from November to May.
Check-in (🏠): 5–11 p.m.
Grade: basic (🏠).
Beds (🛏): 24.
Facilities: equipment storage area, kitchen, linen rental, on-site parking, Heritage programs, **MSA**, open all day.
Groups (▯▯▯▯): welcome.
Reservations advisable (🛏a): always. **By phone:** 403-439-3139. **By FAX:** 403-433-7781.

Credit cards: MasterCard, Visa, (JCB for phone reservations only).
Directions: 90 kilometres south of Jasper and 20 kilometres north of the Columbia Icefield Centre on the west side of Highway 93.

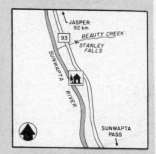

Alberta

Jasper National Park B

Mount Edith Cavell Hostel

The 3363-metre peak of Mount Edith Cavell towers over every other mountain in Jasper National Park. In a cirque valley on the northeast slope of the mountain is the famous Angel Glacier—suspended as if in full flight with its huge icy wings outstretched. In a narrow valley below this spectacular setting is the hostel, providing excellent access to the entire area. Hike to the foot of the glacier and explore the moraines which mark its steady retreat during this century. Experience the brilliant colours of the delicate Cavell Meadows or sit by the turquoise waters of the lake below. At the nearby Tonquin Valley trailhead, descend into magnificent back-country for a day hike or for overnight camping. In winter, fresh powder snow and extensive even grade trails make this area a skier's paradise.

Mail (✉): 10926 88th Avenue, Edmonton, Alberta T6G 0Z1.
Phone (☎): none.
Price (☮): $8 CDN.
Closed (X): October–mid June; road closes in winter, hostel open on a key system.
Check-in (⌂): 5–11 p.m.
Grade: basic (⌂). **Beds (⊨):** 32.
Facilities: equipment storage area, kitchen, linen rental, on-site parking, Heritage programs, **MSA**, open all day.
Groups (⏇): welcome.
Reservations essential (☎●): November–May. **By phone:** 403-439-3139. **By FAX:** 403-433-7781.
Credit cards: MasterCard, Visa (JCB for phone reservations only).

Directions: take Mount Edith Cavell turnoff from Highway 93A, follow road 13 kilometres to hostel (on the left, below Angel Glacier parking area). The road closes in the winter.

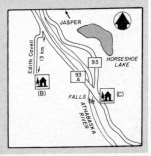

Alberta

Jasper National Park C

Athabasca Falls Hostel

One of the most spectacular sights on the Athabasca River system, the falls have changed very little since the first Europeans viewed its splendor nearly 200 years ago. The step in the valley floor was formed by the glacier that once occupied the Athabasca Valley. This narrow gorge of quartz and sandstone is cut back a few millimetres each year by the rushing water.

With three comfortable sleeping cabins and a large dining and recreational building, Athabasca Falls Hostel is ideally located near many of Jasper National Park's finest attractions, including the columned cliffs of Horseshoe Lake and the hiking trails to Geraldine Lake, Leach Lake, or Fryatt Hut. Enjoy an abundance of cross-country ski trails throughout the valley. Ski the neighbouring alpine slopes of Marmot Basin Resort.

Highway 93.
Mail (✉): 10926 88th Avenue, Edmonton, Alberta T6G 0Z1.
Phone (☎): 403-852-5959.
Price (●): $8 CDN.
Closed (X): Tuesdays (Oct.–April).
Check-in (🏠): 5–11 p.m.
Grade: basic (🏠).
Beds (🛏): 40.
Facilities: equipment storage area, kitchen, linen rental, on-site parking, bicycle shelter, sauna, fully winterized, Heritage programs, volleyball, basketball, horseshoes, campfire pit, barbecue, **MSA**, open all day.
Groups (🏠): welcome.
Reservations advisable (📞): always. **By phone:** 403-439-3139.
By FAX: 403-433-7781.

Credit cards: MasterCard, Visa (JCB for phone reservations only).
Directions: 32 kilometres south of the Jasper townsite and 78 kilometres north of the Columbia Icefield Centre on the east side of Highway 93.

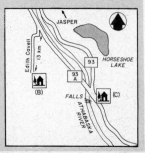

Alberta

Jasper National Park D

Maligne Canyon Hostel

Meaning "wicked" in French, the name Maligne was given to this thundering white-water canyon by a Flemish Jesuit missionary in 1845. Truly an appropriate epithet for this relentless water system which has for thousands of years cut progressively deeper into the earth. Pounding and swirling water and abrasive debris have scoured out the Palliser limestone to its deepest point of more than 55 meters.

Poised alongside the river, just above the spectacular depths of the canyon, this serene hostel is an all-season destination. Enjoy an array of hiking, cycling, and cross-country skiing trails. The nearby Skyline Trail offers one of Jasper National Park's most scenic hikes through an incredible series of mountain landscapes.

Maligne Canyon Road.
Mail (✉): 10926 - 88th Avenue, Edmonton, Alberta T6G 0Z1.
Phone (☎): 403-852-3584.
Price (☺): $8 CDN.
Closed (X): Wednesdays (October–April).
Check-in (🕙): 5–11 p.m.
Grade: basic (♔). **Beds (🛏):** 24.
Facilities: equipment storage area, kitchen, linen rental, on-site parking, fireplace, Heritage programs, barbecue, **MSA**, open all day.
Family rooms (👪): available.
Groups (🎪): welcome.
Reservations advisable (☎a): always. **By phone:** 403-439-3139. **By FAX:** 403-433-7781.
Credit cards: MasterCard, Visa (JCB for phone reservations only).

Directions: 11 kilometres east of Jasper townsite on Maligne Canyon Road. From Highway 16, turn onto Maligne Canyon Road, cross bridge over Athabasca River, follow fork to the left, cross another bridge, and look for sign to the hostel on the right side of the road.

Alberta

Jasper National Park E

Whistler's Mountain Hostel

Whistler's Mountain was once the site of Jasper National Park's only alpine ski area and offered some of Canada's best skiing. With the development of nearby Marmot Basin Ski Resort, a modern world-class facility, skiing was discontinued on Whistler's, a move that ensures the conservation of its unique ecosystem.

Whistler's Mountain Hostel is on the road leading to the Skytram area, overlooking the picturesque Athabasca Valley. Each summer the neighbouring Skytram whisks thousands of visitors to the top of beautiful Whistler's Mountain (elevation 2,285 metres). An interpretive centre at the top describes life in this fragile alpine zone. Hiking trails lead from the hostel right to the summit of the mountain and adjacent mountain trails. In winter, cross-country ski trails weave their way through the scenic valley.

Whistler's Mountain (Syktram) Road.
Mail (✉): 10926 88th Avenue, Edmonton, Alberta T6G 0Z1.
Phone (☎): 403-852-3215.
Price (●): $12 CDN.
Closed (X): never.
Check-in (⌂): 5–11 p.m.
Grade: standard (♠).
Beds (➤): 70.
Facilities: equipment storage area, kitchen, linen rental, lockers, on-site parking, fireplace, Heritage programs, campfire pits, barbecue, mountain bike rentals, **MSA**, open all day.
Family rooms (⌂): available.
Groups (⑪): welcome.
Reservations advisable (⌂a): always. **By phone:** 403-439-3139. **By FAX:** 403-433-7781.

Credit cards: MasterCard, Visa, JCB.
Directions: 7 kilometres southwest of Jasper on Whistler's Mountain (Skytram) Road, off Highway 93, 0.5 kilometre below the Skytram parking area.

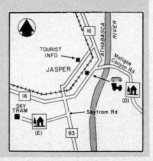

Alberta

Kananaskis Country

Ribbon Creek Hostel

Located midway between Calgary and Banff, Kananaskis Country is a year-round, multi-use recreational area. Visitors can access over 60 mountain biking paths that double as cross-country ski trails in winter. The area also boasts historic sites, rock climbing and downhill skiing at the site of the 1988 Winter Olympics.

The Ribbon Creek Hostel is centrally located in Kananaskis Country, only minutes away from the Nakiska Ski Resort and paved cycling paths. Guests at the hostel can enjoy white water rafting, trail rides, sleigh rides, and outdoor hot tubs. Bicycle rentals are available from nearby outlets.

Mail (✉): Box 1358, Banff, Alberta T0L 0C0.
Phone (☎): 403-591-7333.
Price (💰): $9 CDN.
Closed (X): never.
Check-in (🕐): 4–10 p.m.
Grade: standard (⬆).
Beds (🛏): 44.
Facilities: kitchen, laundry facilities, linen rental, on-site parking, fireplace, Heritage programs, **MSA**, open all day.
Family rooms (👪): available.
Groups (🏛): welcome.
Reservations essential (👥): groups.
Reservations advisable (👥a): always. **By phone:** 403-762-4122 or 237-8282 (within Calgary calling area). **By FAX:** 403-762-3441.
Credit cards: MasterCard, Visa for reservations only.

Directions: 70 kilometres west of Calgary on Highway 1 (Trans-Canada), then 25 kilometres south on Highway 40, turn right at the Nakiska Ski Hill access, cross the Kananaskis River, then left 1.5 kilometres to the hostel.

Alberta

Nordegg

Shunda Creek Hostel

West central Alberta's David Thompson Country offers a landscape of open valleys, clear blue lakes, white water streams and rolling mountains. Deep in the heart of this spectacular area is Shunda Creek Hostel. This four season destination provides the perfect setting for individuals, groups, and families looking for excellent recreational opportunities.

Explore some of the same routes taken by 19th century explorers as you hike or mountain bike over 700 kilometres of trails in the Bighorn area, enjoy some of Alberta's best white fish and trout fishing. Windsurf on Lake Abraham, one of the world's premier freshwater windsurfing sites. There is also great canoeing and rock climbing. In winter, bring your cross-country skis, skates, or snowshoes. Whatever your interests, stay a while and bring a camera.

Shunda Creek
Recreational Area Road.
Mail (✉): 10926 - 88th Avenue, Edmonton, Alberta T6G 0Z1.
Phone (☎): 403-721-2140.
Price (🅾): $10 CDN.
Closed (X): Tuesdays, Wednesdays.
Check-in (🕐): 5–11 p.m.
Grade: standard (♠).
Beds (🛏): 47.
Facilities: equipment storage area, kitchen, linen rental, on-site parking, hostel-based programs, campfire pit, barbecue, **MSA**, open all day.
Family rooms (👪): available.
Groups (🏠): welcome.
Reservations advisable (🔑): always. **By phone:** 403-439-3139.
By FAX: 403-433-7781.

Credit cards: MasterCard, Visa. (JCB for phone reservations only).
Directions: westbound on Highway 11, turn right at Shunda Creek Recreation Area Road, ahead 3 kilometres (keep left at fork in road) to the hostel.

British Columbia

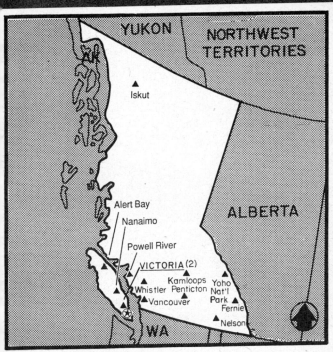

Helpful Organizations

Hostelling International—Canada Regional Office

British Columbia
1515 Discovery Street
Vancouver, British Columbia
V6R 4K5
Phone (☎): 604-224-7177
FAX: 604-224-4852

Provincial Tourism Office

British Columbia
Parliament Buildings
Victoria, British Columbia V8V 1X4
Phone (☎): 604-387-1642
FAX: 800-663-6000

Most British Columbia hostels offer all day access, see individual listings for details.

British Columbia—from the forested landscapes of Vancouver Island, to the spectacular Pacific coastline, to the mountainous interior—this province will take your breath away. In Vancouver, the modern cityscape and bustling cosmopolitan atmosphere blend in with the backdrop of mountains and seaways.

Discounts

Present a valid hostel membership card at the time of purchase to receive the following discounts:

Great Expectations Magazine - Box 8000-411 Abbotsford, V2S 6H1, 1-800-743-3639. 15% discount on 2-year subscription.

Discounts

Fernie

B & N Enterprises Ltd. - 1501-9th Avenue. $15 daily snowmobile rental; 10% discount on motorcycle parts and accessories.

Bubba's Pizza - 701-2nd Avenue, 423-4344. 10% discount on cash purchases of regularly priced food items (5% credit card).

Dorothy's Restaurant - Hwy. #3. 10% discount on all meal purchases.

Fernie Sports Ltd. - Hwy. #3. 10% discount on ski and bicycle rentals.

Fernie Wilderness Adventures - #9 Ridgemont Avenue. 10% discount on hiking, fishing, mountain bike tours, etc.

Gifts 'n' Things - 581-2nd Avenue. 10% discount on everything.

Griz-Inn-Sport Hotel - Located on Ski Area Road. 15% discount on meal purchases.

The Livery 92 - 701-2nd Avenue. 10% discount on cash purchases of regularly priced food items (5% credit card).

Rocky Mountain High Adventure - 10% discount on horseback rides and sleigh rides. Located on Ski Area Road.

Snow Valley Ski School - Box 1745 Fernie, 423-3515. 10% off regularly priced ski lessons.

Taks Home Furnishers - 552-2nd Avenue. 15% discount on all boutique items.

Golden

Whitewater Voyageurs - Box 1983, 344-7335. 20% discount.

Kamloops

Rent-A-Wreck - 2059 East Trans Canada Highway, 374-7788. $5 off per rental or $25 off for a week or more.

Nanaimo

Rent-A-Wreck - 111 S. Terminal Avenue, 753-6461. $5 off per rental or $25 off for a week or more.

Nelson

Rent-A-Wreck - 301 Nelson Avenue, 352-5122. $5 off per rental or $25 off for a week or more.

Smithers

Bear Enterprises Ltd. - P.O. Box 4222, 847-3351 or 847-2854. 10% discount on mountaineering and wilderness trips in NW B.C., both novice and experienced.

Vancouver

Capilano Suspension Bridge - 3735 Capilan Road, 985-7474. Student admission rate.

CNIMAX Theatre - 201-999 Canada Place, 682-6422. $1.00 off one admission to any IMAX matinee performance June - September.

Coast Mountain Sports - 1828 West 4th Avenue, 731-6181. 10% discount on all sports equipment and clothing.

Dr. Sun Yat-Sen Classical Chinese Garden - 578 Carrall Street, 689-7133. 2 for 1, or 50% discount on single admission price.

Gulliver's The Travel Accessories Store - 844 Park Royal, 922-9650. 10% discount on all purchases including books and sale items.

The Harbour Centre Lookout! - 50% discount on adult and student prices.

The Lookout! - located at Harbour Centre, 555 West Hastings, 662-3207. 50% discount on adult and student admissions.

Recreation Rentals - 733-7368 and 273-9176. 15% discount on hiking and camping gear, canoes, and kayaks.

Rent-A-Wreck - 1085 Kingsway, 876-7155. $5 off per rental or $25 off for a week or more.

Rent-A-Wreck - 3031 No. 3 Road (near airport). $5 off per rental or $25 off for a week or more.

Discounts

Vancouver(continued)

Rent-A-Wreck - 180 West Georgia, 688-0001. $5 off per rental or $25 off for a week or more.

The Travel Bug - 2667 W. Broadway, 737-1122. 10% discount on travel accessories (excluding books and maps).

Van Dusen Botanical Gardens - 5251 Oak Street, 266-7194. 2 for 1 admission.

Wanderlust - 1929 West 4th Avenue, 739-2182. The Traveller's Store - 10% discount on travel accessories (excluding books and maps).

Wilderness Equipment Rentals - 2676 West Broadway, 736-0127. 15% discount on all rentals.

Victoria

Budget Discount Cars and Budget Cycle Time - 727 Courtenay Street, 388-4442. 15% discount on regular rental rates of cars and bicycles.

Earth Quest Books - 1286 Broad Street, 361-4533. 10% discount on any regularly priced item.

Ferris' Oyster & Burger Bar - 536 Yates Street, 360-1824. 10% discount on any food item.

Green Cuisine - #5-560 Johnson Street. 10% discount.

Harbour Scooter Rentals - 843 Douglas Street, 384-2133. Low rates for hostel members.

Intertidal Explorations - 2010 Stanley Avenue, 595-4774. 10% discount on wilderness tours in sailing Kayaks; 20% for groups of 3 or more.

Jeune Brothers and Peetz - 570 Johnson Street, 386-8778. 10% off merchandise.

Rent-A-Wreck - 2634 Douglas Street, 384-5343. $5 off per rental or $25 off for a week or more.

The Royal British Columbia Museum - 675 Belleville Street, 387-3014. Student admission rate.

Sea-Trek Sports - 9775-5th Street, Sidney, 656-9888. 10% discount on rentals.

Seacoast Expeditions Ltd. - Inner Harbour, 477-1818. 10% discount on whale watching and marine wildlife tours (May-September when purchased directly).

Seed of Life Natural Foods - 1316 Government Street, 382-4343. 10% off everything except dairy products, sale items, and baked goods.

Whistler

Great Games and Toys - 4114 Golfers Approach. 10% off all regularly priced merchandise with the exception of the month of December.

Wedge Rafting Ltd. - Box 453, 932-7171. 10% discount on rafting trips.

British Columbia

Alert Bay

Pacific Hostelry

Killer whales, sea lions, Kwakiutl Indian culture, and superb fishing can all be experienced from this cedar building on Cormorant Island, approximately 200 miles northwest of Vancouver. Alert Bay is known for the "world's tallest totem pole" and as "home of the killer whale." Visit the U'Mista Cultural Centre, go marine mammal watching, or just simply relax and enjoy the scenery in which blue herons, bald eagles, and small fishing boats abound.

549 Fir Street.
Mail (✉): P.O. Box 302, Alert Bay, British Columbia V0N 1A0.
Phone (☎): 604-974-2026 or 604-974-5363.
Price (●): $13 CDN.
Closed (X): never.
Check-in (🕐): 5–11 p.m.
Grade: standard (♦).
Beds (🛏): 17.
Facilities: equipment storage area, kitchen, on-site parking, hostel-based programs, open all day.
Meals (🍴): breakfast, lunch, dinner (groups only upon request).
Family rooms (👪): available.
Groups (🎎): welcome.
Reservations essential (📅): July-August. **By phone:** 604-974-2026. **By FAX:** 604-974-5300.
Credit cards: not accepted.
Manager: Vivian Marchand.

Directions: from Port Hardy Airport (✈), take bus to Port McNeill, walk downhill (0.25 kilometres) to ferry, take ferry to Alert Bay (approximately 35 minutes), turn right from ferry and go 1 mile to hostel (taxi costs approximately $3).

British Columbia

Fernie

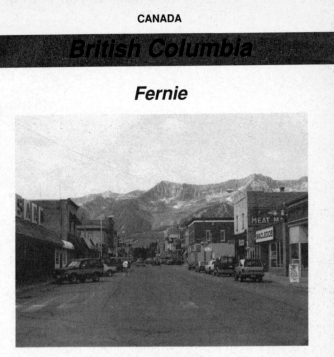

Fernie Hostel

Located in southeastern British Columbia, Fernie was previously a busy mining community. Today, the main attraction here is Fernie Snow Valley, the local ski mountain. However, Fernie is a year round resort offering fantastic hiking, horseback riding, and mountain biking. This is also a popular area for fishing and wildlife observation. The hostel is centrally located, just three blocks from the city centre it offers rooms with ensuite bathrooms. Activities such as ski lessons or guided hiking, fishing and mountain biking tours can be arranged from the hostel.

892 - 6th Avenue
Mail (✉): P.O. Box 580
Fernie, British Columbia
V0B 1M0.
Phone (☎): 604-423-6811.
Price (☎): $9 CDN.
Closed (X): never.
Check-in (⌂): 24 hours.
Grade: standard (♠).
Beds (⊨): 18.
Facilities: equipment storage area, kitchen, laundry facilities, on-site parking, **MSA**, open all day.
Family rooms (⌂): available.
Groups (⫫): welcome.
Reservations essential (☎): December 2–March 1. **By FAX:** 604-423-4397.
Credit Cards: Visa, MasterCard.

Directions: Bus: from station, walk 1 block east on 6th Avenue (to the corner of 9th Street).

British Columbia

Iskut

Red Goat Lodge

Come experience northern hospitality at its very best! The hostel, overlooking Eddontenajon Lake, is situated between two provincial parks—Mount Edziza and Spatsizi—where you'll find some of the finest wilderness trails in North America. The Stikine and Spatsizi Rivers provide unparalleled canoeing adventures in a truly pristine wilderness setting. Both rivers are accessible from the lodge. The ideal facility for the independent outdoors person, the hostel has everything from kitchen and drying room to modern washrooms and a coin-operated laundry.

Highway 37.
Mail (✉): P.O. Box 101, Iskut, British Columbia V0J 1K0.
Phone (☎): 604-234-3261.
Price (💰): $10 CDN.
Closed (X): October–May.
Check-in (🏠): 8 a.m.–noon, 2–10 p.m.
Grade: standard (♠).
Beds (🛏): 10.
Facilities: equipment storage area, kitchen, laundry facilities, lockers, on-site parking, canoe rental, open all day.
Meals (🍴): by special arrangement only.
Family rooms (👪): available.
Groups (👥): welcome.
Reservations essential (📅e): July-August for groups. **Reservations advisable** (📅a): always.

Off-season reservations: mail to Doreen Shaw, 3-29 Menzies Street, Victoria, British Columbia, V8V 2G1.
Credit cards: Visa.
Managers: Tony and Doreen Shaw.
Directions: from Iskut **Airport** (✈), follow Highway 37 south (3 kilometres) to Red Goat Lodge.

British Columbia

Kamloops

Kamloops "Old Courthouse" Hostel

Kamloops is located in the central interior of British Columbia, making it a great place to stop on the TransCanada Highway and a destination in itself. There are a variety of opportunities to enjoy activities such as horseback riding, swimming, fishing, hiking, and skiing. The "Old Courthouse", a former provincial court of law, was built in 1909. It has been renovated to preserve its history and the charm of its former use and to accommodate its new function as a hostel. Hostellers can take in the impressive decor while they enjoy a meal in the dining area, formerly the courtroom, complete with the original prisoner and witness boxes, jury seats, and judge's bench.

7 West Seymour Street
Kamloops, British Columbia
V2C 1E4
Mail (✉): same
Phone (☎): 604-828-7991
Price (●): $12.50 CDN (off-season rates available).
Closed (X): never.
Check-in (🕐): 8–11:30 a.m., 5–11:30 p.m.
Grade: standard (🏠).
Beds (🛏): 92.
Facilities: equipment storage area, kitchen, laundry facilities, lockers, parking on-site, linen rental, **MSA**, open all day.
Family rooms (👨‍👩‍👧): available.
Groups (🏛): welcome.
Reservations essential (📞): groups always, individuals (July 1–August 31) **By FAX:** 604-828-2442.

Credit Cards: Visa, MasterCard, JCB.
Directions: Bus: take bus #3 to West Seymour St. and 3rd Avenue, walk two blocks west. **Train:** 7 km from train station, take taxi to hostel, from airport taxi or shuttle bus.

British Columbia

Nanaimo

Nicol Street Hostel

The hub of Vancouver Island, Nanaimo is the gateway to Tofino and a great location from which to explore many parks and islands, experience bungy jumping, or visit famous petroglyphs. This hostel is centrally located, permits tenting ($7 per person), has a barbecue and, from the backyard, a great view of the ocean and mountains.

65 Nicol Street,
Nanaimo, British Columbia
V9R 4S7.
Mail (✉): same.
Phone (☎): 604-753-1188.
Price (🍴): $12 CDN.
Closed (X): January 1–April 30.
Check-in (🕐): 4–11 p.m.
Grade: standard (🏠).
Beds (🛏): 10.
Facilities: equipment storage area, kitchen, laundry facilities, linen rental, bicycle rentals, tenting space available, nonsmoking, **MSA**.
Groups (🏠): welcome.
Families (👪): welcome.
Reservations: not essential.
Credit cards: MasterCard, Visa.
Manager: Moni Murray.
Directions: Airport (✈): catch the PCL bus to Nanaimo bus station (15 kilometres), travel 1 kilometre north on Highway 1 (Nicol Street) to hostel. **Train:** from the station (1 kilometre) travel south on Selby Road, cross Victoria Road, head south 1 block on Finlayson Road, head north on Island Highway 1 (Nicol Street) to hostel, 1 block south of Harbour Park Mall.

British Columbia

SUPPLEMENTAL ACCOMMODATION

Nelson

Allen Hotel/Hostel

Situated on the shores of Kootenay Lake, Nelson is nestled in the Selkirk Mountains. It has two local ski areas, Whitewater and Morning Mountain, and offers opportunities galore for fishing and hiking. With more than 350 restored heritage buildings, Nelson has become a dream location for filmmakers. The Steve Martin film "Roxanne" and the Christine Lahti film "Housekeeping" were both shot here. The Allen Hotel offers semiprivate rooms and a communal kitchen (you supply your own pots and pans).

171 Baker Street,
Nelson, British Columbia V1L 4H1.
Mail (✉): same.
Phone (☎): 604-352-7573.
Price (◖): $12 CDN.
Closed (X): never.
Check-in (🕐): 5–10 p.m. (must phone first to register).
Grade: (SA).
Beds (🛏): 10.
Facilities: kitchen, laundry facilities, linen rental, on-site parking, air conditioning.

Family rooms (👪): available.
Groups (🏛): welcome.
Reservations essential (☎e): always.
Credit cards: not accepted.
Managers: Pauline and Anna Bowcock.
Directions: 45 kilometres from **Airport (✈)** on Highway 3A. **Bus:** from terminal, walk west on Highway 3A, turn east onto Baker Street, hostel is on the north side of the street.

British Columbia

Penticton

Penticton Hostel

Formerly a 1901 "Bank House", the Penticton Hostel is located in the heart of downtown, close to stores, beaches, and nightlife. Located on the southern tip of the Okanagan Lake, Penticton's recreational facilities include cross country and downhill skiing, ice fishing and snowmobiling in winter. During summer, enjoy golf, hiking, fishing, and a variety of water sports. The region is famous for its sweet peaches and wonderful wines. This is also the home of British Columbia's famous spring Blossom Festival, summer Peach Festival, and Iron Man Triathlon. In the fall, try some local wines at the Wine Tasting Festival.

464 Ellis Street
Penticton, British Columbia
V2A 4M2.
Mail (⌀): same.
Phone (☎): 604-492-3992.
Price (◔): $12.50 CDN (off-season rates available).
Closed (X): never.
Check-in (⏱): 8–11.30 a.m., 5–10 p.m.
Grade: standard (⌂).
Beds (🛏): 45.
Facilities: equipment storage area, kitchen, laundry facilities, lockers, on-site parking , backyard patio with barbecue, bicycle storage, bicycle rentals, **MSA**, open all day.
Family rooms (⌂): available.
Groups (⛺): welcome.

Reservations essential (⌀◔): groups (June–August) **By FAX:** 604-492-8755.
Credit Cards: Visa, MasterCard, JCB.
Directions: from bus station walk south one block, the hostel is on the left.

British Columbia

Powell River

Fiddlehead Farm

Fiddlehead Farm is an enchanting haven surrounded by uninhabited lakes, spectacular mountains, and temperate rain forest. You can walk along a peaceful mountain trail in the morning, swim and canoe in the afternoon, and relax in the steamy cedar sauna in the evening. Due to the hostel's isolated location, one week's stay is preferred. Tenting is permitted for $13. Prices are based on two hours of farm chores (picking fruit, milking the cow, etc.) and include all meals.

Mail (✉): Box 421, Powell River, British Columbia V8A 5C2.

Phone (☎): Call the operator and ask for "Courtney, British Columbia, Marine Operator"; ask the Marine Operator to page the Fiddlehead Courtney Channel 23 #N128507.

Price (●): $18 CDN (includes meals and 2 hours of farm chores; reduced rates for long-term stays).

Closed (X): never.

Grade: simple (⌂). **Beds (🛏):** 18.

Facilities: laundry, wood stove, piano, sauna, canoes, camping, open all day.

Meals (🍴): breakfast, lunch, dinner (included in overnight fee).

Family rooms (👪): available.

Groups (⛺): welcome.

Reservations essential (☎): always.

Credit cards: MasterCard, Visa.

Manager: Linda Scheiber.

Directions: from Powell River go to Powell Lake Marina, hostellers are picked up by private boat (prior arrangement absolutely necessary); accessible only by private boat ($10 return). From Vancouver you must catch the 8:30 a.m. Maverik bus from the greyhound bus terminal.

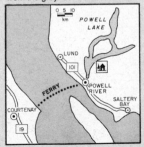

British Columbia

Vancouver

Vancouver International Hostel

Located in Jericho Park, Vancouver International Hostel is next to one of the city's finest beaches and just 15 minutes from downtown by public transportation. The idyllic setting is typical of Vancouver—beautiful waterways, rolling green parklands, and impressive mountains. Gastown, in the downtown core, was where Vancouver began in 1866 as a modest timber community on the shores of the Burrard Inlet, now Vancouver Harbour. Near the hostel, the University of British Columbia's Museum of Anthropology features exceptional displays of Indian culture and history. Stanley Park is one of the largest, most spectacular urban parks in North America with more than 1,000 acres, a variety of hiking and bicycling trails, a small zoo, and a large new aquarium.

1515 Discovery Street,
Vancouver, British Columbia
V6R 4K5.
Mail (✉): same.
Phone (☎): 604-224-3208.
Price (☻): $13.50 CDN (max. member's rate, off-season rates available).
Closed (X): never.
Check-in (⌂): 7:30 a.m.–midnight.
Grade: superior (👤).
Beds (🛏): 282.
Facilities: equipment storage area, kitchen, laundry facilities, linen rental, lockers, safety deposit boxes, on-site parking, bicycle rentals, locked bicycle shed, **MSA**, open all day.
Meals (🍴): breakfast, dinner (March–October).
Family rooms (👪): available.
Groups (🏠): welcome.
Reservations advisable (📠): available via IBN and Pacific Rim Fax-a-bed. **FAX:** 604-224-4852.

Credit cards: MasterCard, Visa, JCB.
Directions: follow West Fourth to NW Marine Drive, right at Jericho Park West. **Airport (✈):** take bus #100 to 70th and Granville, transfer to bus #20 to Sixth Avenue, cross Granville Street (use the underpass) and take bus #4 south to NW Marine Drive, walk downhill and take the first right turn at Jericho Park West.

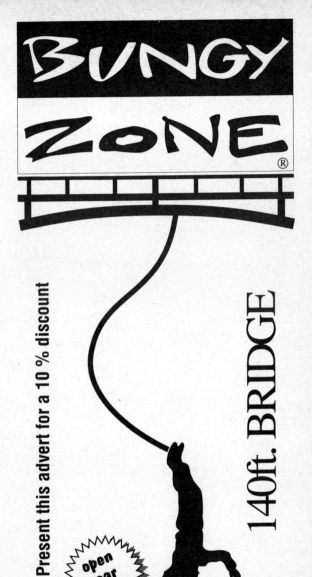

British Columbia

Victoria A

Selkirk Guest House

The Selkirk Guest House is a well-kept heritage building offering accommodation to hostellers visiting Victoria. It is located just outside the city centre on Selkirk Waters, and is still easily accessible to many of Victoria's attractions and outdoor activities. It's just a 20-minute canoe ride to downtown. A private dock at the guest house allows guests to enjoy a variety of watersports including swimming, kayaking and canoeing. A pick-up service from the Yates Street hostel and from the bus station is available.

934 Selkirk Avenue
Victoria, British Columbia
V9A 2V1.
Mail (✉): same.
Phone (☎): 604-389-1213.
Price (●): $12.50 CDN.
Closed (X): never.
Check-in (◻): 4–11 p.m.
Grade: home hostel (🏠).
Beds (🛏): 22.
Facilities: equipment storage area, kitchen, laundry facilities, on-site parking, canoe and rowboat rental, swimming, open all day.
Family rooms (👨‍👩‍👧): available.
Groups (🎪): welcome.
Reservations essential (📠): all year. **By FAX:** 604-389-1313.
Credit Cards: not accepted.
Manager: Norm and Lynn Jackson.

Directions: from the corner of Tillicum and Selkirk continue east on Selkirk, 3–4 km from train and bus station. (Phone for pick up from hostel on Yates St. or from downtown bus station).

British Columbia

Victoria B

Victoria International Hostel

Victoria, which began as a Hudson's Bay fur trading post in 1843, has been the capital of British Columbia since 1871. With its turn-of-the-century heritage exterior restored, the Victoria International Hostel is an important part of Victoria's past. Completely renovated in 1991, the hostel is one of the heritage buildings in Victoria's historic city centre. Walking tours of the nearby heritage buildings are available at the hostel as well as video shows and talks. Most of Victoria's main attractions, including the beautiful waterfront, the historic Parliament buildings, and the incredible Royal British Columbia Museum, which houses 12,000 years of British Columbia history, are within easy walking distance. The hostel makes an excellent base to plan day trips and to gather information about the island's many parks and marine attractions.

516 Yates Street, Victoria, British Columbia V8W 1K8.
Mail (✉): same.
Phone (☎): 604-385-4511.
Price (☕): $13.50 CDN (max. member's rate, off-season rates available).
Closed (X): never.
Check-in (🕐): 7:30 a.m.–midnight (doors open till 2 a.m.).
Grade: superior (👥).
Beds (🛏): 104.
Facilities: equipment storage area, kitchen, laundry facilities, linen rental, lockers, safety deposit boxes, wheelchair accessible (♿), games room, hostel-based programs, **MSA**, open all day.
Family rooms (👶): available.
Groups (🎪): welcome.

Reservations essential (📞): during summer, families and groups always.
Credit cards: MasterCard, Visa, JCB.
Directions: on Yates Street near Wharf Street; close to bus station and train station.

British Columbia

Whistler

Whistler Hostel

Whistler Hostel is a rustic timber cabin on picturesque Alta Lake, a 10-minute drive from the alpine village of Whistler. The Whistler Ski Resort ranked first and second in two recent independent studies. The incredible natural beauty of the surroundings beckons visitors from around the world. Whistler offers a variety of activities from mountain biking, hiking, and river rafting to horseback riding and skiing. At the hostel, go swimming or enjoy a canoe ride on the lake. The village is the spot for nightlife and year-round cultural events, including summer music festivals.

5678 Alta Lake Road.
Mail (✉): P.O. Box 128, Whistler, British Columbia V0N 1B0.
Phone (☎): 604-932-5492.
Price (●): $13.50 CDN (max. member's rate, off-season rates available).
Closed (X): never.
Check-in (◖): 8–10 a.m., 5–10 p.m.
Grade: standard (♠).
Beds (⊨): 33.
Facilities: kitchen, linen rental, free use of canoes and inner tubes, table tennis, pool table, wood stove, piano, guitar, ski tuning room, ski lockers, row boat, sauna, drying room, **MSA**, open all day.
Family rooms (♔): available.
Groups (⏁): welcome.
Reservations essential (⊭e): groups.
Reservations advisable (⊭a): November–March. **By FAX:** 604-932-5492.

Credit cards: MasterCard, Visa, JCB.
Directions: 121 kilometres north of Vancouver off Highway 99 on Alta Lake Road; approximately 5 kilometres from the cutoff, hostel is on the right. **Train:** B.C. Rail will stop at hostel when requested. **Bus:** from loop walk north along the Valley Trail to Rainbow Park, then follow the road to the left and walk 400 metres. The distance is 4 kilometres.

British Columbia

Yoho National Park

Whiskey Jack Hostel

Whiskey Jack Hostel is located in Yoho National Park, 27 kilometres west of Lake Louise. It is within a kilometre of Takakkaw Falls, one of Canada's five highest waterfalls. For solitude and great hiking, in an idyllic setting, Whiskey Jack offers it all. The hostel itself was the staff quarters of an old hotel, which was swept away in an avalanche many years ago. Visitors can lounge on the front porch, with its view of Takakkaw Falls and relax around the campfire at the end of the day.

Yoho National Park
Mail (✉): Box 1358, Banff, Alberta T0L 0C0.
Price (☺): $9 CDN.
Closed (X): October–mid-June.
Check-in (🕐): 4–10 p.m.
Grade: simple (🏠).
Beds (🛏): 27.
Facilities: equipment storage area, kitchen, lockers, on-site parking, **MSA**, open all day.
Groups (🛏🛏): welcome, reservations required.
Reservations advisable (📞): always. **By phone:** 403-762-4122 or 237-8282 (within Calgary calling area). **By FAX:** 403-762-3441.
Credit cards: MasterCard, Visa (reservations only).

Directions: 13 kilometres west along the Yoho Valley Road from Kicking Horse campground, 27 kilometres west of Lake Louise on Highway 1 (Trans-Canada Highway).

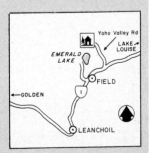

YHA AUSTRALIA

Australia... the friendly way!

In Australia YHA has a network of over 145 friendly hostels in Australia's best locations. YHA offers you:

- comfortable clean low cost facilities
- a friendly, relaxed hostel atmosphere
- self-catering facilities to save you money
- coach and other travel discounts for YHA members
- No Age Limit

The Australian Youth Hostels Association has developed a network of travel agencies servicing its domestic and overseas members. Each office provides facilities for hostel accommodation bookings, bus and airline ticketing and valuable information on Australia's favourite tourist destinations. Visit any of the following offices and you will be greeted by the friendly YHA travel staff.

SYDNEY, 422 Kent Street, NSW 2000 (02) 261 1111
MELBOURNE, 205 King Street, VIC 3000 (03) 670 9611
DARWIN Hostel Complex, Beaton Road via Hidden Valley Road, Berrimah NT0821 (089) 84 3902
BRISBANE, 154 Roma Street, QLD 4000 (07) 236 1680
ADELAIDE, State Office, 38 Sturt Street, SA 5000 (08) 231 5583
HOBART, 1st Floor, 28 Criterion Street, TAS 7000 (002) 34 9617
PERTH, 65 Francis Street, WA 6000 (09) 227 5122

Please send me ☐ general information package plus the full Australian YHA Directory

Name ....

Address ....

.... Postcode ....

Country ....

Send to: **Australian YHA, Level 3, 10 Mallett St, Camperdown NSW 2050**

C.A.H/93

Manitoba

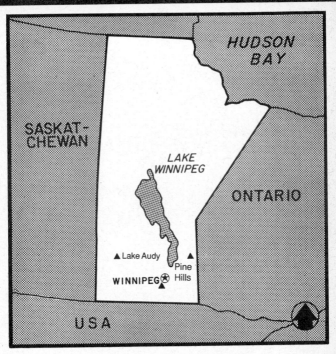

Helpful Organizations

Hostelling International—Canada Regional Office

Manitoba
194A Sherbrook Street
Winnipeg, Manitoba
R3C 2B6
Phone (☎): 204-784-1131
FAX: 204-784-1133

Provincial Tourism Office

Travel Manitoba
Dept. 7020, 7th floor
155 Carlton Street
Winnipeg, Manitoba
R3C 3H8
Phone (☎): 204-945-3777,
800-665-0040

Manitoba hostels offer all day access

Manitoba is a province of lakes, rivers, and vast forests, as well as a rich cultural heritage. Winnipeg, the provincial capital, reflects the multi-cultural background of the 2.5 million immigrants who opened up the prairies in the early years of the 20th century.

Manitoba

Lake Audy, Onanole

Riding Mountain Guest Ranch

Riding Mountain Guest Ranch is nestled in the heart of scenic lake and hill country. The area hosts a mix of prairie, aspen woodland and boreal forest with a diversity of habitats and a wealth of plant and animal life including elk, moose, black bears, beavers, and porcupines. Year-round activities include horseback riding lessons, trail riding, hay rides, hiking, canoeing, and campfire cookouts. Nearby Riding Mountain National Park, with beautiful Clear Lake and Lake Audy, offers further opportunities for outdoor adventure with swimming, fishing, hiking, and cycling trails. The Clear Lake tourist area has shops, a theatre, and an art gallery. The bison enclosure is also a popular spot.

Lake Audy
Onanole, Manitoba
R0J 0Z0.
Mail (✉): same.
Phone (☎): 204-848-2265.
Price (◖): $16 CDN.
Closed (X): September 1–May 30.
Check-in (⏲): 8 a.m.–8 p.m.
Grade: (SA).
Beds (🛏): 24.

Facilities: equipment storage area, laundry facilities, on-site parking, open all day.
Groups (⏍): welcome.
Reservations (r): essential.
Credit cards: not accepted.
Manager: Jim and Candy Irwin.
Directions: from Onanole go west on Highway 270 and then north on Highway 359 to Lake Audy.

Manitoba

Pine Falls (Powerview)

The Maskwa Project

The Maskwa Project Hostel is a rustic retreat on 100 acres of undisturbed wilderness on the banks of the Maskwa River. The project was conceived and developed by a group of concerned citizens during the oil crisis of the 1970s. Water is heated by solar energy. Food is grown organically and the ever-expanding garden offers visitors the opportunity to take part in tending it. Light is generated by solar power. Waste is recycled and wood provides heat in the super-insulated cottage-style buildings. The wide and slow-moving river is perfect for swimming and canoeing. The nearby roads make excellent cross-country ski trails. The northern lights at night, the rapids, and waterfalls nearby make for a wonderful wilderness experience.

Bear River Road.
Mail (✉): General Delivery, Powerview, Manitoba R0E 1P0.
Phone (☎): 204-367-4390.
Price (◔): $9.50 CDN.
Closed (X): never.
Check-in (ⵔ): 24 hours.
Grade: basic (⌂).
Beds (🛏): 35.
Facilities: equipment storage area, kitchen, meeting room, on-site parking, solar-heated bath house and sauna, camping, gazebo, recreational facilities, open all day.
Family rooms (👪): available.
Groups (𝄫): welcome.
Reservations essential (☎e): always. **By mail:** 194 Sherbrook Street, Winnipeg, Manitoba R3C 2B6. **By phone:** 204-784-1131. **By FAX:** 204-784-1133.

Credit cards: not accepted.
Managers: Jill and Ken Phillips.
Directions: north on Highway 59 from Winnipeg, east on Route 304 to Broadlands Road, left on Maskwa Road. **Bus:** Grey Goose provides daily bus service to Peddin's Gas Bar in Powerview, pick-up can be arranged with prior notice.

Manitoba

Winnipeg

Ivey House International Hostel

Ivey House International Hostel, named for Grace Ivey, the founder of hostelling in Manitoba, is an important part of Winnipeg's historic past. A Victorian-style home built in 1908, it is within easy walking distance of the city's many historic and cultural attractions. A number of historic buildings can be found along Main Street and through the Old Market Square. Situated on the river's edge, the Forks National Historic Site offers interpretive programs, including a public archaeological dig. The Museum of Man and Nature traces millions of years of Manitoba's history. The French quarter, St. Boniface, is the largest Francophone community west of Québec. The city celebrates its cultural diversity with the lively Folk Festival and the Fringe Theatre Festival.

210 Maryland Street,
Winnipeg, Manitoba
R3G 1L6.
Mail (✉): same.
Phone (☎): 204-772-3022.
Price (☻): $12 CDN.
Closed (X): never.
Check-in (⌚): 5 p.m.–midnight.
Grade: standard (⚑).
Beds (🛏): 38.
Facilities: equipment storage area, new kitchen and dining room, laundry facilities, limited street parking, sun deck, bicycle rentals, hostel-based programs, **MSA**, open all day.
Family rooms (⚲): available.
Groups (⚏): welcome.
Reservations: not essential.
Credit cards: MasterCard, Visa, JCB.
Manager: Kelly Hartry.

Directions: Bus: walk west on Portage Avenue to Maryland Street, then head south. **Train:** walk west on Broadway or take bus #29 to Broadway and Sherbrook, walk west 1 block to Maryland. **Airport (✈):** take bus #15 to Sargent Avenue and Maryland, transfer to bus #29 to Broadway and Maryland.

New Brunswick

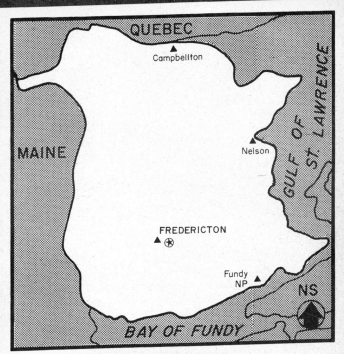

Helpful Organizations

Hostelling International—Canada Regional Office

New Brunswick
c/o Dawna Crosby
150 Leeds Drive
Fredericton, New Brunswick E3B 4S8
Phone (☎): 506-454-9950

Provincial Tourism Office

Tourism New Brunswick
P.O. Box 12345
Fredericton, New Brunswick
E3B 5C3
Phone (☎): 506-453-8745,
800-442-4442 (within province),
800-561-0123

New Brunswick is home to the Bay of Fundy, where the highest tides in the world bring in 100 million tons of sea every 12 hours! It is a land of evergreen forests, meandering rivers, and a coastline of sandy beaches and sheltered coves. The province is still rich in the Acadian traditions brought by the early French settlers.

New Brunswick

Alma

Fundy National Park Hostel

Fundy National Park is centrally located just an hour's drive from Moncton and two hours from Fredericton and Saint John. It's only a few hours from the Maine–Brunswick border and within a day's drive from Montréal or Boston. The area offers a variety of impressive maritime scenery, from fog-shrouded shores to sun-dappled forests, from steep coastal cliffs to tide-washed beaches, from bubbly streams to enchanted waterfalls.

The Fundy National Park Hostel is a 20-bed facility made up of small rustic cabins located right in the park. It is an excellent way to fully experience the surrounding park land. The hostel overlooks the Bay of Fundy, which boasts the world's highest tides (16 metres). Visitors can stroll along the ocean floor at low tide. There's also a swimming pool nearby.

Fundy National Park
Mail (✉): General Delivery, P.O. Box 40 Alma, New Brunswick E0A 1B0.
Phone (☎): 506-887-2216.
Price (⊜): $8.50 CDN.
Closed (X): September 1–May 31.
Check-in (⏰): 8:30–10 a.m., 4:30–10 p.m.
Grade: simple (⌂).
Beds (▬): 20.
Facilities: baggage storage area, kitchen, on-site parking, wheelchair accessible (♿).
Family rooms (👪): available.
Groups (⛺): welcome.
Reservations: not essential. **Off-season:** mail to CHA-Nova Scotia, P.O. Box 3010 South, Halifax, Nova Scotia B3J 3G6.

Credit cards: not accepted.
Directions: Take Highway 2 (Trans-Canada Highway) south, turn onto Route 114 and continue to Fundy National Park.

New Brunswick

Campbellton

Campbellton Lighthouse Youth Hostel

Campbellton is the main centre in this river-rich region. It was named for Sir Archibald Campbell, lieutenant governor of New Brunswick at the time of the city's founding in 1770. The region is famous for its Atlantic salmon, and the fun-filled annual festival pays tribute to this important local delicacy.

Part of Campbellton's recent waterfront development, Canada's only lighthouse hostel is situated on the banks of the Restigouche River, which winds through rolling forested hills to the scenic lowlands bordering the Baie des Chaleurs. The bridge near Campbellton leads to the rugged and beautiful Gaspé region of Québec. Good downhill skiing is available nearby. Explore the many trails that wind through the park lands and shorelines.

1 Ritchie Street.
Mail (✉): P.O. Box 100, Campbellton, New Brunswick E3N 3G1.
Phone (☎): 506-753-7044.
Price (●): $10 CDN.
Closed (X): September–June.
Check-in (⌂): 4 p.m.–midnight.
Grade: standard (♠).
Beds (➤): 20.
Facilities: equipment storage area, kitchen, laundry facilities, lockers, on-site parking, camping, **MSA**.
Groups (⬜): welcome.
Reservations advisable (⬜a): always. Reservation address: same as mailing address.

Credit cards: not accepted.
Contact: Julie Jardine.
Directions: on the city's waterfront, south of Restigouche River.

New Brunswick

Fredericton

York House Hostel

Named in honour of the second son of King George III, Fredericton was at one time an important military centre. Today it is New Brunswick's capital, stretching along the picturesque banks of the Saint John River. The city's military history is relived at the Officer's Square and Compound. The York Sunbury Historical Society Museum has exhibits on the Micmac and Malecite Indians. The renowned Beaverbrook Art Gallery houses works by Dali, Hogarth, and Kreighoff.

First opened in 1893 as Fredericton's grammar school, York House Hostel is a designated heritage property. It has also served as a public library. Close by you'll find an aquatics centre with boat rentals, a craft school, and two universities. In summer, the streets of Fredericton are alive with outdoor theatre, concerts, and festivals.

193 York Street,
Fredericton, New Brunswick
E3B 3N8.
Mail (✉): same.
Phone (☎): 506-454-1233.
Price (◑): $9 CDN.
Closed (X): September–June.
Check-in (🕓): 4 p.m.–midnight.
Grade: standard (⬆).
Beds (🛏): 30.
Facilities: equipment storage area, kitchen, laundry facilities (nearby), linen rental, on-site parking, **MSA**.
Meals (🍴): breakfast, pack lunch, dinner.
Family rooms (👪): available.
Groups (𝗍𝗍𝗍𝗍): welcome.
Reservations: not essential.
Credit cards: not accepted.

Contact: Mike Bravener, 506-458-8348.
Directions: on York Street near George Street; close to bus station and airport transportation.

New Brunswick

Nelson

Beaubear Manor

Overlooking Beaubear Island National Park on the Miramichi River is the charming Beaubear Manor. An historic inn, it offers "antique ambiance" with period pieces, an antique fireplace, well-stocked library and a music room, complete with Steinway piano. From the spacious grounds enjoy spectacular river views and stroll through pleasant gardens. There's also a private beach. Bicycling, nature trail hikes, clam-digging, and heritage home tours are offered. Canoes and motor boat rentals are available. Try salmon fishing or deep sea fishing on local lobster boats. The area hosts a number of festivals, including the National Irish Festival (July 17–19); the Miramichi Jazz Festival (July 1); and the Scottish Provincial Festival (mid-August).

Beaubear Manor
Nelson, New Brunswick
E0C 1T0.
Phone (☎): 506-622-3036.
Price (◐): $15 CDN.
Closed (X): never.
Check-in (◖): all day.
Grade: standard (♠).
Beds (►): 24.
Facilities: kitchen, library and music room, on-site parking, canoe and boat rentals, open all day.
Family rooms (♨): available.
Groups (IIIII): welcome.
Reservations: not essential.
Credit Cards: not accepted.

Directions: on the Miramichi River, opposite the town of New-castle, 5 kilometres from train and bus.

Newfoundland

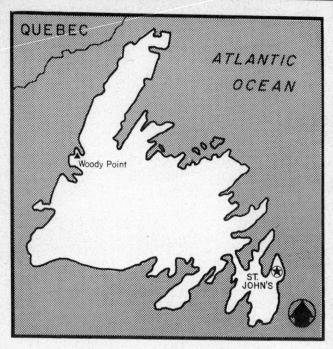

Helpful Organizations

Hostelling International—Canada Regional Office

Newfoundland
P.O. Box 1815
St. John's, Newfoundland
A1C 5P9
Phone (☎): 709-739-5866

Provincial Tourism Office

Department of Tourism
P.O. Box 2016
St. John's, Newfoundland
A1C 5R8
Phone (☎): 709-729-2830,
800-563-6353

Newfoundland's Woody Point Hostel offers all day access

Newfoundland, once a Viking settlement, has a rich history of seafaring and fishing traditions. It is also home to the spectacular landscapes of Gros Morne National Park and a provincial capital that boasts the oldest shopping street in North America. It's Canada's youngest province.

Discounts

Present a valid hostel membership card at the time of purchase to receive the following discounts:

St. John's
Rent-A-Wreck - 43 Pippy Place, 753-2277. $5 off per rental or $25 off for a week or more.

Newfoundland

Woody Point (Bonne Bay)

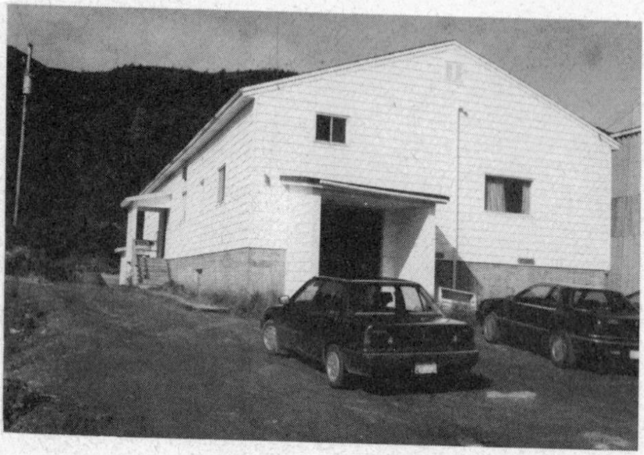

Woody Point Hostel

Woody Point Hostel is situated in the beautiful Bonne Bay Area in Gros Morne National Park. Eons ago this area was honed by glaciers during the Ice Age into a panorama of lakes, deep fjords, and mountains. Add to this the incredible ocean scenery and you have one of the most exciting and beautiful areas in the province. It was designated a UNESCO World Heritage Site in 1988. The park offers hiking trails for all skill levels. Try a challenging full-day hike up to the summit of Gros Morne Mountain or follow meandering trails to the marine exhibits at Lobster Cove Head. The most unique activity in the area is whale-watching. Local boat tours are available. In the town of Woody Point, learn more about local history with a visit to Pioneer Village.

Community Hall, School Road.
Mail (✉): c/o Bonne Bay Development Association, P.O. Box 159, Bonne Bay, Newfoundland A0K 1P0.
Phone (☎): 709-453-2442 (hostel) or 709-453-2470 (office).
Price (☎): $10 CDN.
Closed (X): October–May.
Check-in (c): 10 a.m.–11 p.m.
Grade: simple (⌂). **Beds (━):** 10.
Facilities: equipment storage areas, kitchen, laundry services available, on-site parking, boat rentals, **MSA**, open all day.
Groups (ⅢⅢ): 10 maximum.
Reservations essential (⌂e): groups.
Credit cards: not accepted.
Manager: Emma Gillam.
Directions: take Highway 430 from Deer Lake to Wiltondale, take Route 431 into Woody Point, the hostel is on School Road, close to bus station.

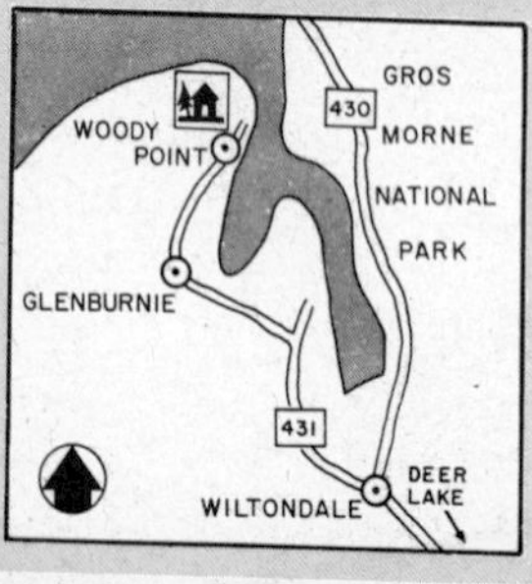

Come way down under
if you can stand the excitement!

This is the latest craze in New Zealand — jumping off a bridge with only a rubber band to stop your fall.

Its called bungee jumping and it is just one of the many exciting attractions New Zealand has to offer.

Rafting, jet boating, skiing and some of the best hiking in the world are just a few of the others.

Another feature New Zealand has to offer is one of the finest

YHA Hostel chains — in 50+ convenient locations, open all day, superb facilities, with the friendliest managers and hard to beat prices. And, of course, for YHA members there are discounts available on most of the attractions mentioned.

So why don't you come way down under this year? You'll be pleased you did.

YHA
NEW ZEALAND

For more information contact your local YHA or write for a free copy of our "Good Bed Guide" to:
YHANZ, P.O. Box 436, Christchurch, New Zealand
Telephone 64 33 799 970. Fax 64 33 654 476.

Nova Scotia

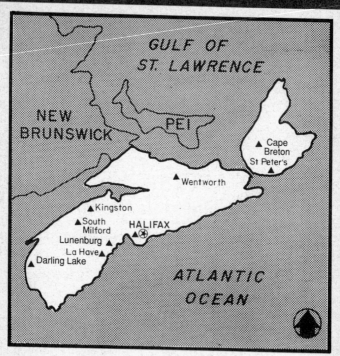

Helpful Organizations

Hostelling International—Canada Regional Office

Nova Scotia
Sport Nova Scotia Centre
5516 Spring Garden Road
P.O. Box 3010 South
Halifax, Nova Scotia B3J 3G6
Phone (☎): 902-425-5450
FAX: 902-425-5606

Provincial Tourism Office

Nova Scotia Department of Tourism
P.O. Box 456
Halifax, Nova Scotia
B3J 2R5
Phone (☎): 902-425-5781,
800-565-0000

Nova Scotia, with its spectacular coastal drives and uncrowded beaches, is Canada's ocean playground. The world's second-largest natural harbour is located in Halifax, and the province is a lively mix of seafaring traditions and Scottish and French ancestry.

Discounts

Present a valid hostel membership card at the time of purchase to receive the following discounts:

Halifax
Rent-A-Wreck - 2823 Robie Street, 454-2121. $5 off per rental or $25 off for a week or more.

Nova Scotia

Cape Breton

Glenmore International Hostel

Cape Breton is an island where past and present live side by side and where people are as down-to-earth as the land itself. Spend a day at one of the fine sandy beaches on the shores of Lake Ainslie or picnic at Trout Brook Provincial Park, located on Route 395. Also on Route 395, overlooking Lake Ainslie, is the MacDonald House Historic site. This site includes a restored Gothic-style 1839 farmhouse, carpentry tools, crafts, a housing loom, a spinning wheel, and a one-room schoolhouse.

The Glenmore International Hostel has recently been expanded and offers 11 beds, indoor bathrooms, and a kitchen. Visitors can buy fresh vegetables, bread, and eggs. Recreational opportunities in the area include hiking and boating. It is advisable to call ahead before checking in.

R.R. #1, Whycocomah,
Twin Rock Valley,
Cape Breton, Nova Scotia
B0E 3M0.
Mail (✉): same.
Phone (☎): 902-258-3622.
Price (●): $10 CDN (June 15–September 30); $13 (October 1–June 14).
Closed (X): never.
Check-in (🕐): 7–9 a.m., 4–10 p.m.
Grade: simple (🏠).
Beds (🛏): 11.
Facilities: baggage storage area, kitchen, on-site parking.
Groups (🏠): welcome.
Reservations essential (☎●): for more than 5 people.
Credit cards: not accepted.
Manager: Jeff Feigin.

Directions: take Trans-Canada Highway to Route 395, turn right immediately after second bridge onto Twin Rock Valley Road, go 1-3/4 miles to hostel.

Nova Scotia

Darling Lake

The Ice House Hostel

Located just 22 kilometres from Yarmouth, this unique hostel once stored ice for Churchill Mansion, the Victorian summer home of shipping magnate Aaron (Rudder) Churchill. Churchill Mansion is a registered Nova Scotia heritage property and has retained much of its original charm. The beautiful country estate overlooks picturesque Darling Lake. The Widow's Walk Cupola offers a spectacular view of two lakes and the Bay of Fundy. Nearby attractions include quaint fishing villages, salt water beaches, canoeing, antique shops and museums.

Highway 1 (Evangeline Trail)
Mail (✉): R.R. 1,
Yarmouth, Nova Scotia B5A 4A5.
Phone (☎): 902-649-2818.
Price (💲): $8.50 CDN.
Closed (X): October 15–May 10.
Check-in (🕐): 1–9 p.m.
Grade: home hostel (🏠).
Beds (🛏): 4.

Facilities: baggage storage area, kitchen, on-site parking.
Credit cards: MasterCard, Visa.
Manager: Connie Nicholl.
Directions: from Yarmouth, north-east 22 kilometres on highway 1, turn of at Darling Lake.

Nova Scotia

Halifax

Halifax Heritage House Hostel

Founded in 1749 to establish British strength in the North Atlantic, Halifax is a city full of history and culture. It has been a thriving seaport and naval station from its earliest days. The capital of Nova Scotia, it is known as the "City of Trees" because of its eight major parks. Halifax also boasts an active community of local performing arts groups and plays host to a great variety of festivals and cultural events, including the renowned Nova Scotia International Tattoo, held in July.

Centrally located, the Halifax Heritage House Hostel is within easy walking distance of downtown shopping, historic sites like Citadel Hill, and Point Pleasant and Cornwallis parks. It is near the trendy waterfront, which is a picturesque mixture of renovated 18th-century buildings housing contemporary shops and restaurants.

1253 Barrington Street,
Halifax, Nova Scotia B3J 1Y3.
Mail (✉): same.
Phone (☎): 902-422-3863.
Price (⬤): $12 CDN.
Closed (X): never.
Check-in (🕐): 7–10 a.m., 4–11 p.m.
Grade: standard (♦).
Beds (🛏): 50.
Facilities: baggage storage area, kitchen, laundry facilities, linen rental, on-site parking, small store, Heritage programs, **MSA**.
Family rooms (👪): available.
Groups (🎪): welcome.
Credit cards: Visa.

Directions: on Barrington Street, 500 meters from train station, 7 km from bus station.

Nova Scotia

Kingston

Bishop Mountain Hostel

Bishop Mountain Hostel is situated amidst rich dairy and fruit country. It's a rural Canadian farmstead located just outside the town of Kingston in a secluded, peaceful setting on the North Mountain. A car or at least a mountain bike is needed to travel the 11-kilometre dirt road that leads to the hostel. Plan on arriving during daylight.

This farm hostel offers a unique opportunity to experience rural Canadian life in the Maritimes. Friendly farm animals greet visitors upon their arrival. Kingston is the site of Nova Scotia's annual steer barbecue, the largest in the province. Nearby Clairmont Provincial Park offers delightful picnic areas in a scenic natural setting of red pine forest. Hiking, mountain biking, canoeing, and fishing can all be enjoyed in the area. The spectacular Bay of Fundy is just minutes away.

Bishop Mountain Road.
Mail (✉): P.O. Box 433, Kingston, Nova Scotia B0P 1R0.
Phone (☎): 902-765-3555.
Price (⬤): $6 CDN.
Closed (X): September 1–May 31.
Check-in (◍): any time before 10 p.m.
Grade: basic (⌂).
Beds (⊨): 12.
Facilities: equipment storage area, kitchen, on-site parking, swimming pond, open all day.
Groups (⊞): welcome.
Reservations essential (☎): groups.
Credit cards: not accepted.

Manager: Peter Gubbins.
Directions: 11 kilometres north of Kingston on Bishop Mountain Road (exit off Highway 101).

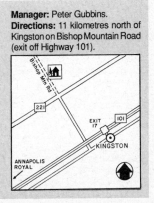

Nova Scotia

LaHave

LaHave Marine Hostel

LaHave is a small community with an important historical background. It was here that the French explorer de Monts first landed in 1604 and established Fort Sainte-Marie-de-Grâce. The name comes from Cap LaHève, a cape in France near de Monts' departure point. It is believed that the first school in Canada was started here in the 1630s by the Capuchin fathers. The actual site of de Monts' landing is commemorated by the Fort Point Museum, housed in a former lighthouse keeper's home. Just a few hundred yards away is LaHave Marine Hostel. It's located in a building that served as the headquarters of the original LaHave Outfitting Company on an historic wharf overlooking the LaHave River. For a special treat, visit the hostel manager's bakery for fresh breads, rolls, cakes, and cookies.

Mail (✉): c/o LaHave Outfitters, P.O. Box 92, LaHave, Nova Scotia B0R 1C0.
Phone (☎): 902-688-2908.
Price (💰): $9 CDN.
Closed (X): October–May.
Check-in (🕐): noon–7 p.m.
Grade: simple (🏠).
Beds (🛏): 8.
Facilities: equipment storage area, kitchen, laundry facilities, on-site parking, scuba equipment rental, coastal excursions by boat, open all day.
Family rooms (👪): available.
Reservations: not essential.
Credit cards: Visa.

Managers: Michael and Gael Watson.
Directions: 15 minutes from Bridgewater on Route 331.

Nova Scotia

HOME HOSTEL

Lunenburg

Lunenburg Hostel

Lunenburg is Canada's oldest German settlement. It was hailed for its distinctive architecture as "Canada's prettiest town" by *Equinox* magazine, and has been named a national heritage site. Lunenburg is also known as the home of the tall ships. The HMS Rose, the largest tall ship in the world, was built here.

Built in 1879, the Lunenburg Hostel is in the historic part of town. The four-bed rooms have ensuite bathrooms. The scenic harbourfront is a short walk away, and the Knot Pub is a favourite for its good fare and low prices. Hostel manager, David Callan, speaks English, "Deutsch", and "Français". Boat tours are available for seal and whale watching.

9 King Street,
Lunenburg, Nova Scotia B0J 2C0.
Mail (✉): same.
Phone (☎): 902-634-9146.
Price (☞): $12.50 CDN.
Closed (X): October–April.
Check-in (⏰): 4–8 p.m.
Grade: home hostel (🏠).
Beds (🛏): 8.
Facilities: baggage storage area, cold kitchen, laundry facilities, linen rental, some on-site parking, free use of bicycles.
Meals (🍴): breakfast.
Family rooms (👪): available.
Groups (👥): not accepted.
Reservations: not essential.
By FAX: 902-634-3019.
Credit cards: not accepted.
Manager: David Callan.
Directions: centrally located in the town of Lunenburg.

St. Peter's

Joyce's Motel and Cottages

Joyce's Motel and Cottages is located just 1 mile east of the town of St. Peter's. There are a variety of recreational activities available, including boating, swimming, hiking and fishing. The nearby Bras d'Or Lake offers all of these pastimes and is also a perfect spot for wildlife watching. Historic landmarks in the area include Provincial Battery Park with its historic old fort. Visitors can also explore MacAskill House and Nicholas Denny's Museum.

Mail (✉): Box 193
St. Peters, Nova Scotia
B0E 3B0.
Phone (☎): 902-535-2404.
Price (◓): $10 CDN.
Closed (X): October 1–June 15.
Check-in (🕐): 1–11 p.m.
Grade (SA).
Beds (🛏): 6.

Facilities: baggage storage area, kitchen, laundry facilities, linen rental, on-site parking, swimming pool, horse shoe pit, outdoor fireplace, all day access.
Reservations : not essential.
Credit Cards: Visa, MasterCard.
Manager: Ralph Robertson.
Directions: 2.5 kilometres east of St. Peters on Highway 4. 1.5 kilometres from bus terminal.

Nova Scotia

South Milford

Sandy Bottom Lake Hostel

Located in South Milford between the historic town of Annapolis Royal and scenic Kejimkujik National Park, Sandy Bottom Hostel is perfect for those who love the outdoors. The hostel offers a complete canoe outfitting rental service. Swimming is available nearby, and a good network of cross-country ski trails leads through the picturesque surroundings. The region is dotted with small communities, most of which are located near rivers or lakes. Annapolis Royal, founded in 1605, is the oldest settlement in Canada. A walking tour of downtown, with buildings dating back to 1712, provides glimpses of the area's rich history.

Virginia Road.
Mail (✉): R.R. 4, Annapolis Royal, Nova Scotia B0S 1A0.
Phone (☎): 902-532-2497.
Price (●): $8.
Closed (X): November–April.
Check-in (🕐): 5–10 p.m.
Grade: simple (🏠).
Beds (🛏): 9.
Facilities: baggage storage area, laundry facilities, kitchen, on-site parking, showers, canoe rentals, hostel-based programs.
Family rooms (👪): available.
Groups (𝄃𝄃𝄃): small groups welcome.
Reservations: not essential.
Credit cards: not accepted.
Managers: Granville and Maggie Nickerson.

Directions: South from Annapolis Royal on Route 8 (27 kilometres), in South Milford turn west onto Virginia Road, the hostel driveway is 3.2 kilometres on the right (follow hut and tree signs).

Nova Scotia

Wentworth

Wentworth Hostel

Cumberland County, named after Fort Cumberland, is one of Nova Scotia's largest counties. The area is a collage of fertile agricultural land, large tracts of woodlands, and extensive stone quarries. It also boasts over 200 kilometres of scenic coastline. The Wallace River winds its way through the county's Wentworth Valley past the small farming community of Wentworth.

Wentworth Hostel is a quaint, 100-year-old country farmhouse set amidst the rolling hills and green fields of the valley. There are over 75 kilometres of hiking trails beginning right at the hostel's door. A nearby native campsite is reputed to be over 10,000 years old, the oldest excavation yet found in Canada. Higgin's Brook Waterfall and Warwick Mountain Waterfall are also local attractions. For a special treat, take in blueberry harvest time in late summer. The area is also famous for excellent downhill skiing.

Valley Road,
Wentworth Station.
Mail (✉): R.R. 1,
Wentworth, Nova Scotia B0M 1Z0.
Phone (☎): 902-548-2379.
Price (☺): $9.50 CDN.
Closed (X): never.
Check-in (🕐): 4–10 p.m.
Grade: simple (🏠).
Beds (🛏): 44.
Facilities: equipment storage area, kitchen, on-site parking, **MSA**.
Family rooms (👪): available.
Groups (🏛): welcome.
Reservations advisable (📞a): groups.
Credit cards: not accepted.
Manager: Gaby Hutton.

Directions: at Wentworth Station in Cumberland County, Take Route 104 (Trans-Canada Highway) to Wentworth Valley, exit on Valley Road, follow signs to hostel.

Ontario

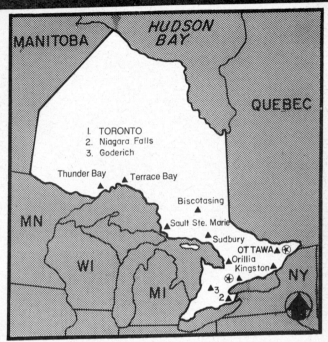

1. TORONTO
2. Niagara Falls
3. Goderich

Helpful Organizations

Hostelling International—Canada Regional Offices

Ontario East
18 Byward Market
Ottawa, Ontario K1N 7A1
Phone (☎): 613-230-1200
FAX: 613-230-6986

Great Lakes
209 Church Street
Toronto, Ontario M5B 1Y7
Phone (☎): 416-862-2665
FAX: 416-368-6499

Provincial Tourism Office

Ontario Travel
Queen's Park
Toronto, Ontario M7A 2E5
Phone (☎): 416-314-0944;
800-668-2746 (English) or
416-314-0956;
800-268-3736 (Français)

Most Ontario hostels offer all day access, see listings for details.

Ontario is home to one of the world's great wonders and to the country's capital. Niagara Falls attracts millions of visitors each year. In Ottawa the gothic spires of Parliament Hill rise high above the banks of the Ottawa River. Cosmopolitan Toronto is a sophisticated city rich in ethnic influences and a vibrant modern atmosphere.

Discounts

Present a valid hostel membership card at the time of purchase to receive the following discounts:

Kingston

The Canadian Shop - 219 Princess Street. 10% off on footwear and crafts (not books).

Frontenac Cycling Shop - 397 Princess Street, 542-4455. 10% off all items (only on non-sale).

John's Deli - 507 Princess Street, 548-7638. 10% off all items other than specials. Gratuities not included.

The Hostel Houseboat Shuttle - 5-day cruise between Ottawa and Kingston. July and August only. Reservations, 613-230-1200. 20% discount for Hostelling International members.

Kingston Boardsailing Academy - 347 Wellington Street, 541-1189.
- 2-hr. step on board lesson - min. 3 people $15/person
- 3-hr. introductory lesson - min. 3 people $25/person
- 6-hr. lesson - min. 3 people $60/person

Kingston's Deli - 91 Princess Street. 10% discount on meals (breakfast/lunch/supper) not on drinks.

Kingston International Hostel - 210 Bagot Street, 546-7203. 10% discount on IYHF retail items.

Kingston Windsurfing - Behind Pump House Steam Museum at 23 Ontario Street. 20% off all rentals and lessons.

North Ridge Wilderness - 80 Queen Street, 546-4757. 10% discount on all regular priced goods (canoes and kayaks not included).

Wood's Marina Canoe Center - 400 Bath Road. 1/3 off all rentals - canoe and accessories.

Ottawa

Allsport Rentals and Sales - 512 Bank Street. 10% off the published rates for 1992–93

The Bike Stop - 1223 Bank Street. 10% discount on regularly priced items.

Black's Camping International - 901 Bank Street. 10% discount off regular prices except Eureka tents.

Bytowne Cinema - 325 Rideau Street. Special admission rate, must present Bytowne Cinema membership card obtained from hostel.

The Expedition Shoppe - 43 York Street. 10% off on regularly priced items (except on tents and promotional red tag items or sale items).

The Hostel Houseboat Shuttle - 5-day cruise between Ottawa and Kingston. July and August only. Reservations, 613-230-1200. 20% discount for Hostelling International members.

Hostel Shop - Canadian Hostelling Association - 18 Byward Market, 230-1200. 10% discount on travel essentials and books.

In Sync Hair Studio - 18 Byward Market. 15% discount on haircuts only.

Japan Camera Centre - Rideau Centre location and 135 Bank Street (at Slater). 15% discount on regular price of 1 hour print film photofinishing and up to 11x14 enlargements from negatives.

Mexicali Rosa's - 207 Rideau Street. 20% off food. Gratuities not included. Hostelling International card must be shown.

Ottawa International Hostel - 75 Nicholas Street, 235-2595. 10% on travel essentials and books.

Ottawa Valley Field Trips - 85 Abbeyhill Drive, 591-1722. 10% off any day trips (not to be used in conjunction with other discounts).

Rentabike - Chateau Laurier Hotel, 1 Rideau Street, 233-0268. 10% off rentals, except Saturday and Sunday.

Rideau Photo Studio - 1-78 Georges Street. 10% off on passport, citizenship, and visa photos. Black and white only.

Riverrun - Box 179 Beachburg. 15% discount on 1 and 2 day rafting - raft tour.

Discounts

Ottawa(continued)
Walkley Bowling Centre - 2092 Walkley Road, 521-0132. Please call for reservations: 3 games of bowling for $5.00 shoes included.

Pembroke
Esprit Rafting - P.O. Box 463, 683-3241. 15% discount on rafting excursion packages: food, transportation, and rafting. Transportation and trip available from May to September, 7 days a week subject to booking. Booking can be made at Ottawa International Hostel.

Sudbury
Anderson Farm Museum - Box 910, Lively, 692-4448. 10% discount in souvenir shop.
Discount Car & Truck Rentals - 865 Kingsway, Sudbury and 192 Lakeshore Drive North Bay. 10% off all rates upon presenting valid membership card.
Science North - 100 Ramsey Lake Road. $1.00 off regular admission to Science North or Big Nickel Mine (cannot be used in conjunction with other coupons or discounts).

Toronto
Passport Cafe - 217 Church Street, 862-0399. Special member discounts. Be sure to visit Hostelling International Travel Services for regular discounted products.
Rent-A-Wreck - 374 Dupont Street, 961-7500. $5 off per rental or $25 off for a week or more.
Rent-A-Wreck - 102 Gerrard Street E., 599-1230. $5 off per rental or $25 off for a week or more.
Rent-A-Wreck - 175 Ossington Avenue, 532-8640. $5 off per rental or $25 off for a week or more.
Rent-A-Wreck - 4200 Weston Road, 744-9910. $5 off per rental or $25 off for a week or more.

Ontario

Biscotasing

Air Base Island International Hostel

After your adventures at Sudbury's Rocky Mountain Ranch Hostel, catch the train for a wonderfully scenic trip, or drive, to Biscotasing for another kind of Canadian experience. Your hosts, Brian and Kim, will meet you with their boat to escort you to Air Base Island. Explore the six acres of wilderness and visit the mainland. There's swimming, boating, hiking, canoeing, fishing, snorkelling and scuba diving. The A-frame cabin, complete with kitchen, sleeps four adults comfortably, and there are 6 tent sites with cooking areas. Meal plans are also available. This is a wilderness environment; guests are requested to behave in an environmentally sensitive manner regarding wildlife, fire, pollution, and hygiene. Biodegradable personal products and sleep sheet are mandatory.

Biscotasing, Ontario P0M 1C0.
Mail (✉): same.
Phone (☎): 705-674-0104 (September–May); 613-230-1200 (June–August).
Price (⬤): $8 CDN.
Closed (X): August 31–May 31.
Check-in (🏠): 7 a.m.–9 p.m.
Grade: basic (⌂).
Beds (🛏): 8.
Facilities: baggage storage area, kitchen, **MSA**, open all day, store and phone 5 min. by boat at Biscotasing.
Reservations essential (☎): must reserve in advance in order to book the boat shuttle that takes you from Biscotasing to Air Base Island.
Credit Cards: not accepted.

Manager: Brian and Kim Phillips.
Directions: located 90 miles northwest of Sudbury. Access by train from Sudbury or via Highway 144, or directly by charter float plane. The island is a short boat ride downstream from the town of Biscotasing.

72

Ontario

Goderich

Goderich International Hostel

Goderich is a gracious city laid out in a cartwheel plan, with wide tree-lined streets radiating from a picturesque central park. The city is situated on a bluff overlooking Lake Huron. It is said that one can watch the sunset twice in Goderich; first from the boardwalk on the waterfront and then from the clifftop where the town itself lies.

Goderich International Hostel is a cozy log cabin located on the eastern shore of Lake Huron, next to a secluded sand and pebble beach. Goderich contains a number of interesting historic buildings, which add to its pioneer charm, such as the Huron Historic Gaol, built in 1842. The beautiful lakeshore is the place to enjoy swimming, boating, fishing, waterskiing, windsurfing, hiking and cross-country skiing.

Mail (✉): R.R.#2 Goderich, Ontario N7A 3X8.
Phone (☎): 519-524-8428.
Price (☻): $10 CDN.
Closed (X): late October–late April.
Check-in (🕐): 8 a.m.–11 p.m.
Grade: simple (🏠).
Beds (🛏): 8.
Facilities: kitchen, on-site parking, open all day.
Groups (▥): welcome
Reservations essential (✆): groups.
Reservations advisable (✆): always.
Credit cards: not accepted.
Manager: Jamie Sutherland.

Directions: on the shores of Lake Huron. **Bus:** take a taxi from the bus station (6.5 kilometres).

Ontario

Kingston

Kingston International Hostel

Kingston, on Lake Ontario, is one of the many towns located along the famous Rideau Canal system, a water transportation route built after the War of 1812 in order to keep supplies moving between Kingston and Ottawa. A Houseboat Hostel takes five days to travel between these two cities going through 34 of the 44 scenic town locks. This special adventure is available in July and August with reservations only. Kingston, Canada's first capital, is full of history, beautiful architecture, boutiques, and charming restaurants. There are 15 museums and art galleries, and Old Fort Henry which relives Kingston's colonial history through mock battles with period costumes. Boat tour the famous Thousand Islands or snowshoe, cross-country ski, or hike the 300-km Rideau Trail to Ottawa. Members receive discounts for sailboarding and windsurfing lessons. It's excellent cycling country and home of Queen's University.

210 Bagot Street.
Kingston, Ontario
K7L 3G1.
Mail (✉): same.
Phone (☎): 613-546-7203
Price (◑): $11 CDN.
Closed (X): December 15–January 15.
Check-in (⏱): 7–10 a.m., 5 p.m.–1 a.m.
Grade: standard (⌂).
Beds (🛏): 30 (summer); 12 (winter).
Facilities: equipment storage area, kitchen, showers, barbecue, **MSA**.
Meals (✎): breakfast (summer).
Family rooms (👪): available.
Groups (🏛): welcome.
Reservations advisable (☎): always.
By FAX: 613-546-3715.
Credit cards: Visa.

Directions: from Johnson St., south on Bagot. **Train:** from station take bus #1 to Brock Street (Hospital) walk 2 blocks to Johnson and Bagot. **Bus:** from station take bus #2 to Bagot and Brock St. Walk 2 blocks south on Bagot to Johnson.

HANG OUUUUT!

WWWWWITH US!

...enjoy ropeswinging, fishing, snorkelling, swimming. Visit a blacksmith shop, explore villages, hike, dine for 5 days and 5 nights while cruising the 200km RIDEAU CANAL, internationally acclaimed as the most scenic canal system in the world linking Ottawa, Canada's Capital, and old historic Kingston. Both cities offer first-class Hostelling International hostels to begin and end your adventure on land! Discover Canada's natural beauty, learn our history, and be charmed by our hospitality! Book Now!

You and your 9 mates will share a 14m houseboat a BBQ, sundeck, galley, waterslide, music, fun...and a *unique hostelling experience!*

Ottawa Dep. Mondays: July 05, July 19, Aug 02, Aug 16
Kingston Dep. Mondays July 12, July 26, Aug 09, Aug 23

$250 CDN per person or
$200 CDN each for group of 9 people
Credit cards accepted: VISA, MASTERCARD, JCB

Reservation advisable: *confirmed upon receipt of $100CDN deposit. Refunded if fully booked. Balance is due before departure date.*

Fee includes: *bedding, towels, continental breakfasts, fishing and snorkelling gear.*

for information and reservation contact :
Hostelling International - Ontario East
18 Byward Market, Ottawa,
Ontario, Canada, K1N 7A1
Phone (613) 230-1200 Fax: (613) 230-6986

HOSTELLING
INTERNATIONAL

Ontario

Niagara Falls

Niagara Falls International Hostel

Niagara Falls International Hostel is located in a quiet residential part of the city near the city centre, site of the world famous Horseshoe Falls. The city of Niagara Falls is located at the centre of a beautiful 40-kilometre park system that stretches from the falls down river to the quaint colonial town of Niagara-on-the-Lake. The beautiful Niagara Parkway winds its way along the river, past vineyards and orchards and the Brock Monument, a tribute to General Brock who died leading his troops to victory over American forces at the Battle of Queenston Heights in 1813. From the top of the monument view a spectacular panorama of Lake Ontario and the surrounding lakeshore.

4699 Zimmerman Avenue, Niagara Falls, Ontario L2E 3M7.
Mail (✉): same.
Phone (☎): 416-357-0770 (effective Oct. 1, 93 area code changes to "905").
Price (☻): $12 CDN.
Closed (X): never.
Check-in (🛏): 9–11 a.m., 5–11 p.m.
Grade: standard (♠).
Beds (🛏): 58.
Facilities: kitchen, laundry facilities, linen rental, lockers, street parking, outdoor patio, woodstove, bicycle rentals, hostel-based programs, **MSA**, open all day.
Family rooms (👪): available.
Groups (🏠): welcome.
Reservations essential (☎e): groups.
Reservations advisable (☎a): summer.

Credit cards: MasterCard, Visa, JCB.
Manager: Laurie Jackson.
Directions: on Zimmerman Avenue, between Queen and Huron Streets, approximately 1 kilometre from the falls, close to bus station and train station.

Ontario

Orillia
Orillia Home Hostel

Situated on the narrows between Lake Couchiching and Lake Simcoe, Orillia was an important centre of native life before the arrival of the early explorers in 1615. In the early 1900s, the town was home to Canada's foremost humorist Stephen Leacock. His 19-room lakeshore mansion is now a museum. The Orillia Home Hostel is close to downhill and cross-country skiing, swimming, water skiing, and sailing. Houseparents Guenther and Rita Grotsch organize four to eight-day canoe trips to Algonquin Park and Lake Temagami from June through mid-September.

198 Borland Street East,
Orillia, Ontario L3V 2C3.
Mail (✉): same.
Phone (☎): 705-325-0970.
Price (◐): $11 CDN.
Closed (X): never.
Check-in (⏰): 8–10 a.m., 5–9 p.m.
Grade: home hostel (🏠).
Beds (🛏): 20.
Facilities: equipment storage area, kitchen, laundry facilities, linen rental, on-site parking, fireplace, hostel-based programs, **MSA**, open all day.

Meals (🍴): breakfast, light meals.
Family rooms (👪): available.
Groups (🎋): welcome.
Reservations essential (•🔔e): groups (June 15–October 15).
Reservations advisable (•🔔a): summer.
Credit cards: not accepted.
Managers: Guenther and Rita Grotsch.
Directions: on Borland Street East, close to bus station and train station.

Ontario

Ottawa

Ottawa International Hostel

Originally an 1860's county jail, Ottawa International Hostel offers public tours of the building's penal and transition history. Ottawa, Canada's National Capital, is at one end of the Rideau Canal, a heritage water system built after the War of 1812 to move supplies between Kingston and Ottawa. Ask about the new "Houseboat Hostel" that makes the five-day journey between the two cities each week (see our ad in this book for full details).

Ottawa offers an abundance of activities minutes away from the hostel, from museums and galleries, to marketplaces and parks and year round festivals. Cycling paths dissect the city, as do waterways for canoeing. Recreational programming is offered in all seasons, and white-water rafting excursions leave from the hostel on a regular basis (May–September).

75 Nicholas Street,
Ottawa, Ontario K1N 7B9.
Mail (✉): same.
Phone (☎): 613-235-2595.
Price (●): $13 CDN.
Closed (X): never.
Check-in (🕐): 7 a.m.–2 a.m.
Grade: standard (♦).
Beds (🛏): 150.
Facilities: kitchen, laundry, parking, equipment storage area, reading room, TV lounge, courtyard with barbecue and games, canoe rentals, Hardlock Café (summer), historic guided tours, **MSA** open all day.
Meals (🍴): available for groups.
Family rooms (👪): available.
Groups (🏛): welcome.
Reservations essential (📞e): families, groups.
Reservations advisable (📞a): summer, February (winterlude). **By FAX:** 613-569-2131. Reservations accepted via IBN and Pacific Rim Fax-a-bed.

Credit cards: MasterCard, Visa, JCB.
Directions: Bus: take local bus #4 (St. Laurent) from corner of Arlington and Kent to Nicholas Street and Rideau; walk 2 blocks south. **Train:** take bus #95 (Baseline) to Eaton's Rideau Shopping Centre. (the hostel is behind you, on the shopping centre side).

Ontario

SUPPLEMENTAL ACCOMMODATION

Sault Ste. Marie

Algonquin Hotel

Known as "The Sault" (pronounced "soo"), Sault Ste. Marie is located at the link between Lake Huron and Lake Superior. The canals here are the most active in the entire St. Lawrence Seaway system, maneuvering some 80 or more steamers each day. Established in 1669 by French missionaries, the city retains much of its historic charm. The Algonquin Hotel is located close to the scenic harbourfront, the museum, and the art gallery. Excellent downhill skiing and world-class cross-country ski trails are also nearby. In summer, hiking, cycling, canoeing and many other outdoor activities are available. The Algoma Central Railway offers a scenic ride through the surrounding wilderness past waterfalls, mountains, ravines and forests to the spectacular Agawa Canyon.

864 Queen Street East, Sault Ste. Marie, Ontario P6A 2B4.
Mail (⋇): same.
Phone (☎): 705-253-2311.
Price (◓): $19 CDN.
Closed (X): never.
Check-in (ⵂ): 24 hours.
Grade: (SA).
Beds (⊨): 45.

Facilities: private rooms, baggage storage area, restaurant bar on site, pool table, dart board, TV, on-site parking, **MSA**, open all day.
Meals (✎): lunch and dinner.
Credit cards: not accepted.
Manager: David Stanghetta.
Directions: downtown on Queen Street, 2 km from train and bus station.

Ontario

Sudbury

Rocky Mountain Ranch Hostel

Nestled in a fertile valley, just 10 minutes north of Sudbury, this 230 acre horse ranch has something for everyone. Saddle up for a trail ride, enjoy an evening bonfire with wieners and marshmallows, pet the farm animals, and tour NOAH (Northern Ontario Animal Hospital), a wildlife refuge centre and hospital. Swim at nearby Lake Whitson, go for a hike, go mountain-biking, and play baseball and volleyball. Once you've worked up an appetite, enjoy a home-cooked meal in the Ranch's own licensed country dining lounge. Hostel-based activity packages are also available. The city of Sudbury lies in a vast geological basin surrounded by 30 lakes and 6,000 acres of protected woodland. One can travel 20 metres down a nickel mine, visit Science North, or take in one of the many festivals. Sudbury is five hours northwest of Ottawa en route to Manitoba.

2881 Valleyview Road.
Mail (✉): P.O. Box 219 Sudbury, Ontario P0M 1E0.
Phone (☎): 705-897-4931.
Price (💲): $12 CDN.
Closed (X): never.
Check-in (⌂): 9 a.m.–11 p.m.
Grade: standard (♠).
Beds (🛏): 20.
Facilities: baggage storage area, kitchen, laundry facilities, linen rental, lockers, on-site parking, TV room and tourist information, wheelchair accessible (♿), **MSA,** open all day.
Family Rooms (👪): available.
Groups (👫): welcome.
Meals (🍴): breakfast, lunch, dinner.

Reservations essential (☎): groups.
Credit Cards: Visa, MasterCard.
Directions: from Highway 69 north exit on to Valleyview Road.

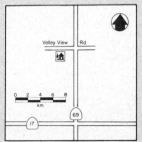

Ontario

Terrace Bay

Aguasabon Falls International Hostel

Located at the northernmost point of Lake Superior, Terrace Bay is known as the "gem of the North Shore." Relax on the long sandy beaches, marvel at the huge rocky cliffs, and hike to the breathtaking Aguasabon Falls (only 15 minutes from the Aguasabon Falls International Hostel). The entire region is an outdoorsman's dream! Discover miles of unspoiled wilderness and beautiful scenery along the Casque Isles Hiking Trail. Make Terrace Bay your home away from home in northern Ontario.

Highway 17.
Mail (✉): P.O. Box 1106 Terrace Bay, Ontario P0T 2W0.
Phone (☎): 807-825-3802, or 807-825-9295.
Price (☮): $12 CDN.
Closed (X): October 15–May 15.
Check-in (🕙): 9 a.m.–11 p.m.
Grade: standard (♠).
Beds (🛏): 10.
Facilities: baggage storage area, kitchen, cafeteria, **MSA**, open all day.
Family rooms (👪): available.
Groups (🏛): welcome.
Reservations: not essential.
Credit cards: Visa.

Manager: Chris and Judy Joubert.
Directions: on the western edge of Terrace Bay on Highway 17.

Ontario

Thunder Bay

Confederation College - Sibley Hall Residence

Thunder Bay is a virtual playground for outdoor enthusiasts, offering everything from fishing and skiing to beautiful parks and wildlife. For an unparalleled look into Canada's past, visit Old Fort William and step back 175 years to a time when voyagers paddled thousands of miles by canoe to gather here for the fur trade. In 1815, it was known as the "Great Rendez-vous," and its spirit lives on at Old Fort William. The Thunder Bay Art Gallery houses one of the country's largest collections of work by Canada's premier native artists. Other attractions include the majestic Kakabeka Falls, Ouimet Canyon, the Terry Fox Monument, and the largest amethyst mine in North America.

960 William Street.
Mail (✉): Confederation College Sibley Hall Residence P.O. Box 398 Thunder Bay, Ontario P7C 4W1.
Phone (☎): 807-475-6381.
Price (◒): $19.50 CDN (shared), $24.50 (single).
Closed (X): August 16–May 14.
Check-in (◖): 9 a.m.–4 p.m. (weekdays), 1–4 p.m. (weekends).
Grade: standard (♠).
Beds (▸━): 100.
Facilities: baggage storage area, kitchen, laundry facilities, linen provided, on-site parking, cafeteria, safety deposit boxes, wheelchair accessible (&), **MSA**, open all day.
Meals (✎): breakfast, lunch, dinner.
Groups (▥): welcome.

Reservations essential (☎e): May 15–August 15.
Manager: Lorna Pearson.
Directions: West Main Street turns into Harbour Expressway, continue west on Fort William Road, turn south on Balmoral Street to William Street.

Ontario

Toronto

Toronto International Hostel

Toronto is an international gateway to Canada with a picturesque skyline and such unique buildings as City Hall, the Royal Ontario Museum, the Ontario Art Gallery, and the new Skydome stadium, home of the Blue Jays, 1992 World Series champions. The fashionable harbourfront area overlooks the beautiful Lake Ontario shoreline. The world's tallest free-standing structure, the CN Tower, stands high above the lake. Toronto International Hostel is a few minutes from the Eaton's Centre, one of the largest North American-style shopping centres in Canada. Centrally located, it's within easy walking distance to major attractions, shopping areas, nightclubs, cinemas, and restaurants.

223 Church Street,
Toronto, Ontario M5B 1Y7.
Mail (✉): same.
Phone (☎): 416-368-0207.
Price (◒): $14.29 CDN.
Closed (X): never.
Check-in (⌂): 7 a.m.–2 a.m.
Grade: standard (♠).
Beds (🛏): 154.
Facilities: kitchen, laundry facilities, linen provided, lockers, large sun deck, cafe, travel store, hostel-based programs, **MSA**, open all day.
Meals (✎): breakfast, lunch, dinner.
Family rooms (👪): available.
Groups (🎪): welcome.
Reservations essential (🔑e): groups.
Reservations advisable (🔑a): summer. **By FAX:** 416-368-6499. Reservations accepted via IBN and Pacific Rim Fax-a-bed.

Credit cards: MasterCard, Visa, JCB.
Manager: Robert Bisson.
Directions: on Church Street near Dundas. **Airport (✈):** take airport bus to downtown, ask to be let off at hostel. **Bus:** walk east along Dundas to Church Street. **Train:** take subway to Dundas, walk east to Church Street.

Prince Edward Island

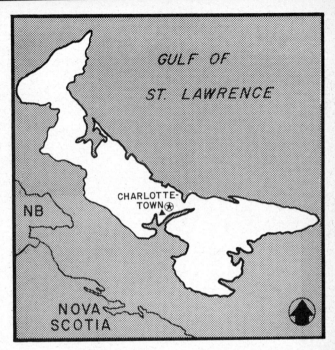

Helpful Organizations

Hostelling International—Canada Regional Office

Prince Edward Island
P.O. Box 1718
Charlottetown
Prince Edward Island C1A 7N4
Phone (☎): 902-894-9696 (summer),
800-663-5777(winter)

Provincial Tourism Office

Department of Tourism
P.O. Box 940
Charlottetown
Prince Edward Island C1A 7M5
Phone (☎): 902-368-4444,
800-565-7421 (from New Brunswick
and Nova Scotia),
800-565-0267

Prince Edward Island is Canada's smallest province and boasts a gentle beauty with its rich red earth, rolling green hills, and endless beaches. The island was also made famous by the Anne of Green Gables tales, which are immortalized at the charming farmhouse replica of Anne's childhood home.

Discounts

Present a valid hostel membership card at the time of purchase to receive the following discounts:

Charlottetown

Rent-A-Wreck - 114 St. Peter's Road, 894-7039. $5 off per rental or $25 off for a week or more.

Prince Edward Island

Charlottetown

Charlottetown Hostel

Charlottetown is Canada's smallest capital but one of the most important in Canadian history. In 1864, the Fathers of Confederation met here for the first time. The Confederation Centre for the Arts was built in 1964 to commemorate the historic event. Each summer, the Charlottetown Festival takes place at the centre, with regular performances of the famous musical, "Anne of Green Gables." The Charlottetown Hostel is modeled after a typical rural island dairy barn. Located near the University of Prince Edward Island, it is outside the city itself but still close to major attractions in Charlottetown and around the island. Prince Edward Island also has more than 30 provincial parks offering beautiful red and white sand beaches and pleasant wooded trails for hiking and bicycling.

153 Mount Edward Road.
Mail (✉): P.O. Box 1718, Charlottetown, Prince Edward Island C1A 7N4.
Phone (☎): 902-894-9696 summer, 1-800-663-5777 winter.
Price (💰): $13 CDN.
Closed (X): September 6–May 28.
Check-in (🕐): 4 p.m.–midnight.
Grade: standard (🏠).
Beds (🛏): 55.
Facilities: lockers, kitchen, linen rental, on-site parking, wheelchair accessible (♿), snack canteen, bicycle rentals, volleyball, **MSA**.
Family rooms (👪): available.
Groups (🎪): welcome.
Reservations essential (📞): families, groups.

Reservations advisable (📞): always.
Credit cards: Visa, MasterCard, JCB.
Directions: on Mount Edward Road behind Mount St. Mary's Convent and across the field from the University of Prince Edward Island, close to airport.

Québec

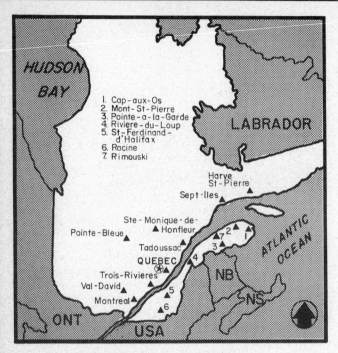

1. Cap-aux-Os
2. Mont-St-Pierre
3. Pointe-a-la-Garde
4. Riviere-du-Loup
5. St-Ferdinand-
   d'Halifax
6. Racine
7. Rimouski

Helpful Organizations

Hostelling International—Canada Regional Office

Tourisme Jeunesse
4545 Pierre De-Coubertin
Montréal, Québec
H1V 3R2
Phone (☎): 514-252-3117
FAX: 514-252-3119
800-461-8585 (for reservations)

Provincial Tourism Office

Tourisme Québec
C.P. 20,000
Québec, Québec
G1K 7X2
Phone (☎): 514-873-2015
800-363-7777

Québec hostels offer all day access

Québec with its French culture and "joie-de-vivre" is truly unique in North America. It is home to world-famous Montréal, the second-largest French-speaking centre in the world, and historic Québec City, North America's only walled city. The cosmopolitan flair of its big cities is matched by the beauty of its mountains, rivers, and rugged shoreline.

Québec

Cap-aux-Os (Gaspé)

Auberge de Cap-aux-Os

Auberge de Cap-aux-Os is located in the heart of beautiful Forillon National Park in the spectacular Gaspé region. The name Gaspé comes from the Micmac Indian word Gespeg, meaning "land's end." Gaspé overlooks an immense natural harbour into which three salmon-rich rivers flow. Forillon National Park contains three distinct ecological zones: the dry Penouille dunes, the briny marshes of the bay, and the arctic alpine zones, whose flora are remnants of the last ice age. There is a great diversity of plant and animal life in this small area. Hike through conifer and hardwood forests, rolling fields, lush marshes, or along the ocean-side. Thousands of seabirds make their home on the coastal cliffs. From May to October, a variety of whales can be seen.

2095 boul. Grande-Grève, Cap-aux-Os, Gaspé, Québec G0E 1J0.

Mail (✉): same.
Phone (☎): 418-892-5153.
Price (●): $12 CDN.
Closed (X): never.
Check-in (◑): 11 a.m.–midnight.
Grade: standard (♠).
Beds (🛏): 56.
Facilities: equipment storage area, cafeteria (summer), kitchen (winter), linen rental, on-site parking, bicycle rental, hostel-based programs, **MSA**, open all day.
Meals (🍴): breakfast, lunch, dinner (summer).
Family rooms (👪): available.
Groups (👥): welcome.
Reservations essential (✦): groups, reservations accepted at 418-892-5153 and 1-800-461-8585 (toll free inside Québec).

Reservations advisable (✦a): individuals (June 15–August 31).
Credit cards: not accepted.
Manager: Gilles Shaw.
Directions: on Route 132 in Cap-aux-Os. **Bus:** bus stops at the hostel June 24–September 30. During the off-season take bus or train to Gaspé (25 kilometres from hostel).

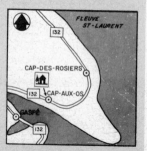

Québec

Havre-St-Pierre

Auberge de la Minganie A.J.

Founded in 1887 by fishermen from the Magdalene Islands, Havre-St-Pierre is the capital of the Minganie region. The nearby fishing village of Mingan and the Montagnais reserve are reminders of the area's rich heritage. The informative exhibits at the historic Hudson Bay Company store really bring the area's cultural and natural history to life. The name Mingan is derived from the Basque word meaning "strip of land," referring to the unique and beautiful body of islands making up the Archipel-de-Mingan. Boats to the islands depart regularly from the town of Havre-St-Pierre. The Auberge de la Minganie consists of five small cabin-style buildings just 15 kilometres from the town of Havre-St-Pierre along the last accessible route on Québec's north shore.

Route 138,
Havre-St-Pierre, Québec
G0G 1P0.
Mail (✉): same.
Phone (☎): call 514-252-3117 outside Québec province or in Montréal area, or 1-800-461-8585 in rest of Québec.
Price (☺): $12 CDN (Oct. 15–May 1).
Closed (X): Sept. 15–June 15.
Check-in (⌂): 10 a.m.–11 p.m.
Grade: standard (♦).
Beds (🛏): 24.
Facilities: equipment storage area, linen rental, on-site parking, camping, open all day.
Family rooms (♦): available.
Groups (⛺): welcome.
Reservations essential (⌂e): groups, reservations accepted at 514-252-3117 and 1-800-461-8585 (toll free inside Québec).

Reservations advisable (⌂a): always.
Manager: Andrew Coutts.
Directions: 200 kilometres east after Sept-Îles on Route 138 east. **Bus:** take bus from Sept-Îles to Havre-St-Pierre and ask to be let off at the hostel in La Minganie (Romaine River).

Québec

Montréal

Auberge de Montréal

Located at the junction of the St. Lawrence and the Ottawa Rivers, Montréal is actually on an island. It was a major fur-trading centre, as well as an outpost for the exploration of the North American continent by European settlers. Today, the city is a major gateway into eastern Canada with world-class theatres, art galleries, international boutiques, and restaurants. The modern underground "Metro" provides easy access to many important sites, including the botanical gardens and the Olympic Stadium, with its renowned "leaning" tower. Situated in the heart of Montréal, Auberge de Montréal is within easy walking distance of downtown attractions. The hostel offers an impressive list of programs, including free city walking tours and guided tours to local events.

3541 rue Aylmer,
Montréal, Québec H2X 2B9.
Mail (✉): same.
Phone (☎): 514-843-3317.
Price (💰): $15 CDN.
Closed (X): never.
Check-in (🕐): 9:30 a.m.–2 a.m.
Grade: superior (👫).
Beds (🛏): 275 (summer), 100 (winter).
Facilities: equipment storage area, kitchen, laundry facilities, linen rental, lockers, limited street parking, free walking tours, **MSA**, open all day.
Family rooms (👪): available.
Groups (🏠): welcome.
Reservations essential (☎): groups always, reservations accepted at 514-843-3317 and 1-800-461-8585 (toll free inside Québec); also on IBN and Pacific Rim Fax-a-bed.

Reservations advisable (☎): always.
Credit cards: MasterCard, Visa.
Directions: take subway to McGill Station (Union Street exit), turn right and walk to Sherbrooke Street, turn right on Sherbrooke, left on Aylmer; close to bus and train station.

Québec

Mont St-Pierre

Auberge Les Vagues

Auberge Les Vagues is situated in the Mont St-Pierre on the shores of the St. Lawrence River. Nestled amidst incredible scenery, this pleasant village sits in a valley surrounded by mountains and overlooking a bay. For thrilling views of the surrounding area, visit nearby Parc de la Gaspésie. Mont St-Pierre, the mountain from which the village takes its name, is unique in that it has five glider launch pads at its summit. Hiking, biking, and cross-country skiing are available on 500 km of trails. Because of the different levels of altitude and various climatic regions on the peaks of Mont Jacques-Cartier and Mont Albert, plants that are usually found only in Québec's far north thrive here. Unique wildlife can also be found, including moose, wood caribou, and deer. Enjoy local seafood at the hostel's own restaurant and café.

84 rue P. Cloutier (Route 132), Mont St-Pierre, Québec G0E 1V0.
Mail (✉): C. P. 58.
Phone: (☎): 418-797-2851.
Price (●): $12 CDN.
Closed (X): never.
Check-in (🕙): 8 a.m.–1 a.m.
Grade: standard (♦).
Beds (🛏): 90 (summer), 20 (winter).
Facilities: equipment storage area, laundry facilities, linen rental, on-site parking, camping, nature interpretation centre, food supplies, hang gliding information; linen, bicycle, ski equipment, snowmobile, and car rentals; **MSA**; debit cards accepted (CDN bank cards).
Meals (🍴): restaurant open all day in summer; breakfast, lunch, and dinner in winter.
Family rooms (🛏): available in summer.
Groups (🏛): welcome.

Reservations essential (📞): groups always, reservations accepted at 418-797-2851 and 1-800-461-8585 (toll free inside Québec).
Reservations advisable (📞): always.
Credit cards: MasterCard, Visa.
Manager: Denis Fortier.
Directions: take Route 132 to the centre of Mont St-Pierre, follow sign to the hostel; close to bus station.

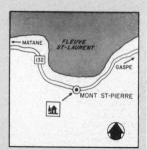

Québec

Pointe-à-la-Garde

Auberge de Pointe-à-la-Garde

When Jacques Cartier arrived in 1534, the warm currents of the bay led him to name this area "chaleur," the French word for warmth. The fertile land led settlers to concentrate on farming more than fishing. However, the rivers do provide salmon and other local delicacies.

Auberge de Pointe-à-la-Garde is a quaint hostel which can accommodate up to 22 people. Enjoy hiking, swimming, horseback riding, relaxing on the beach, or searching for fossils. Two major museums, Miguasha and Restigouche, attract thousands of visitors each year. The area also has several major ski hills.

152 boulevard Perron
Pointe-à-la-Garde, Québec
G0C 2M0.
Mail (✉): same.
Phone (☎): 418-788-2048.
Price (◉): $12 CDN.
Closed (X): never.
Check-in (🏠): 24 hours.
Grade: standard (♦).
Beds (🛏): 22.
Facilities: equipment storage area, laundry facilities, linen rental, on-site parking, camping, open all day.
Meals (🍴): breakfast included; banquet served every summer evening in castle behind hostel.
Family rooms (👪): available.
Groups (🏚): welcome.
Reservations essential (🔑e): groups always, reservations accepted at 418-788-2048 and 1-800-461-8585 (toll free inside Québec).

Reservations advisable (🔑a): always.
Credit cards: not accepted.
Manager: Jean Roussy.
Directions: on Route 132 in Pointe-à-la-Garde. **Bus:** bus stops by request 100 metres from hostel.

Québec

Pointe-Bleue-Mashteuiatsh

Auberge Kukum

When the first European settlers to the Saguenay–Lac St-Jean region of Québec arrived 150 years ago, they imposed their ways on the nomadic Montaignais peoples who inhabited the area. Since then the natives have been striving to keep their traditions, customs, and language alive. Auberge Kukum ("grandmother" in the Montagnais language) is located in Pointe-Bleue-Mashteuiatsh Native Reserve and recently underwent extensive renovations. The only Montaignais museum in Canada is found here. Enjoy canoeing, sailing, bicycling, hiking, camping, cross-country skiing, dog sledding, snowmobiling, sledding, and ice fishing, as well as guided excursions and a chance to live in the forest with a native family (minimum five days).

241 Ouiatchouan,
Village Amérindien de Pointe-Bleue-Mashteuiatsh,
Lac St-Jean, Québec G0W 2H0.
Mail (✉): same.
Phone (☎): 418-275-0697.
Price (⊖): $14 CDN.
Closed (X): never.
Check-in (🔟): 10 a.m.–11 p.m.
Grade: standard (♠).
Beds (🛏): 48.
Facilities: equipment storage area, laundry facilities, linen rental, on-site parking, snowmobile rental, camping, hostel-based programs, **MSA**.
Meals (🍴): breakfast, lunch, dinner.
Family rooms (👪): available.
Groups (🎪): welcome, reservations required.
Reservations advisable (📠): summer. **By FAX:** 418-275-6481.

Credit cards: MasterCard, Visa.
Manager: Guylaine Duhamelle.
Directions: on the main street of the village of Pointe-Bleue-Mashteuiatsh, follow route signs for Roberval. **Bus:** take bus to Roberval (6 km from Pointe-Bleue-Mashteuiatsh) and phone the hostel for directions.

Québec

Centre International de Séjour de Québec

The most important hostel in Québec is located in the heart of Québec's "Old City". Strategically located above the St. Lawrence River, it played an essential role in the defense of northeastern America. The only fortified city north of Mexico, it is a designated UNESCO World Heritage Site. Located outside the city's walls are the Plains of Abraham. Once the sight of the battle between the English and the French over Québec, today it offers more than 250 acres of picturesque woodlands and walkways. The European flair of the city is evident in the colourful café-lined streets, fashionable boutiques, and craft shops. Winter and summer, the city is alive with music, theatre, street performers, and festivals. The hostel offers cultural and historic programs and walking tours. Great alpine skiing, hiking, and cycling routes are all nearby.

19 rue Ste-Ursule,
Québec, Québec G1R 4E1.
Mail (✉): same.
Phone (☎): 418-694-0755.
Price (●): $15 CDN.
Closed (X): never.
Check-in (⌚): 11 a.m.–2 a.m.
Grade: Hostel. **Beds (🛏):** 273.
Facilities: equipment storage area, laundry facilities, linen provided, lockers, safety deposit boxes, limited street parking, wheelchair accessible (♿), meeting rooms, hostel-based programs, **MSA**, open all day.
Meals (🍴): breakfast, lunch, dinner.
Family rooms (👪): available.
Groups (🏨): welcome.
Reservations essential (✆): groups, reservations accepted at 418-694-0755 and 1-800-461-8585 (toll free inside Québec). **By FAX:** 418-694-2278.

Reservations advisable (✆): always.
Credit cards: MasterCard, Visa.
Directions: follow Laurier Boulevard to the walls of Old Québec, Ste-Ursule is the second street on the left.
Bus: take city bus #3 from the bus station toward Haute-ville, get off at corner of Dauphine and Ste-Ursule; close to bus station and train station.

Québec

Racine

Auberge de la grande ligne

Auberge de la grande ligne is a small hostel with 21 beds but offers a wide variety of activities. The proximity to Mount Orford makes the hostel an excellent base for cross-country and downhill skiers. Snowshoeing is another popular winter sport. Explore the region by bicycle or enjoy a variety of water sports. The hostel is also close to many picturesque hiking trails. Parachuting is available for the more adventurous. Another unique attraction is the Crystal and Quartz Mine.

318 Chemin de la grande ligne, Racine, Québec J0E 1Y0.
Mail (✉): same.
Phone (☎): 514-532-3177.
Price (☺): $14 CDN.
Closed (X): never.
Check-in (◖): 10 a.m.–11 p.m.
Grade: standard (⚑).
Beds (⊨): 21.
Facilities: equipment storage area, laundry facilities, linen rental, safety deposit boxes, on-site parking, camping, **MSA**, open all day.
Meals (⚄): breakfast, lunch (for groups with advance notice), dinner.
Family rooms (⚲): available.
Groups (⊞): small groups only.
Reservations essential (⚲☺): groups always, reservations accepted at 514-532-3177 and 1-800-461-8585 (toll free inside Québec).
Credit cards: not accepted.
Manager: Gilles Veilleux.

Directions: from Highway 10 turn onto Route 243 North to Racine (30 kilometres), turn right onto Route 222 East, then follow La grande ligne on your right (2.4 kilometres) to the hostel. **Bus:** at Waterloo, Eastman, Richmond, Sherbrooke, or Magog, phone hostel for pick-up (please reserve in advance).

Québec

Rimouski

Auberge la Voile

Rimouski is located midway between Québec and Gaspé on the St. Lawrence River. The town extends from the shores of the river uplands to a point overlooking the whole area. It is a religious, educational, and cultural centre with museums, galleries, parks, and nature trails to enjoy. Each year there are a number of large-scale events, such as Festi-Jazz (August), Carrousel international de Film (September), and Festival d'Automne, which celebrates the beautiful fall colours (October). There are three nearby parks, Park Beauséjour, Park "du Bic", and Parc Rimouski, offering a variety of outdoor activities. Auberge la Voile organizes guided visits to points of interest in the area. There is also a well-marked walking tour highlighting Rimouski's architectural heritage.

58 St-Germain Est
Rimouski, Québec
G5L 1A4.
Mail (✉): same.
Phone (☎): 418-722-8002.
Price (●): $13 CDN.
Closed (X): never.
Check-in (🕐): 7 a.m.–1 p.m., 4:30–11 p.m.
Grade: standard (♠).
Beds (🛏): 34.
Facilities: equipment storage area, kitchen, laundry facilities, linen rental, on-site parking, small food counter, bicycle rental, **MSA**, open all day.
Meals (🔧): breakfast
Family rooms (👪): available.
Reservations essential (🔒e): groups always.

Reservations advisable (🔒a): reservations accepted at 418-722-8002 and 1-800-461-8585 (toll free inside Québec).
Credit Cards: not accepted.
Manager: Nathalie Caron.
Directions: from Route 132 north, continue 38 kilometres past Ste-Flavie, hostel is near the cathedral. 500 metres from bus station and train station.

Québec

Rivière-du-Loup

Auberge Internationale de Rivière-du-Loup

Rivière-du-Loup is located at an important crossroads between the regions of Gaspé, Québec, Charlevoix, Saguenay–Lac St-Jean, and New Brunswick. Situated at the top of a rocky cliff overlooking the Gulf of St. Lawrence, the town offers fascinating scenery, pleasant beaches, and a variety of outdoor excursions.

Auberge Internationale de Rivière-du-Loup is situated in the heart of the town near many sites of interest, including the Rivière-du-Loup waterfalls. From the hostel you can take part in a variety of local activities including excursions to Île Verte Island, lighthouse tours, star-gazing at the observatory, forest hikes, tours of the scenic waterways, and whale watching. For a local treat, try the hostel's "cabane à sucre", a summer celebration of the delights of maple syrup, including a meal and maple toffee. Outdoor barbecues are also offered.

46 Hotel de ville,
Rivière-du-Loup, Québec
G5R 1L5.
Mail (✉): same.
Phone (☎): 418-862-7566.
Price (💲): $12 CDN
Closed (X): November 1–March 31 (open upon reservation only during this time).
Check-in (🕐): 10 a.m.–2 a.m.
Grade: standard (🏠).
Beds (🛏): 60.
Facilities: equipment storage area, kitchen, laundry facilities, linen rental, lockers, on-site parking, bicycle rental, **MSA**, open all day.
Family rooms (👪): available.
Groups (🏘): welcome.
Reservations essential (🔑e): groups always.
Reservations advisable (🔑a): always.

reservations accepted at 418-862-7566 and 1-800-461-8585 (toll free inside Québec).
Credit cards: MasterCard, Visa.
Manager: Vincent Berubé.
Directions: take Cartier Boulevard to Lafontaine Street and Hotel de ville; 1 kilometre to bus station and train station.

Québec

Ste-Monique-de-Honfleur

Auberge Île-du-Repos de Péribonka

Auberge Île-du-Repos is situated in the village of Ste-Monique, overlooking the Péribonka River. In 1912, this historic region inspired the author Louis Hémon to write his world-famous novel, "Maria Chapdelaine." The museum in Péribonka displays articles of his personal life and his writing. The surrounding woodlands and waterways offer picturesque scenery as well as opportunities for hiking and swimming. The hostel is the only one in Canada located on a private island. Along with the comfortable cabins, camping is available. The hostel's cafeteria and café are good places to meet with local residents; local music and special live performances are presented in the evening.

Ste-Monique-de-Honfleur,
Lac St-Jean, Québec G0W 2T0.
Mail (✉): same.
Phone (☎): 418-347-5649 summer, 418-668-5679 winter.
Price (●): $12 CDN.
Closed (X): September 30–May 30 (Groups accepted year round, minimum 15 persons).
Check-in (🕐): 10 a.m.–11 p.m.
Grade: simple (🏠). **Beds (🛏):** 50.
Facilities: equipment storage area, laundry facilities, linen rental, safety deposit boxes, on-site parking, bar/lounge, **MSA**, open all day.
Meals (🍴): breakfast, lunch, dinner.
Family rooms (👪): available.
Groups (🏘): welcome.
Reservations essential (☎e): groups always, reservations accepted at 418-347-5649 (summer),

418-668-5679 (winter) and 1-800-461-8585 (toll free inside Québec).
Reservations advisable (☎a): always.
Credit cards: MasterCard, Visa.
Manager: Micheline Beaupré.
Directions: off Route 169, on the northern border of the village of Ste-Monique.

Québec

St-Ferdinand

Le Domaine Fraser

Saint-Ferdinand is a small community nestled in the lush green Appalachian Mountains. This region, located midway between Montréal and Québec, is call the "coeur-du-Québec" or the "heart of Québec." The landscape is spectacular with the forested Canadian Shield, plains bordering on the St. Lawrence River, and the mountains to the south. Le Domaine Fraser was once the Fraser estate. Today it is a modern, fully equipped outdoor recreation centre. A wide range of activities are available, from canoeing and horseback riding to skiing, snowshoeing, and tobogganing.

684 Route 265,
St-Ferdinand d'Halifax, Québec
G0N 1N0.
Mail (✉): same.
Phone (☎): 418-428-9551 or 1-800-263-9551 (toll free in Québec).
Price (●): $12 CDN
Closed (X): never.
Check-in (🕐): 10 a.m.–11 p.m.
Grade: standard (♠).
Beds (🛏): 62.
Facilities: equipment storage area, kitchen, linen rental, laundry, on-site parking, camping, hostel-based programs, **MSA**, open all day.
Meals (🍴): breakfast, lunch, dinner.
Family rooms (👪): available.
Groups (🎭): welcome, reservations required.
Reservations advisable (👤a): always.
Reservations essential (👤e): groups.

Credit cards: Visa.
Manager: Clément Prince.
Directions: take Highway 20 (Trans-Canada Highway) to exit #228 (from Montréal) or exit #253 (from Québec), then take Route 265 15 kilometres past Plessiville.
Bus: ask to be let off at Domaine Fraser.

Québec

Sept-Îles

Auberge internationale le tangon

Once an important meeting place for Montagnais bands, Sept-Îles began as a French trading post in the 18th century. Situated on a bay which is almost completely circular, Sept-Îles is Canada's second largest port and the last major centre before Havre-St-Pierre, the last accessible town in the rugged north. Eight deep-water wharves operate year-round. The scenic boardwalk is a centre for summertime activity. The Auberge internationale le tangon offers easy access to nearby beaches. The nearby island park of Sept-Îles is home to a wide variety of marine birds and animals. At the Native Cultural Centre, local craftsmen sell moccasins, mittens, snowshoes, and other traditional items.

555 Cartier.
Mail (✉): C. P. 902.
Sept-Îles, Québec G4R 4L2.
Phone (☎): 418-962-8180.
Price (●): $12 CDN.
Closed (X): September–June.
Check-in (🕐): 8 a.m.–midnight.
Grade: simple (⌂).
Beds (⊨): 36.
Facilities: equipment storage area, kitchen, laundry facilities, linen rental, safety deposit boxes, on-site parking, camping, wheelchair accessible (♿), **MSA**, open all day.
Family rooms (f): available.
Groups (⊞): welcome.
Reservations essential (✦●): groups.
Credit cards: not accepted.

Manager: Jaques Bergeron.
Directions: behind new school on Cartier Street, take Laure Boulevard (Route 138) to Regneault, continue down Regneault to Cartier (east); close to train station and bus station.

Québec

Tadoussac

La Maison Majorique

Located at the mouth of the Saguenay, La Maison Majorique is the perfect base for exploring the port town of Tadoussac. The friendly staff accompany visitors on outdoor excursions to the surrounding forest and network of waterways. Tadoussac (meaning "knoll") is one of the oldest settlements on the North American continent, dating to 1599, when a French fur trader erected a trading post here. The area's two main attractions are the Saguenay Fjord, the largest in eastern North America, and the beluga, blue, and finback whales that feed in the St. Lawrence from June to October. Don't miss the winter activities, like dog sledding, snowmobiling, cross-country skiing, snowshoeing, etc.

154 Bateau Passeur, Tadoussac, Québec G0T 2A0.
Mail (✉): same.
Phone (☎): 418-235-4372.
Price (☺): $12 CDN.
Closed (X): never.
Check-in (🗓): 10 a.m.–11 p.m.
Grade: standard (🏠).
Beds (🛏): 46.
Facilities: laundry facilities, linen rental, lockers, on-site parking, wheelchair accessible (♿), camping, car rental, **MSA**.
Meals (🍴): breakfast, dinner.
Family rooms (👪): available.
Groups (🎪): welcome.
Reservations essential (📞): groups. **By FAX:** 418-235-4449.
Credit cards: not accepted.

Manager: Marthe Boulianne.
Directions: 700 metres past the boat and 300 metres from the bus station.

Québec

Trois-Rivières

Auberge la Flottille

Trois-Rivières is a prosperous industrial town. Located half-way between Montréal and Québec at the mouth of the St-Maurice River, it is the second oldest city in Canada. Auberge la Flottille is in the centre of town and provides easy access to many interesting historic sites, restaurants, cafés, and lounges. The hostel is recognized by the tourism bureau under its sign "l'hospitalité québecoise." There are a variety of festivals and special events year-round, including the International Poetry Festival.

497 rue Radisson,
Trois-Rivières, Québec G9A 2C7.
Mail (✉): same.
Phone (☎): 819-378-8010.
Price (💰): $13 CDN.
Closed (X): never.
Check-in (🕐): 10 a.m.–11 p.m.
Grade: standard (🏠).
Beds (🛏): 41 (summer), 22 (winter).
Facilities: equipment storage area, kitchen, laundry facilities, linen rental, on-site parking; **MSA**, open all day in summer, 8 a.m.–noon and 4–10:30 p.m. in winter.
Meals (🍴): breakfast.
Family rooms (👪): available.
Groups (🎪): welcome, reservations required.
Reservations advisable (📞): always.
Credit cards: not accepted.

Manager: Paul Gauthier.
Directions: take Route 138 east or Highway 40 along the north bank east from Montréal, follow signs to the city centre (centre-ville).

Québec

Val-David

Le Chalet Beaumont

The Chalet Beaumont in the Laurentian mountains resembles a pioneer-style log cabin. It contains many special features and comforts, including two large stone fireplaces. Just north of Montréal, the Laurentian mountains are reputed to be the region with the largest concentration of alpine ski hills in North America. Excellent cross-country ski trails and scenic forest glades for snowshoeing compliment the many downhill ski centres. It is an all-season area with popular summer activities including hiking, climbing, swimming, sailing, canoeing, horseback riding, and bicycling. The village of Val-David is a haven for artists and artisans, many of whom have set up residence within the area. Visitors can watch them at work in the local craft shops.

1451 Beaumont,
Val-David, Québec J0T 2N0.
Mail (✉): same.
Phone (☎): 819-322-1972.
Price (💰): $13 CDN.
Closed (X): never.
Check-in (🏠): 10 a.m.–10 p.m.
Grade: superior (🏠).
Beds (🛏): 65.
Facilities: equipment storage area, kitchen, linen rental, meeting rooms, on-site parking, hostel-based programs, ski, canoe, bicycle rental, **MSA** open all day.
Meals (🍴): breakfast; other meals for groups only.
Family rooms (👨‍👩‍👧): available.
Groups (🎠): welcome.
Reservations essential (📞e): groups always, reservations accepted at 819-322-1972 and 1-800-461-8585 (toll free inside Québec).

Reservations advisable (📞a): always. **By FAX:** 819-322-1972.
Credit cards: MasterCard, Visa.
Managers: Bernard and Francine De Pierre.
Directions: exit off Route 117 to Val-David, pass through town on Doncaster Road, turn left onto Beaumont Street, hostel is on the right.

Saskatchewan

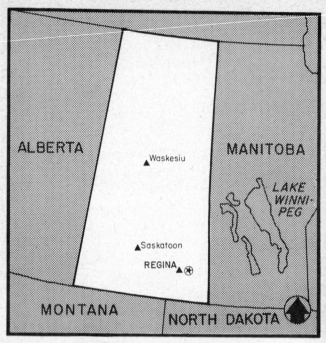

Helpful Organizations

Hostelling International—Canada Regional Office

Saskatchewan
2341 McIntyre Street
Regina, Saskatchewan S4P 2S3
Phone (☎): 306-791-8160
FAX: 306-721-2667

Provincial Tourism Office

Tourism Saskatchewan
2103 11th Avenue
Regina, Saskatchewan S4P 3V7
Phone (☎): 306-787-2300,
800-667-7538 (within province),
800-667-7191

Saskatchewan is Canada's "bread basket" and home to some of the largest wheat farms in the world. It also hosts 1.3 million hectares of park lands with more than 200 national, provincial, and regional parks. Regina, its capital, is an elegant city named after Queen Victoria.

Saskatchewan

Regina

Turgeon International Hostel

With the coming of the railway, Regina, a mere settlement in 1882, grew to become today's bustling provincial capital. The city hosts a renowned symphony orchestra and a wealth of natural and cultural history contained in museums, galleries, parklands, and recreational centres. Turgeon International Hostel, a designated "Municipal Heritage Property", is situated among the stately homes of the city's first families, adjacent to the beautiful Wascana Centre, an urban park in the heart of the city. On its grounds are a man-made lake, bicycle and hiking trails, a waterfowl park, museums, the Saskatchewan Science Centre, galleries, and the Saskatchewan Legislature. A few short blocks away, a wide range of entertainment, shopping, and restaurant services are available in Regina's downtown core.

2310 McIntyre Street,
Regina, Saskatchewan S4P 2S2.
Mail (✉): same.
Phone (☎): 306-791-8165.
Price (💰): $10 CDN.
Closed (X): never.
Check-in (🕐): 7–10 a.m., 5 p.m.–midnight.
Grade: superior (👫).
Beds (🛏): 50.
Facilities: equipment storage area, kitchen, laundry facilities, linen rental, lockers, limited street parking, travel library, hostel-based programs, **MSA**.
Meals (🍴): for groups upon request.
Family rooms (👪): available.
Groups (🏘): welcome.
Reservations advisable (📞): always.
Credit cards: MasterCard, Visa.

Directions: 1 block east of Albert Street on McIntyre Street, between 15th Avenue and College. From Highway 1 (Trans-Canada Highway), Highway 6, and Highway 11, follow Albert Street to 15th Avenue; near bus station.

Saskatchewan

Saskatoon
Patricia Hotel

Saskatoon hosts a wide range of festivals and events, including "Folkfest", a 3-day multicultural extravaganza of food, dancing and culture; the "Fringe", a wacky celebration of live theatre with entertainers from around the world; and the Pro Tour Rodeo. The city also offers activities for all tastes, from racing to golf, and theatres to drive-in movies. For outdoor fun, there's the Forestry Farm and Zoo and the Beaver Creek Conservation Area. Culture buffs can explore the Western Development Museum, the Ukrainian Museum of Canada, the Sport Hall of Fame and the Diefenbaker Centre at the University of Saskatchewan. The Patricia Hotel is in the centre of it all—shopping, dining, and sightseeing—with friendly staff eager to make your visit the best it can be. Just outside the city, enjoy Batoche Historical Park, Pike Lake Provincial Park, and Wanuskewan, a native word for "peace of mind".

345 Second Avenue North, Saskatoon, Saskatchewan S7K 2B8.
Mail (✉): same.
Phone (☎): 306-242-8861.
Price (●): $10 CDN.
Closed (X): never.
Check-in (⏷): 24 hours.
Grade: (SA). Beds (▬): 20.
Facilities: equipment storage area, lockers, on-site parking, laundry facilities nearby, open all day.
Meals (✎): breakfast, lunch, dinner.

Family rooms (⚘): available.
Groups (🏛): welcome.
Reservations advisable (🛎a): always.
Credit cards: all major credit cards accepted.
Manager: Murray Sadownick.
Directions: on the corner of Second Avenue and 25th Avenue.
Bus: go 1.5 blocks east from station to Second Avenue and 2 blocks north to 25th Avenue.

Saskatchewan

Waskesiu Lake

Waskesiu International Hostel

Waskesiu is a busy town in the middle of 388,000 hectares of Canadian wilderness known as Prince Albert National Park. Waskesiu International Hostel is situated in the town site, just minutes from a superb beach and many wondrous natural attractions.

Prince Albert National Park was once home to Grey Owl, one of the world's most famous park naturalists and impostors. Born Archibald Belaney, Grey Owl was an Englishman who came to Canada to fulfill a boyhood dream of living in the wilderness. He dyed and braided his hair, donned traditional buckskin clothing, changed his name, and presented himself to the world as the son of an Apache woman. His cabin on the shores of Lake Ajawaan can still be reached by a 20-kilometre overnight hike.

Montreal Road.
Mail (✉): P.O. Box 85, Waskesiu Lake, Saskatchewan S0J 2Y0.
Phone (☎): 306-663-5450.
Price (●): $10 CDN.
Closed (X): October–May.
Check-in (🕐): 7–10 a.m., 5 p.m.–midnight.
Grade: standard (♠).
Beds (🛏): 60.
Facilities: equipment storage area, kitchen, laundry facilities, linen rental, lockers, on-site parking, hostel-based programs, **MSA**.
Meals (🍴): for groups by request.
Family rooms: available.
Groups (🎪): welcome.

Reservations advisable: always. **Off-season:** mail to 2341 McIntyre Street, Regina, Saskatchewan S4P 2S3, or call 306-791-8160.
Credit cards: MasterCard, Visa.
Directions: take Route 264 to the town of Waskesiu, turn left onto Montreal Road, look for hostel sign.

Yukon

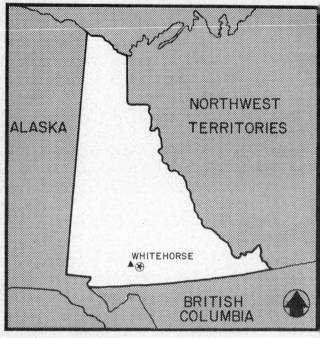

Helpful Organizations

Hostelling International—Canada Regional Office

Inquiries about Yukon Territory
c/o **British Columbia Region**
1515 Discovery Street
Vancouver, British Columbia V6R 4K5
Phone (☎): 604-224-7177
FAX: 604-224-4852

Territory Tourism Office

Tourism Yukon
P.O. Box 2703
Whitehorse, Yukon Y1A 2C6
Phone (☎): 403-667-5340
800-661-0494

Yukon's Whitehorse hostel offers all day access.

The Yukon is part of Canada's northland—the land of the midnight sun—where a
day can last 24 hours! It's home to some of Canada's mightiest rivers, lakes, vast
forests, and tundra landscapes. It is also rich with history and the lively heritage of
the Klondike Gold Rush.

Discounts

Present a valid hostel membership card at the time of purchase to receive the
following discounts:

Rent-A-Wreck - 668-7554. $5 per rental or $25 off for a week or more.

Yukon

SUPPLEMENTAL ACCOMMODATION

Whitehorse

Fourth Avenue Residence

After the building of the Alaska Highway in 1942, Whitehorse quickly grew from a small town of 500 to a modern city of more than 20,000. In 1953, Whitehorse became the capital of the Yukon, but it still retains much of its historic character. Many attractions date back to the gold rush days. The Yukon Historical and Museums Association offers free walking tours of downtown during July and August. Fourth Avenue Residence is within walking distance of the major points of interest. With long summer days (daylight lasts until midnight), visitors have more time to enjoy bicycling, canoeing, and fishing. Hike to Grey Mountain or follow the scenic trails of Miles Canyon and Hidden Lake.

4051 Fourth Avenue,
Whitehorse, Yukon
Y1A 1H1.
Mail (✉): same.
Phone (☎): 403-667-4471.
Price (◒): from $16.20 CDN.
Closed (X): never.
Check-in (🕐): after 1 p.m.
Grade: (SA) Beds (🛏): 122.
Facilities: baggage storage area, kitchen, laundry facilities, lockers, on-site parking, limited wheel-chair accessible (♿); adjacent to city pool with sauna and whirlpool, open all day.
Family rooms (👪): available.
Groups (🎎): small groups welcome.
Reservations advisable (🖐a): always. **By FAX:** 403-667-6457.
Credit cards: MasterCard, Visa.
Manager: Marg Rose.
Directions: on Fourth Avenue near Lowe Street, close to bus station.

United States of America

Population:	234 million
Area:	3.6 million sq. mi., 9.4 million km^2
Capital:	Washington, D.C.
Language:	English
Currency:	U.S. dollar ($) = 100 cents
Total hostels:	180

The USA is variety. It is tundra where the soil is frozen year round in Alaska. It is temperate zone rain forests in Oregon and Washington. It is majestic Rocky Mountains spanning several states and Canada. It is the Grand Canyon in Arizona. It is hot deserts in the Southwest. It is broad prairies in the central region, where half of the world's corn and one third of its wheat are grown. It is quaint New England villages. It is sunny beaches. It is wilderness protected parks and preserves. It is New York City and Los Angeles.

HOSTELLING INTERNATIONAL ®

Hostelling International–USA
National Office
733 15th Street, Northwest
Suite 840
Washington, D.C. 20005
Telephone: 202-783-6161
Fax: 202-783-6171

You'll find hostels in and near some of the most beautiful and most interesting parts of the country. You'll find each hostel a unique experience, whether in a nationally recognized and AYH-preserved historic property or a simple shelter. And to help you gain the most from each and every place you visit, there's a wide array of programs, from architectural walking tours to environmental programs, designed to introduce you to the wonders of nature. Hike, bike, ski, trek, sail, or photograph—just take full advantage of the programs and local discounts AYH offers.

Alaska

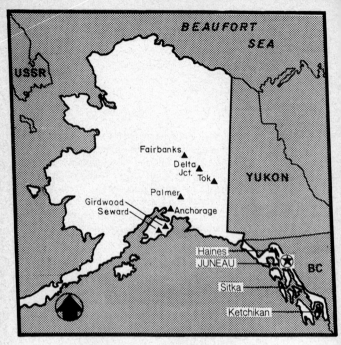

Helpful Organizations

AYH Council Office

Alaska Council
700 H Street
Anchorage, AK 99501
Phone (☎): 907-562-7772
(phone answered by machine)

State Tourism Office

Alaska Division of Tourism
P.O. Box E
Juneau, AK 99811-0800
Phone (☎): 907-465-2010

Discounts

Present a valid hostel membership card at the time of purchase and receive the following discounts:

Tok

First Gallery - 10% off all wood, fiber, glass, ceramic, and graphic arts; 10% off German–English translating service - Mile 1313 Alaska Highway, 907-883-5600.
Gateway Salmon Bake - 10% off on dinner for AYH members.
Huck Hobbit's Homestead Retreat - 20% off canoe trips and guided fishing trips (20% discount is also available on cabin rental & camping fees - no AYH-Hostel in nearby area)
Mukluk Land - 10% off admission price.
Northern Energy Corp. - 5¢ discount per gallon for AYH members and groups.

Alaska

Anchorage

Anchorage International AYH-Hostel

Located in the heart of Alaska's largest city, just blocks away from the bus and train stations, the Anchorage International AYH-Hostel is near the Alaska Center for Performing Arts, Anchorage Museum of History, and the Visual Arts Center. The hostel sponsors van trips to see the stunning blue ice of Portage Glacier and the Kenai Peninsula.

Anchorage is famous for Fur Rendezvous, one of the biggest winter festivals in the country. But there are plenty of other attractions. Those looking for more unique ways to see the sights can enjoy flightseeing and dog sled tours. And, of course, the skiing is terrific. Alpine skiing is available at Hilltop Ski Area, Alpenglow, and Alyeska (35 miles south).

700 H Street,
Anchorage, AK 99501.
Mail (✉): same.
Phone (☎): 907-276-3635.
Price (☺): $12 U.S.
Closed (X): never.
Office Hours: 8 a.m.–noon, 5 p.m.–midnight.
Grade: Hostel.
Beds (🛏): 95.
Facilities: equipment storage area, information desk, kitchen, laundry facilities, lockers/baggage storage, linen rental, limited street parking, wheelchair accessible. (♿), **MSA.**
Family rooms (🛏): available.
Groups (🏫): welcome.
Reservations essential (☎e): May 15–September 15. **By phone:** not accepted.
Credit cards: not accepted.

Manager: Walt Morgan.
Directions: downtown on H Street between Seventh and Eighth, across from Arco Tower; short walk from train station. **Airport (✈):** take People Mover bus #6 to the corner of Seventh and H Streets.
Bus: 1 block from the hostel.

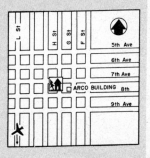

Alaska

Delta Junction

Delta International AYH-Hostel

Situated at the end of the Alaska-Canadian Highway, Delta Junction is the perfect place to stop and enjoy the vast Alaskan wilderness. Spend a day fishing or canoeing on the Delta and Tanana rivers, just minutes from the hostel. Cameras and hiking boots are a must for those who wish to get a closer look at the spectacular mountains that highlight the area.

Also bring the camera to Clearwater State Recreation Site; it's a good spot to see the spring and fall migrations of sandhill cranes, geese, and other waterfowl. For the cyclist, mountain biking in this area provides an exhilarating challenge.

After a sun-soaked day in the great outdoors, join in a game of volleyball at the hostel or cuddle up in your sleeping bag and drift off to sleep in a smoke-free environment.

Main Street USA.

Mail (✉): P.O. Box 971, Delta Junction, AK 99737.
Phone (☎): 907-895-5074.
Price (☺): $7 U.S.
Closed (X): September–May.
Office Hours: 8–11 a.m., 3–11 p.m.
Grade: Hostel.
Beds (⊨): 10, sleeping bag required.
Facilities: information desk available, kitchen, on-site parking.
Family rooms (👪): available.
Groups (👪): welcome.
Reservations: not essential.
By phone: accepted.
Credit cards: not accepted.
Manager: Marsha Fulton.

Directions: 10 miles north of Delta Junction, off Alaska Route 2 at milepost 272.

Alaska

Fairbanks
Fairbanks Home Hostel

This is the northernmost hostel facility in the USA. In Fairbanks, view the Trans-Alaska Pipeline which transverses the area. The University of Alaska-Fairbanks has an excellent museum and its Geophysical Institute has a great deal of information on the Aurora Borealis. There are also plentiful lakes for canoeing and fishing and hot springs nearby.

Call for reservations.
Phone (☎): 907-456-4159
Price (●): $6.25 U.S.
Closed (X): September 15–May 15.
Grade: home hostel (🏠).
Beds (🛏): 5.
Facilities: kitchen, linen rental, deck and gazebo, **MSA**.

Reservations essential (⋅🏠●): always; groups of less than 6 are welcome. **By phone:** call for information.
Credit cards: not accepted.
Managers: Paul G. Schultz.
Directions: available upon reservation confirmation.

Alaska

Girdwood
Alyeska Home Hostel

This cabin, with wood heat and gas lights, is in a picturesque valley surrounded by mountains and glaciers. Although there's no hot water, the sauna more than makes up for it. For those who love downhill skiing, Alyeska Resort and Ski Area is a half-mile away.

Mail (✉): P.O. Box 10-4099, Anchorage, AK 99510.
Phone (☎): 907-783-2099.
Price (●): $8 U.S.
Closed (X): never.
Grade: home hostel (🏠).
Beds (🛏): 8.
Facilities: equipment storage area, kitchen, linen rental, on-site parking, sauna instead of shower, **MSA**.

Family rooms (👪): available.
Reservations essential (☎●): always. **By phone:** 907-276-3635.
Credit cards: not accepted.
Directions: available upon reservation request.

Haines
Bear Creek Camp and Hostel

The Bear Creek Camp and Hostel offers wood-heated cabins near the frequently traveled Haines Highway, making it easily accessible to travelers. Haines' most famous citizens are the thousands of American bald eagles that nest in Chilkat State Park between November and February. Tour this quaint fishing village on the spectacular Chilkat Peninsula. Be sure to stop at Fort William Seward and see the Native American village. Outdoor enthusiasts can wander the area's four first-class trails or fish in the clear blue streams.

Lot 36A, Small Tract Road.
Mail (✉): P.O. Box 1158, Haines, AK 99827.
Phone (☎): 907-766-2259.
Price (●): $10 U.S.
Closed (X): November 1–March 1.
Office Hours: 8–10 a.m., 5–10 p.m.
Beds (🛏): 20. **Grade: (SA)**.
Facilities: 6 cabins, information desk, kitchen, laundry facilities, on-site parking.
Family rooms (👪): available.

Groups (🎚): welcome; reservations required March–November.
Reservations essential (☎●): June 1–September 1. **By phone:** accepted.
Credit cards: not accepted.
Managers: Alan and Lucille Miller.
Directions: 90 miles northwest of Juneau on Alaska Highway 7, south on Third Avenue to Mud Bay Road, veer left onto Small Tract Road, hostel is on the left.

Alaska

Ketchikan

Ketchikan AYH-Hostel

The Ketchikan AYH-Hostel, located in a local church, provides floor mattresses, free hot drinks, and home-baked sweets for hostellers. The best way to see Alaska's southernmost city is on foot. The Ketchikan Visitors Bureau can help plan a memorable trip to Tongass National Forest and the gorgeous Misty Fiords National Monument.

The Tongass Historical Society Museum offers background on the Native Americans, the fishing industry, and the more colorful parts of Ketchikan's history. The Totem Heritage Center and the Saxman Native Village have many totem poles made by the Tlingit and Haida tribes. Hike up Deer Mountain for a panoramic view of the Prince of Wales Island.

Grant and Main.
Mail (✉): P.O. Box 8515, Ketchikan, AK 99901.
Phone (☎): 907-225-3319, 907-225-3780.
Price (⊖): $7 U.S.
Closed (X): September 2–May 23.
Office Hours: 7–9 a.m., 6–11 p.m.
Grade: Hostel.
Beds (⊨): 33 floor mats; bring a sleeping bag.
Facilities: information desk, linen rental, kitchen, showers, on-site parking at night only, **MSA**.
Family rooms (⌂): limited availability.
Groups (▥): welcome; reservations required.
Reservations essential (☎): always for groups. **By phone:** accepted.
Credit cards: not accepted.

Directions: downtown in First United Methodist Church at Grant and Main, 2 miles south of ferry from airport or Marine Highway; accessible only by boat or airplane.

Alaska

Seward

Snow River AYH-Hostel

The Snow River AYH-Hostel, with stone-terrace gardens, is in the park near a waterfall. The hostel is a favorite of those wishing to explore the Kenai Peninsula. Explore the park's breathtaking coastal mountain ranges on foot or by boat through a charter service.

Alaska Highway 9, milepost 16.
Mail (✉): HCR 64, Box 425 Seward, AK 99664.
Phone (☎): none; call 907-276-3635 for information.
Price (☺): $10 U.S.
Closed (X): never.
Office Hours: 8–10 a.m., 5–10 p.m.
Grade: Hostel
Beds (🛏): 10.
Facilities: equipment storage area, information desk, kitchen, linen rental, on-site parking, shower, **MSA**, sleeping bags required
Family rooms (🏠): available.
Groups (🍴): welcome; reservations required.
Reservations essential (☎): always for groups. **By phone:** not accepted.
Credit cards: not accepted.
Managers: Woody and Denise Walker.

Directions: 16 miles north of Seward off Alaska Highway 9 at milepost 16, follow the signs.

Alaska

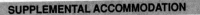

Sheep Mountain (Palmer)
Sheep Mountain Lodge

The historic Sheep Mountain Lodge is nestled between the Chugach and Talkeetna Mountains, near the headwaters of the Matanuska River. The great Matanuska Glacier is just 10 miles away. Cycle, hike, take a guided rafting tour and glacier walk, view Dall sheep, or go horseback riding in the Alaskan wilderness. Although there is no kitchen, the lodge provides meals in a dining room overlooking the mountains.

Alaska Highway 1, milepost 113.
Mail (✉): HC03 Box 8490, Palmer, AK 99645.
Phone (☎): 907-745-5121.
Price (☻): $8 U.S.
Closed (X): October–April.
Office Hours: call ahead.
Beds (▬): 12. **Grade: (SA).**
Facilities (mixed use): information desk available, on-site parking, cafe.
Meals (🍴): at cafe.

Family rooms (♨): available.
Groups (▥): welcome.
Reservations advisable (👤a): always. **By phone:** with credit card confirmation.
Credit cards: MasterCard, Visa.
Managers: David Cohen, Diane Schneider.
Directions: 70 miles northeast of Palmer, on Alaska Highway 1 at milepost 113.

Alaska

Sitka
Sitka Youth Hostel

Situated on the Alaskan Panhandle, Sitka is connected to the mainland by a ferry system. Staying at the Sitka Youth Hostel, located three miles from Sitka, is the best way to enjoy both the city and the lush countryside. Picturesque Mount Edgecumbe and the Pacific Ocean coastline offer limitless opportunities for swimming, scuba diving, fishing, and hiking. The Sitka National Historical Park is noted for its excellent collection of totem poles, and don't miss Castle Hill, where the transfer of Alaska from the Russians occurred.

303 Kimsham Street.
Mail (✉): P.O. Box 2645, Sitka, AK 99835.
Phone (☎): 907-747-8356.
Price (●): $7 U.S.
Closed (X): September–May.
Office Hours: 8–10 a.m., 6–10 p.m.
Grade: (SA).
Beds (⊨): 20; bring a sleeping bag.
Facilities: on-site parking, **MSA**.

Groups (▥): welcome; reservations required.
Reservations essential (⊷●): always. **By phone:** accepted.
Credit cards: not accepted.
Directions: at the corner of Kimsham Street and Edgecumbe Drive. **Ferry:** take Halibut Point Road, left on Peterson Street to Kimsham.

Alaska

Tok

Tok International AYH-Hostel

Tok (pronounced TOKE) International AYH-Hostel, hours away from any large city, offers clean air, solitude, and starry skies. For those who enjoy backwoods ruggedness, this tent hostel is clean and comfortable, with managers who know the area well.

Spend the afternoon fishing in the Tanana River or just exploring the ecosystem that surrounds it. The historic Eagle Trail, which is only two miles from the hostel, is a great way to see the area as the early settlers did. The nearby town of Tok, located 94 miles from the U.S.-Canadian border, is the gateway to Alaska.

Mile 1322 1/2 Alaska Hwy.
Mail (✉): Box 532, Tok, AK 99780.
Phone (☎): (907)883-3745.
Price (●): $7.50 U.S.
Closed (X): September 16–May 14.
Office Hours: 8–10 a.m., 5–10 p.m.
Grade: Rustic.
Beds (🛏): 10; bring a sleeping bag.
Facilities: kitchen, limited linens, lockers/baggage storage, on-site parking, **MSA**.
Family rooms (👪): available.
Groups (👥): welcome.
Reservations: not essential.
Credit cards: not accepted.
Managers: Michelle and Wayne Stout.

Directions: 8 miles west of Tok on Alcan Highway at Mile 1322-1/2, turn south on Pringle Drive and follow signs to the hostel.

Arizona

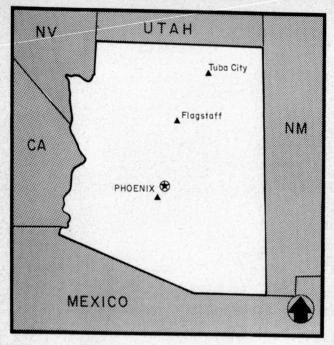

Helpful Organizations

AYH Council Office

Arizona-Southern Nevada Council
1046 East Lemon Street
Tempe, AZ 85281-3904
Phone (☎): 602-894-5128

State Tourism Office

Arizona Office of Tourism
1100 West Washington Street
Phoenix, AZ 85007
Phone (☎): 602-542-8687

Discounts

Present a valid hostel membership card at the time of purchase and receive the following discounts:

Flagstaff

Admiral's Rent A Car - guaranteed lowest rates on car rentals in Flagstaff exclusively for hostel guests (contact hostel for details) - 602-774 2731.
Charley's Restaurant - 15% off food purchase, downstairs; 50% off entertainment charge at Charley's pub. Performances live on stage every Tuesday night - 23 North Leroux.

Phoenix

Arizona Center Plaza - guarantees all year a free buffet dinner from 5–7 p.m., Monday–Friday - Arizona Center (downtown) Sports Bar.
Mystery Castle - offers reduced entry fees for hostellers - 1301 E. Mineral.

Arizona

Flagstaff
Weatherford Hotel

Enjoy the charm of yesterday and the convenience and comfort of today at the Weatherford Hotel, which is listed on the National Register of Historic Places. Close to the train and bus stations, the hotel is a convenient stop for Grand Canyon visitors.

23 North Leroux,
Flagstaff, AZ 86001.

Mail (✉): same.
Phone (☎): 602-774-2731.
Price (●): $10 U.S.
Closed (X): never.
Office Hours: 7 a.m.–noon, 5–10 p.m.
Beds (🛏): 52. **Grade: (SA)**.
Facilities: equipment storage area, information desk, kitchen, linen rental, lockers/baggage storage, on-site parking, pub with live music on premises.
Family rooms (🛏): available.

Groups (👪): welcome; reservations required.
Reservations essential (☎): June–October. **By phone:** accepted with credit card confirmation.
Credit cards: American Express, MasterCard, Visa.
Managers: Pamela Green, Margaret Rees.
Directions: 1/2 block east from Greyhound station, 4 blocks north Milton Road, 3 blocks east Santa Fe Avenue, 1 block north Leroux Street.

Arizona

Phoenix

Metcalf House AYH-Hostel

The Metcalf House AYH-Hostel, located in the heart of Phoenix, is a short distance from the airport, bus, and train stations, and within walking distance of downtown, parks, museums, and shopping centers.

Arizona's capital city, Phoenix, has much to offer. The Desert Botanical Gardens at Papago Park features Sonoran Desert plant life. Visit the anthropological exhibits in the Heard Museum, tune in to the Phoenix Symphony, or join in the fun at the Hello Phoenix Festival in March.

Hike in nearby Squaw Peak, Camelback, and South Mountain parks, ride down the Salt River on an inner tube, or explore the city by bicycle. The Arizona–Southern Nevada Council of American Youth Hostels also sponsors many weekend activities.

1026 North Ninth Street,
Phoenix, AZ 85006.
Mail (✉): same.
Phone (☎): 602-254-9803.
Price (💰): $10 U.S.
Closed (X): never.
Office Hours: 7–10 a.m., 5–11 p.m.
Grade: Hostel.
Beds (🛏): 40.
Facilities: common room open for day use, late key available, equipment storage area, kitchen, laundry facilities, linen rental, lockers/baggage storage, street parking only, **MSA**.
Family Rooms (🏠): must reserve.
Groups (🎪): welcome.
Reservations: not essential.
Credit cards: not accepted.
Manager: Susan Gunn.

Directions: downtown on Ninth between Portland and Roosevelt, 2 blocks east of Seventh Street.
Airport (✈): take Super Shuttle (downtown) to hostel.

Arizona

Tuba City
Greyhills Inn

A former Bureau of Indian Affairs dormitory, the Greyhills Inn is on a Navajo reservation. Learn about the history, culture, and modern-day lifestyle of Navajo and Hopi tribes. Nearby attractions include beautiful Pasture Canyon and several dinosaur tracks. Tuba City is convenient to the Grand Canyon, Lake Powell Recreation Area, and Monument Valley National Park.

160 Warrior Drive.
Mail (✉): P.O. Box 160, Tuba City, AZ 86045.
Phone (☎): 602-283-6273, ext. 41.
Price (💰): $10 U.S.
Closed (X): never.
Office Hours: 8–10 a.m., 1–10 p.m.
Beds (🛏): 64. **Grade: (SA)**.
Facilities: information desk, laundry facilities, linen rental, on-site parking, wheelchair accessible (♿).
Family rooms (👪): available.
Groups (🏛): welcome.

Reservations essential (🔑): May 15–August 31. **By phone:** accepted.
Credit cards: not accepted.
Manager: Marie R. Morales.
Directions: from U.S. Highway 160 and 264 Junction, go east 1 mile on U.S. Highway 160, turn north at Tuba City post office, go 1/4 mile on Warrior Drive, (on the east side of the road).

California

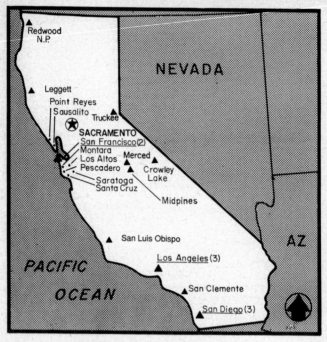

Helpful Organizations

AYH Council Offices

Central California Council
P.O. Box 3645
Merced, CA 95344
Phone (☎): 209-383-0686

Golden Gate Council
425 Divisadero Street #301
San Francisco, CA 94117
Phone (☎): 415-863-9939
FAX: 415-863-3865

Los Angeles Council
1434 Second Street
Santa Monica, CA 90401
Phone (☎): 310-393-3413
FAX: 310-393-1769

San Diego Council
335 West Beech Street
San Diego, CA 92101
Phone (☎): 619-338-9981
FAX: 619-338-0129

State Tourism Office

California Office of Tourism
P.O. Box 189
Sacramento, CA 95812-0189
Phone (☎): 800-862-2543

Discounts

Present a valid hostel membership card at the time of purchase and receive the following discounts:

Crescent City

Undersea World - 20% discount on admissions to aquarium - 304 Highway 101, South, 707-464-3522.

Discounts

Crowley Lake

Alpine Adventures Tours & Guides - 15%-25% discount on hot air ballooning, jeep rides, waterskiing, and riding - Old Mammoth Road & Highway 203, Mammoth Lakes, 934-7188.

Mammoth Sporting Goods - 15% to 25% discount on bicycle, ski, and snowboard rentals - Old Mammoth Road, Mammoth Lakes, 619-934-3239.

Redwood National Park

Trees of Mystery - 20% admission discount, 1550 Highway 101, Klamath, 707-482-2251 or toll-free 1-800-638-3389.

Undersea World - 20% admission discount, 304 Highway 101 South, Crescent City, 707-464-3522.

Leggett

Garske's Leggett Market - 10% discount on all grocery items except milk, cigarettes, or alcohol - 67660 Drive-Thru Tree Road, 707-925 6279.

The Peg House Delicatessen - 10% discount on all deli case items, including salads, ice cream, cheeses, and our world-famous Big Mouth sandwiches (outdoor picnic area available) - 69500 North Highway 101, 707-925-6444.

Palo Alto

Country Sun Natural Foods - 10% discount coupon available at Hidden Villa Hostel. Store located at 440 California Avenue, 415-324-9190.

Hidden Villa Nature Store - 10% discount of all items with hostel overnight receipt. 26870 Moody Road, Los Altos Hills, 415-949-8658.

San Pedro

Kings Bicycle Store - 10% discount on clothing, shoes, accessories; 5% discount on tires; 10% discount on labor for bicycle tune-ups. 1209 South Pacific Avenue, 310-833-2835.

Lighthouse Deli - 10% discount on purchase of meal (breakfast, lunch, or dinner). 508 W. 39th Street, 310-548-3354.

Sacred Grounds - 10% discount on all items. 399 W. 6th Street, 310-514-0800.

Sailboards West - 10% discount and transportation to the beach. 2128 South Pacific Avenue, 310-548-3537.

Wallaby Darned - 10% discount on total of check. 617 South Centre Street, 310-833-3629.

Santa Cruz

Adventure Sports Unlimited (scuba diving, kayaking, swimming) -10% discount - 303 Potrero Street, 408-458 3648.

Bicycle Trip Shop - 1201 Soquel Avenue at Seabright, 408-427-2580.

Guaranga's Vegetarian Restaurant - 503 Water Street, 408-427-0294.

Heartwood Spa (hot tub and sauna garden) - 10% discount - 3150-A Mission Drive, 408-462-2192.

Pacific Parasail - $5 off - Municipal Wharf, 408-423- 3545.

Roaring Camp & Big Trees - 20% discount; narrow gauge railroad - Graham Hill Road, Felton, CA, 408-335-4484.

Santa Cruz Health Club - 1212 17th Avenue, 408-462-2544.

Los Angeles (Santa Monica)

Mike Photo and Sound - discount on equipment, purchases, and repairs (must show hostel receipt) - 1259 Third Street Promenade, 393-9371.

California

Crowley Lake

Hilton Creek International AYH-Hostel

Located on the eastern slopes of California's Sierra Nevada Mountains, the Hilton Creek International AYH-Hostel is halfway between Yosemite and Death Valley in Inyo National Forest. Take advantage of the hostel's free guided mountain bike tours to historic mines. Explore the backcountry on skis with the hostel's "Intro to Ski-Touring" program. Ski Mammoth Mountain, California's highest ski area. Explore nearby Mono Lake, visit the ghost town of Bodie, and wander through the rugged high country of the John Muir Wilderness Area.

Crowley Lake Drive.
Mail ()): R.R. 1, P.O. Box 1128, Crowley Lake, CA 93546.
Phone (☎): 619-935-4989.
Price (◒): $9 U.S. + tax (summer), $11 U.S. + tax (winter).
Closed (X): never.
Office Hours: 7–10 a.m., 4–11 p.m.
Grade: Hostel. **Beds (▭):** 22.
Facilities: cross-country ski equipment rental, hot tub, day use of common room, information room, kitchen, laundry facilities, lockers/baggage storage, linen rental, on-site parking, **MSA.**
Meals (✎): breakfast.
Family rooms (👪): available.
Groups (▥): welcome; reservations required November 15–April 30.
Reservations advisable (◑a): November 15–May 15. **By phone:** not accepted.
Credit cards: not accepted.
Managers: Robert Berwyn, Sue Judson.

Directions: 14 miles southeast of Mammoth Lakes; take U.S. Highway 395 south to McGee Creek exit, turn left at stop sign onto Crowley Lake Drive, go exactly two miles to hostel sign; turn right; take U.S. Highway 395 north to Crowley Lake/Hilton Creek exit, left on South Landing Road for 1/2 mile, right on Crowley Lake Drive for 1 mile to hostel sign, turn left.

132

California

Leggett

Eel River Redwoods AYH-Hostel

The Eel River Redwoods AYH-Hostel sits on the banks of the twisting Eel River in the midst of a redwood and fir forest. Managers Gene and Sandra Barnett give insiders' tips on where to find black sand beaches. Go whale watching, ride on a steam locomotive, swim in the river's water hole, relax in the all-night sauna. Hike through Standish and Hickey State Park. The world-famous tree house and drive-through tree are only two miles away. And it's an easy drive to the Avenue of the Giant Redwoods and the coastal towns of Mendocino and Fort Bragg.

70400 North U.S. Highway 101, Leggett, CA 95585.
Mail (✉): same.
Phone (☎): 707-925-6469.
Price (💰): $10 U.S. + tax.
Closed (X): never.
Office Hours: 24 hrs.
Grade: Hostel.
Beds (🛏): 40.
Facilities: bicycles and sporting equipment, family and couples cabins, Indian tipi, equipment storage area, information desk, kitchen, laundry facilities, linen rental, lockers/baggage storage, on-site parking, bistro (dinner only), free sauna, **MSA**.
Meals (🍴): at bistro.
Family rooms (👪): available.
Groups (👥): welcome; reservations required.
Reservations advisable (📞): April–October. **By phone:** accepted with credit card confirmation.
Credit cards: accepted for reservations only.

Managers: Gene and Sandra Barnett.
Directions: 2 miles north of Leggett on U.S. Highway 101 at Bell Glen Eel River Inn; **Bus:** take Greyhound Line #607 to Standish-Hickey stop, walk 1/2 mile north (driver may let you off at hostel driveway).

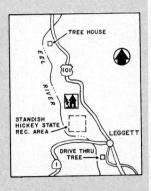

California

Los Angeles (Disneyland Area)

Fullerton Hacienda AYH-Hostel

Only five miles from the magic of Disneyland, the Fullerton Hacienda AYH-Hostel offers an inexpensive, fun, and friendly place to rest after seeing Tomorrowland and Space Mountain. The romantic Spanish-style house was once a part of an old California dairy farm. Take advantage of the many day tours offered by local operators to most Southern California attractions: Universal Studios, Knotts Berry Farm Amusement Park, and Tijuana, Mexico.

1700 North Harbor Boulevard, Fullerton, CA 92635.

Mail (✉): same.
Phone (☎): 714-738-3721.
Price (☺): $12 U.S. + tax.
Closed (X): never.
Office Hours: 7:30 a.m.–11 p.m.
Grade: Hostel.
Beds (🛏): 24.
Facilities: equipment storage area, large fireplace, information desk, kitchen, laundry facilities, linen rental, lockers/baggage storage, on-site parking, wheelchair accessible (&), **MSA.**

Reservations essential (⬛e): October 15–March 15 for groups.

Reservations advisable (⬛a): summer. **By phone:** accepted with credit card confirmation 24 hours in advance. **By FAX:** 714-738-0925.
Credit cards: MasterCard, Visa, JCB.
Manager: Rob Delamater.

Directions: 3 miles north of California Highway 91 on Harbor Boulevard, in Brea Dam Park.
Airport (✈): Take a "Golden Star" or "Airway" bus shuttle from LAX directly to the Hostel's front door (only $15 - excellent price!). **Bus or Train:** from Fullerton Transporation Center take bus #41 West north on Harbor Boulevard to Brea Dam Park.

California

Los Angeles (San Pedro)

Los Angeles International AYH-Hostel

Situated on a bluff in Angels Gate Park, Los Angeles International AYH-Hostel overlooks the Pacific Ocean, Santa Catalina Island, and the port of Los Angeles. Spend your day biking, swimming, sunning, fishing, or hiking, then spend the evening socializing on the hostel's patio or relaxing in the common rooms. Take a walk down to one of the area's beaches and examine the interesting tide pools and unique sea life. To get a closer look at Los Angeles Harbor, take an evening cruise. From Christmas to April, observe gray whales on their annual Alaska–Baja journey.

3601 South Gaffey Street #613.
Mail (✉): P.O. Box 5345, San Pedro, CA 90733.
Phone (☎): 310-831-8109.
Price (⊖): $11.25 U.S.
Closed (X): never.
Office Hours: 7 a.m.–midnight.
Grade: Hostel.
Beds (🛏): 60.
Facilities: information desk, kitchen, laundry facilities, linen rental, lockers/baggage storage, free on-site parking, sorry - no sleeping bags allowed, **MSA**.
Family rooms (⚥): available.
Groups (🏛): welcome.
Reservations essential (☎): June-August. **By phone:** accepted with credit card confirmation. **By FAX:** 310-831-4635 with credit card confirmation.
Credit cards: MasterCard, Visa, JCB.

Directions: 5 miles south of Interstate 110 on Gaffey, in Angels Gate-Park. **Airport (✈):** take parking lot C bus to bus terminal #8, take RTD #232 to Avalon Boulevard, take RTD #446 south on Avalon (using transfer ticket from #232) to Angels Gate Park.

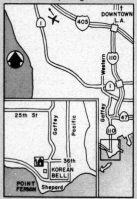

California

Los Angeles (Santa Monica)

Santa Monica International AYH-Hostel

The Santa Monica International AYH-Hostel, a modern four-story facility, is located just two blocks from the beach and the Santa Monica Pier. Built around a lovely courtyard, the hostel features 37 dorm rooms (including twins and quads), lots of common areas, and a full-service travel store. The hostel also includes the old Rapp Saloon, circa 1875, which has been restored and furnished in period style and is now used as a common room. Good public transport makes the hostel easily accessible from L.A. International Airport and area attractions.

1436 Second Street,
Santa Monica, CA 90401.
Mail (✉): same.
Phone (☎): 310-393-9913.
Price (●): $14 U.S. + tax.
Closed (X): never.
Office Hours: 24 hours.
Beds (🛏): 200. **Grade:** Hostel.
Facilities: bicycle storage, open-air courtyard, couples rooms, information desk, kitchen, laundry facilities, library, linen rental, lockers/baggage storage, TV lounge, travel store, wheelchair accessible (♿), **MSA.**
Family rooms (🛏): available at higher rate. **Groups (🛏):** welcome; reservations required.
Reservations essential (📞e): May–October; always for groups. **Reservations advisable (📞a):** always. By phone: accepted with credit card confirmation and 24-hour advance notice. **By FAX:** 310-393-1769 with credit card confirmation. IBN global reservation system available.
Credit cards: MasterCard, Visa, JCB.

Managers: Melissa Kelley, Chris Fencl.
Directions: 2 blocks east of beach and Santa Monica Pier.
Airport (✈): take LAX shuttle bus #C to city bus terminal, take Santa Monica municipal bus #3 (blue bus) to Fourth and Broadway, walk 2 blocks west to Second Street, turn right, 1/2 block to hostel. **Train:** take RTD bus #33 from Los Angeles and Arcadia streets to Second and Broadway, walk 1/2 block north.

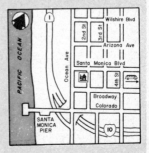

California

HOME HOSTEL

Merced
Yosemite Gateway Home Hostel

The Yosemite Gateway Home Hostel provides a friendly homestay experience in Merced, only 80 miles from Yosemite National Park. Buses leave for the park three times daily from town. Explore the park's spectacular Yosemite Valley, with its massive granite domes and waterfalls, and take in the view from Glacier Point. Enjoy Castle's Air Museum and the local museum in Merced. Walk or cycle past the tranquil dairy farms, orchards, and cotton fields.

Call hostel for reservations.
Mail (✉): P.O. Box 3755, Merced, CA 95344.
Phone (☎): 209-725-0407.
Price (●): $10 U.S.
Closed (X): rarely.
Grade: home hostel (🏠).
Beds (🛏): 4.
Facilities: equipment storage area, information desk, kitchen, laundry facilities, linen provided, on-site parking, **MSA**; call for free pick-up from Greyhound and Amtrak stations.
Family rooms (👪): available. private rooms also available.
Reservations essential (📞●): always. **By phone:** accepted.
Credit cards: not accepted.
Directions: available upon reservation confirmation.

HOME HOSTEL

Midpines
Midpines Home Hostel

The Midpines Home Hostel uses gas for lighting and cooking (plan to arrive before dark). Plumbar Creek, behind the hostel, is the place to try your luck at gold panning with the hostel's equipment. Hike in nearby Yosemite, 37 miles away, or visit the gold rush town of Mariposa.

Call hostel for reservations.
Mail (✉): P.O. Box 173, Midpines, CA 95345.
Phone (☎): 209-742-6318.
Price (●): $7.50 U.S.
Closed (X): November 1–April 14.
Grade: home hostel (🏠).
Beds (🛏): 5.
Facilities: no electricity, unisex sleeping room, kitchen, on-site parking, **MSA**; arrive before dark.
Groups (🏛): welcome.
Reservations essential (📞●): always. **By phone:** accepted.
Credit cards: not accepted.
Manager: Mitch Terkildsen.
Directions: available upon reservation confirmation.

California

Montara

Point Montara Lighthouse AYH-Hostel

On the rugged California coast, just 25 miles south of San Francisco, sits the Point Montara Fog Signal and Light Station. Established in 1875, the historic lighthouse and turn-of-the-century buildings have been preserved and restored by American Youth Hostels and California Department of Parks and Recreation, in cooperation with the U.S. Coast Guard.

Explore the coastline and watch the annual migration of gray whales between November and April. The James Fitzgerald Marine Reserve, a four-mile stretch of tidepools full of starfish, crabs, mussels, abalone, and sea anemones, is also nearby. There are several great beaches for swimming, surfing, jogging, horseback riding, and windsurfing. Cycle along the shore on the Bikecentennial California Coast Bicycle Route.

16th Street at California Highway 1.
Mail (✉): P.O. Box 737, Montara, CA 94037.
Phone (☎): 415-728-7177.
Price (◔): $9 U.S.
Closed (X): never.
Office Hours: 7:30–9:30 a.m., 4:30–9:30 p.m.
Beds (⊨): 45. **Grade:** Hostel.
Facilities: outdoor hot tub, equipment storage area, information desk, kitchen, laundry facilities, linen rental, on-site parking, wheelchair accessible (♿), **MSA**; day use by groups available by reservation.
Family rooms (⚲): available.
Groups (⛺): welcome (up to 25 people).
Reservations essential (⌖): April–September and weekends; mail $9 U.S. deposit. **Reservations advisable (⌖):** always; mail 1 night deposit. **By phone:** With credit card only.

Credit cards: Mastercard, Visa.
Manager: Rich Lilley
Directions: 25 miles south of San Francisco on California Highway 1 between Montara and Moss Beach, look for hostel signs.

California

Palo Alto (Los Altos Hills)

Hidden Villa Ranch AYH-Hostel

In 1937 Frank and Josephine Duveneck opened the West's first hostel at their ranch in the foothills of the Santa Cruz Mountains in Los Altos Hills. Today Hidden Villa Ranch is an actual working farm with farm animals, oak-studded grasslands, organic gardens, and Adobe Creek's woodland watershed. During the summer, Hidden Villa serves as a multicultural camp for children (the hostel is closed during this period). There are more than 20 miles of trails for guests to roam in the hills behind the hostel. San Francisco, San Jose, Stanford University, and the towns of "Silicon Valley" are all close by. For the young at heart, Great America Amusement Park is just 12 miles away.

26870 Moody Road,
Los Altos Hills, CA 94022.
Mail (✉): same.
Phone (☎): 415-949-8648.
Price (💰): $8.50 U.S.
Closed (X): June–August.
Office Hours: 7:30–9:30 a.m., 4:30–9:30 p.m., no curfew.
Grade: Hostel.
Beds (🛏): 33.
Facilities: heated cabins, equipment storage area, information desk, kitchen, linen rental, on-site parking, **MSA**.
Family rooms (👪): available.
Groups (🏨): welcome; reservations required.
Reservations essential (📞💳): weekends; always for groups.
By phone: accepted with credit card confirmation.
Credit cards: not accepted for payment of overnight fee.

Manager: Diny van der Velden.
Directions: 45 miles south of San Francisco, 12 miles north of San Jose, and 2 miles west of Interstate 280 in Los Altos Hills.

California

Pescadero

Pigeon Point Lighthouse AYH-Hostel

Perched on a cliff on the central California coast, 50 miles south of San Francisco, the 110-foot Pigeon Point Lighthouse AYH-Hostel, one of the tallest lighthouses in America, has been guiding mariners since 1872. The associated keepers' housing was restored as a hostel by American Youth Hostels, California Department of Parks and Recreation, and the U.S. Coast Guard. From the boardwalk behind the fog signal building, watch for gray whales on their annual migration. Walk through the tidepool area, 100 yards north of Pigeon Point, or through the amazing 1,000-year-old redwoods nearby. Explore Pescadero Marsh, the feeding and nesting place for more than 150 species of birds, and Ano Nuevo State Reserve, the breeding site of northern elephant seals.

Pigeon Point Road and California Highway 1, Pescadero, CA 94060.
Mail (✉): same.
Phone (☎): 415-879-0633.
Price (💲): $9 U.S.
Closed (X): never.
Office Hours: 7:30–9:30 a.m., 4:30–9:30 p.m.
Beds (🛏): 52. **Grade:** Hostel.
Facilities: outdoor hot tub, equipment storage area, kitchen, linen rental, on-site parking, wheelchair accessible (♿), **MSA**.
Family rooms (👪): available.
Groups (🛏🛏): welcome.
Reservations essential (📞e): May–September, weekends.
Reservations advisable (📞a): always with 1 night deposit.

By phone: accepted 1 week in advance of arrival, or with credit card.
Credit cards: MasterCard, Visa.
Manager: Janice Keen.
Directions: 20 miles south of Half Moon Bay and 27 miles north of Santa Cruz on California Highway 1.

California

Point Reyes National Seashore

Point Reyes AYH-Hostel

The Point Reyes AYH-Hostel is two miles from the ocean in a secluded valley on Point Reyes National Seashore. The seashore is known for its abundant flora and fauna, including bobcats, fox, deer and elk herds, harbor seals, and sea lions. The varied habitat, unique coastal climate, and location draw a rich and diversified array of breeding and migrating birds. The Point Reyes National Seashore juts far out into the path of migrating gray whales. Point Reyes Lighthouse, 25 miles from the hostel, is the best place in the Bay Area for whale watching January-April. Bear Valley Visitor Center, eight miles away, has informative displays on the area's geological, natural, and native history.

Off Limantour Road.
Mail (✉): Box 247, Point Reyes Station, CA 94956.
Phone (☎): 415-663-8811.
Price (💰): $9 U.S.
Closed (X): never.
Office Hours: 7:30–9:30 a.m., 4:30–9:30 p.m., no check-in after 9:30 p.m.
Beds (🛏): 44. **Grade:** Hostel.
Facilities: information desk, kitchen, linen rental, on-site parking, wheelchair accessible (♿).
Family rooms (👪): available for parents with child/children age 5 or younger. **Groups (🏃):** welcome.
Reservations advisable (📞a): always with 1 night deposit, full deposit within 2 weeks of arrival.
By phone: with credit card only.

Credit cards: MasterCard, Visa.
Manager: Bob Baez.
Directions: from flashing traffic light in Olema, go north 100 yards on California Highway 1, turn left on Bear Valley Road, go 1-1/2 miles to second possible left turn, go 5-1/2 miles to first crossroad and turn left.

California

Redwood National Park

Redwood AYH-Hostel

The northernmost link in the California coastal chain of hostels, Redwood AYH-Hostel is located in mist-shrouded Redwood National Park. Just a stone's throw from the ocean, the hostel was the pioneer home of Louis DeMartin, built in 1908. The hostel promotes active recycling and conservation of our natural resources. Information is available on hiking trails, park attractions, and the ecology, economy and history of the local area. Redwood National Park, a World Heritage Site, contains sections of the spectacular Coast Trail as well as day and half-day hikes through the immense trees of the primordial Redwood Forest. Hostellers can also cycle on the Bikecentennial Coastal Route, surf, swim, and warm themselves by a driftwood fire on the beach or the wood stove in the cozy common room.

14480 California Highway 101 at Wilson Creek Road.
Mail (✉): 14480 California Highway 101, Klamath, CA 95548.
Phone (☎): 707-482-8265.
Price (☺): $9 U.S.
Closed (X): never.
Office Hours: 7:30–9:30 a.m., 4:30–9:30 p.m.
Beds (🛏): 30. **Grade:** Hostel.
Facilities: wood heat, bicycle/equipment storage area, information desk, kitchen, laundry facilities, linen rental, lockers/baggage storage, on-site parking, wheelchair accessible (♿), **MSA**.
Family rooms (👪): available.
Groups (⛺): welcome.
Reservations advisable (📞a): May–September with 1 night deposit.

By phone: with credit card only.
Credit cards: MasterCard, Visa.
Manager: C.L. Hale Caldwell.
Directions: 12 miles south of Crescent City and 7 miles north of Klamath off California Highway 101 at Wilson Creek Road.

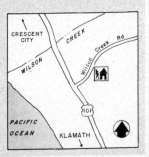

California

San Clemente

San Clemente Beach AYH-Hostel

A former library, the San Clemente Beach AYH-Hostel promises visitors plenty of fun in the sun. Set midway between Los Angeles and San Diego, and a short drive from Disneyland, San Clemente boasts "the world's finest climate", with average temperatures near 70 degrees in the cooler months. Swimming, volleyball, and surfing are all favorite beach sports. Cycling on the coastal Bikecentennial route is also popular. The serious fisherman can hop on a boat at nearby Dana Point Harbor. The wharf around the harbor has some quaint shops with one-of-a-kind wares. The Mission San Juan Capistrano, near San Clemente, is the summer nesting spot of thousands of migrating swallows. The mission houses the Serra Chapel, California's oldest building.

233 Avenida Granada,
San Clemente, CA 92672.
Mail (✉): same.
Phone (☎): 714-492-2848.
Price (●): $9 U.S.
Closed (X): never.
Office Hours: 8–10 a.m., 4:30–10 p.m.
Grade: Hostel.
Beds (⊨): 45.
Facilities: patios, kitchen, laundry facilities, linen rental, lockers/baggage storage, on-site parking, wheelchair accessible (♿), **MSA**.
Groups (⬛): welcome.
Reservations essential (☎): August; mail 1 night deposit. **By phone:** accepted with credit card confirmation and 24-hour notice (fee nonrefundable).
Credit cards: MasterCard, Visa, JCB.
Manager: Catharina Eñbar-Salo.

Directions: from Interstate 5 southbound, exit at Palizada, turn west and go 2 blocks, turn south on El Camino Real, go 5 blocks then turn west on Avenida Granada; from Interstate 5 northbound, exit at Presidio, turn west and go 1 block, turn north on El Camino Real, go 2 blocks then turn west on Avenida Granada.

California

San Diego (Downtown)

AYH-Hostel on Broadway

The hostel, covering the entire second floor of the Armed Services YMCA, is conveniently located downtown. Seaport Village, San Diego Bay, and the nightlife of the historic Gaslamp district are just a few blocks away.

Don't forget Balboa Park with its famous San Diego Zoo and museums. Sea World is close by, too, and Mexico is just twenty minutes away by trolley.

Catch the ferry to Coronado and have lunch at the Hotel Del Coronado, or spend the afternoon trying to count the waves on one of the world's great beaches.

We'd love to help you visit San Diego!

500 West Broadway,
San Diego, CA 92101.
Mail (✉): same.
Phone (☎): 619-525-1531.
Price (⊖): $11 U.S.
Closed (X): never.
Office Hours: 8–10 a.m., 4:30–11 p.m.
Grade: Hostel.
Beds (⊨): female, 45, male, 67.
Facilities: equipment storage area, laundry facilities; lockers/baggage storage; restaurant.
Reservations essential (☎e): July–September. **By phone:** accepted.
Credit cards: MasterCard, Visa., JCB.
Manager: Chuck Ehrensperger.

Directions: By car from Fwy 5: Take Front St. exit. Turn right on Broadway. Between Columbia St. and India St. By train: Walk east 1 block on Broadway. By bus: Walk west 3 blocks on Broadway.

145

California

San Diego (Imperial Beach)

Imperial Beach International AYH-Hostel

Hey, amigos! The Imperial Beach International AYH-Hostel is only five miles from Tijuana, Mexico, so practice that Spanish before arriving here. Visit great Mexican restaurants on both sides of the border and listen to lively Mexican music.

If the sights of the Mexican border town don't sound exciting, don't worry. San Diego is overflowing with things to do and see. The hostel is just one block from the beach. Surf or play beach volleyball against some of the best. Spend time whale watching on the beach. For a close-up view of these huge mammals, head for Sea World and its impressive animal shows starring creatures of the deep.

170 Palm Avenue,
Imperial Beach, CA 91932.
Mail (✉): same.
Phone (☎): 619-423-8039.
Price (💲): $9 U.S. + tax.
Closed (X): never.
Office Hours: 8–10 a.m., 5:30–11 p.m.
Beds (🛏): 36. **Grade:** Hostel.
Facilities: equipment storage area, kitchen, laundry facilities, linen rentals, lockers/baggage storage, on-site parking, **MSA**.
Groups (🏠): welcome.
Reservations essential (📞): June–October; mail 1 night deposit.
By phone: accepted with credit card confirmation and 48-hour notice (fee nonrefundable).
Credit cards: MasterCard, Visa, JCB.

Manager: Michael Wade.
Directions: 10 miles south of downtown, 2-1/2 miles west off Interstate 5. **Airport (✈):** take city bus #2 to downtown, transfer to city bus #901. **Bus:** take city bus #901, get off at Rainbow and Palm. alternate route available.

California

San Diego (Point Loma)

Elliott International AYH-Hostel

The Elliott International AYH-Hostel is an airy two-story building with a spacious outdoor courtyard. Located in the Point Loma neighborhood, the hostel is just a hop, skip, and jump away from the ocean. The famous San Diego Zoo, a must-see for all visitors, is in gigantic Balboa Park, along with several major museums featuring art, history, photography, space, and science exhibits. Those looking for performance art will find it at the Old Globe Theatre and the Spreckels Organ Pavilion. Cyclists arriving by the coastal Bikecentennial route will find that San Diego is easy to tour on two wheels.

3790 Udall Street,
San Diego, CA 92107.
Mail (✉): same.
Phone (☎): 619-223-4778.
Price (☺): $12 U.S.
Closed (X): never.
Office Hours: 8–10 a.m., 5:30–11 p.m.
Grade: Hostel.
Beds (⊨): 60.
Facilities: outdoor courtyard, travel library, equipment storage area, kitchen, linen rentals, lockers/baggage storage, **MSA**.
Family rooms (⚶): available.
Groups (⬛): welcome.
Reservations essential (✉e): April–September; mail $12 U.S. deposit 2 weeks in advance. **By phone:** accepted with credit card confirmation and 48-hour notice (fee nonrefundable).
Credit cards: MasterCard, Visa, JCB.
Manager: Jeff Raisch.

Directions: take interstate 5 to Sea World Drive exit. Go west, bear right onto Sunset Cliffs Blvd. Turn left on Voltaire. Turn right on Worden. Go one block to Udall.
Airport (✈): take city bus #2 to Broadway, transfer to city bus #35 westbound to Ocean Beach, get off at Voltaire and Poinsettia. **Bus:** take city bus #35 westbound to Ocean Beach, get off at Voltaire and Poinsettia.

California

San Francisco (Fort Mason)

San Francisco International AYH-Hostel

Ah, San Francisco! Cable cars climbing steep fog-shrouded hills and the famous Golden Gate Bridge make the "city by the bay" one of America's most intriguing and popular destinations.

The San Francisco International AYH-Hostel is located at Fort Mason in the Golden Gate National Recreation Area, an urban national park right on the bay. Fort Mason is also home to museums, galleries, and theaters. The nearby Bikecentennial route makes this hostel a perfect stop for cyclists. Fisherman's Wharf, Chinatown, and Ghirardelli Square are all within easy walking distance.

Fort Mason, Building 240, San Francisco, CA 94123.
Mail (✉): same.
Phone (☎): 415-771-7277.
Price (◔): $13 U.S.
Closed (X): never.
Office Hours: 7 a.m.–1 a.m.
Beds (🛏): 150. **Grade:** Hostel.
Facilities: equipment storage area, information desk, kitchen, laundry facilities, linen rental, lockers/baggage storage, on-site parking, wheelchair accessible (♿), **MSA.**
Family rooms (👪): available.
Groups (🏠): welcome; reservations required.
Reservations essential (✉e): groups; mail 1 night deposit 2–3 months in advance. **Reservations advisable (✉a):** always, mail 1 night deposit 2 weeks in advance. Advance reservations nonrefundable.
By phone: accepted with credit card confirmation and 48-hour notice. **Note only:** IBN global reservation system available.
Credit cards: MasterCard, Visa, JCB.
Manager: Jeanne Comaskey.
Directions: 2 miles north of downtown. **Bus, Train:** take MUNI bus #42 from Trans Bay Terminal to Bay and Van Ness, walk 1 block west to Franklin and Fort Mason entrance, follow signs to hostel. **Airport (✈):** take shuttle vans to hostel.

California

San Francisco (Union Square)

AYH-Hostel at Union Square

A block from the excitement of Union Square, in the theater district, this new hostel (formerly the Hotel Virginia) provides double and triple rooms. In most cases, two rooms share a bath. Right outside the front door are a variety of restaurants, shops, and art galleries. Union Square is a great place to people-watch or enjoy a picnic under the palm trees. Just two blocks away at Powell and Market streets are the world-famous cable cars, which will give you a breathtaking ride to Fisherman's Wharf and the Bay. You'll also find public transportation here to most areas of the city.

312 Mason Street,
San Francisco, CA 94102.
Mail (✉): same.
Phone (☎): 415-788-5604.
Price (●): $14 U.S.
Closed (X): never.
Office Hours: 23 hours daily (closed 11 a.m.–noon).
Grade: Hostel.
Beds (⊨): 200.
Facilities: baggage storage area, kitchen, linen rental, lockers, showers, vending machines, **MSA**.
Family rooms (⌂): available.
Groups (⊞): welcome, reservations required.
Reservations essential (☎●): June–September. **By phone:** accepted with credit card confirmation and 48-hour notice. Advance reservations nonrefundable.
Credit cards: MasterCard, Visa, JCB.
Manager: Mike Reed.

Directions: downtown on Mason Street, between Geary and O'Farrell; from U.S. Highway 101 (Van Ness), go east on O'Farrell 7 blocks to Mason Steet. **Airport (✈):** take shuttle van to hostel or catch SAM-TRANS bus #7B or #7F on upper level in front of Delta or United. Get off at Fifth and Mission, walk 5 blocks north (Fifth becomes Mason). **Bus, train:** from Transbay Terminal, take 38 Geary bus to Mason Street., look downhill for Virginia Hotel sign.

California

San Jose (Saratoga)

Sanborn Park AYH-Hostel

Just west of San Jose, the Sanborn Park AYH-Hostel is tucked away amid a forest of redwoods and madrones in Sanborn County Park in Saratoga. This log house, constructed in 1908 and listed on the National Register of Historic Places, is an excellent starting point for hiking in the Santa Cruz Mountains and to the ocean. Visit San Jose's famous Winchester Mystery House, Rosicrucian Egyptian Museum, Technology Center Museum, and Historical Museum park.

15808 Sanborn Road,
Saratoga, CA 95070.
Mail (✉): same.
Phone (☎): 408-741-0166.
Price (●): $7:50 U.S.
Closed (X): never.
Office Hours: 7–9 a.m., 5–11 p.m.
Grade: Hostel.
Beds (🛏): 39.
Facilities: equipment storage area, information desk, kitchen, laundry facilities, linen rental, lockers/baggage storage, on-site parking, wheelchair accessible (♿), **MSA**.
Family rooms (👪): available.
Groups (👥): welcome.
Reservations advisable: weekends and for groups. **By phone:** accepted.
Credit cards: not accepted.
Managers: Sylvia Carroll, Don Wilkinson.
Directions: from Interstate 280, take Saratoga Avenue or Saratoga-Sunnyvale exit to Saratoga; from California Highway 17, take Highway 9 exit. Take California Highway 9 (Big Basin Way) 2 miles past Saratoga Village, turn left on Sanborn Road, and follow the signs to the hostel. **Train:** from San Francisco, take CalTrain to Sunnyvale station, then bus #54 to Saratoga Village. **Bus:** from Santa Cruz, take any bus to Los Gatos, then bus #27 to Saratoga Village. From San Jose, ask bus drivers the way to Saratoga. From Saratoga Village, call the hostel for a ride.

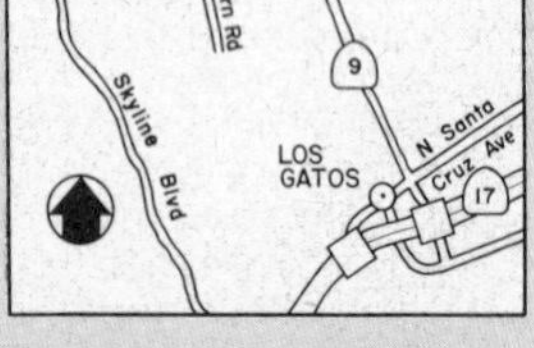

California

HOME HOSTEL

San Luis Obispo
Alana's Home Hostel

Alana Buckley's home hostel is just minutes from Pismo Beach and the beautiful and secluded Montana de Oro State Park. The famous Hearst Castle is less than an hour's drive from the hostel. Enjoy clamming, fishing, horseback riding, and hiking at the beach. And don't miss the farmers market every Thursday evening!

Call for reservations.
Phone (☎): 805-541-5510.
Price (◔): $11 U.S. + tax.
Closed (X): September 13–March 31.
Grade: home hostel (🏠).
Beds (🛏): 5.
Facilities: baggage storage area, laundry facilities, linen rental, kitchen, on-site parking, showers, **MSA**.
Family rooms (🛏): available.
Meals (🍴): breakfast.

Reservations essential (📞e): always. **By phone:** accepted with 2-day advance notice, with credit card only, 48-hour cancellation charge.
Credit cards: MasterCard, Visa (50¢ surcharge).
Manager: Alana Buckley.
Directions: available upon reservation confirmation.

HMC—Hostel Management Course—HMC

DON'T JUST
GET A JOB...
PURSUE A LIFESTYLE—

HOSTELLING INTERNATIONAL offers training opportunities that cover:

- The philosophy and spirit of hostelling

- Hostel guest services and activities
- Organizational structure and opportunities

HOSTELLING
INTERNATIONAL
American Youth Hostels

- Practical operational activities, and more

Turn to page 302 for more details.

California

Santa Cruz

Santa Cruz AYH-Hostel

The Santa Cruz AYH-Hostel is an 1890s Victorian house close to downtown and the beach. In the true hostelling tradition, guests are urged to arrive by bicycle, public transportation, or on foot.

The Santa Cruz climate is very mild year-round. Spend balmy, carefree days on the vast stretches of sandy beaches. The boardwalk has many amusement rides and games. Along the coast lies fisherman's wharf and the yacht harbor. Steamer Lane is one of the best surfing spots along the coast. The University of California at Santa Cruz features modern buildings nestled among redwood trees. Beautiful Capitola Village is just four miles away and historic Monterey is 45 minutes by car. An extensive local bus system makes Santa Cruz an ideal starting point to several state parks in the nearby mountains.

511 Broadway.
Mail (✉): P.O. Box 1241, Santa Cruz, CA 95061.
Phone (☎): 408-423-8304.
Price (◐): $12 U.S.
Closed (X): never.
Office Hours: 7–9 a.m., 5–10 p.m.
Grade: Hostel.
Beds (🛏): 18 + annex.
Facilities: information desk, kitchen, linen rental, lockers/baggage storage, limited parking, 28-bed Victorian Annex due to open Spring 1993, **MSA**; preference given to those arriving on foot, by bicycle, or public transportation.
Groups (▥): welcome.
Reservations essential (✆): June–September. **By phone:** not accepted.

Credit cards: not accepted.
Manager: Bill Jones.
Directions: 76 miles south of San Francisco, 40 miles west of San Jose, 40 miles north of Monterey. Near the city center.

California

Sausalito

Golden Gate AYH-Hostel

The Golden Gate AYH-Hostel sits on a hillside in the serene Marin Headlands, just across the Golden Gate Bridge from San Francisco, in the Golden Gate National Recreation Area. These turn-of-the-century military quarters at Fort Barry are surrounded by beaches, forests, and rolling hills. The Rodeo Lagoon and Beach provide an abundance of wildlife and native plant life to study. Scenic trails are available at Mount Tamalpais State Park, Muir Woods National Monument, and in the Marin Headlands.

Fort Barry, Building 941, Sausalito, CA 94965.

Mail (✉): same.

Phone (☎): 415-331-2777.

Price (⬤): $9 U.S.

Closed (X): never.

Office Hours: 7:30–9:30 a.m., 4:30–11 p.m.

Grade: Hostel.

Beds (🛏): 66.

Facilities: equipment storage area, information desk, kitchen, laundry facilities, linen rental, lockers/baggage storage, on-site parking, **MSA**.

Family rooms (👪): available.

Groups (🏚): welcome; reservations required September 15– June 30.

Reservations essential (✦e): always, mail 1 night deposit. **By phone:** with credit card only.

Credit cards: MasterCard, Visa.

Manager: Brian McHugh.

Directions: 11 miles north of San Francisco; take U.S. Highway 101 north just past Golden Gate Bridge to Alexander Avenue exit, bear left, turn left at stop sign and cross under freeway to "Marin Headlands" sign; traveling from the north on U.S. 101 take second Sausalito exit, turn left off ramp to "Marin Headlands" sign. From "Marin Headlands" sign take first right for 1 mile, take first right onto McCullough Road, turn left at bottom of hill onto Bunker Road, go 1-1/2 miles, take left fork, follow signs to the hostel. Call for details on public transportation.

California

Truckee

North Lake Tahoe AYH-Hostel

The hostel is part of a European-style hotel that has been in continuous operation for more than a century. Located in the historic preservation district, the hostel is convenient to many recreational activities in Tahoe-Truckee area.

Skiers can enjoy resorts such as Northstar or Squaw Valley. Many places have night skiing and cross-country ski trails. In summer, the sparkling water of Lake Tahoe and Donner Lake tempts all to go swimming and boating. Hike the surrounding mountains or rent a bike or a horse. Visit Donner Memorial State Park with its excellent walking trails and museum.

10015 West River Street.
Mail (✉): P.O. Box 1227 Truckee, CA 96160.
Phone (☎): 916-587-3007.
Price (◔): $10 U.S. + tax.
Closed (X): never.
Office Hours: 6–9 a.m., 4–9:30 p.m.
Grade: Hostel.
Beds (🛏): 14.
Facilities: linen rental, wheelchair accessible (♿), **MSA**.
Reservations essential (☎e): July–September, November–April.
By phone: with Visa/MasterCard.
Manager: Terry Puccini.

Directions: on West River Street and California Highway 267, 1/2 block from bus/train depot.

Colorado

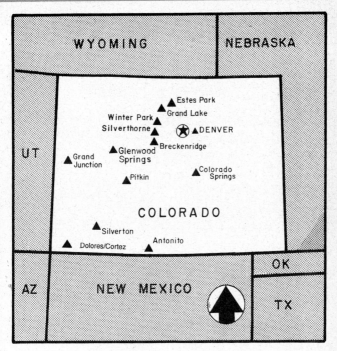

Helpful Organizations

AYH Council Office

Rocky Mountain Council
P.O. Box 2370
Boulder, CO 80306
Phone (☎): 303-442-1166

State Tourism Office

Colorado Tourism Board
1625 Broadway, Suite 1700
Denver, CO 80202
Phone (☎): 800-433-2656

Discounts

Present a valid hostel membership card at the time of purchase and receive the
following discounts:

Breckenridge

The Adventure Company - 10% on regular river trips. P.O. Box 3876, 303-453-0747.

Lone Star Sports - 10% on storewide merchandise, including rentals and repair. $5.00 off major ski tune-ups in winter. $2.00 off daily on mountain bike rentals in summer. 200 W. Washington, 303-453-2003; 1-800-621-9733.

Rebel Sports - 4 or more days rental, get one day free. 315 North Main Street, 303-453-2526; 1-800-228-4757.

Estes Park

Colorado Bicycling - 10% discount on cycling accessories and bicycle rentals. 184 E. Elkhorn Ave., 303-586-4241.

Sombrero Ranches, Inc.- 10% discount for members for horseback riding and combination horseback riding with meals. 1895 Big Thompson Avenue, 303-586-4577.

Discounts

Grand Lake

Sombrero Ranches, Inc. - 10% discount for members for horseback riding and combination horseback riding with meals. W. Portal Road, 303-627-3514.

Winter Park

Active Images - 10% discount on clothing.
Hernando's Pizza - 10% discount until 6:00 p.m. U.S. Hwy 40.
Lani's Place - 10% discount. Cooper Creek Square.
Last Waltz - 10% discount on all food. Kings Crossing.
Le Ski Lab - 25% discount on bike and ski rentals; 10% discount on all purchases. U.S. Hwy 40. Call hostel for details.
Rudi's Deli - 10% discount. Park Plaza.

YOU HAVE TO SEE THE WORLD TO UNDERSTAND IT.

American Youth Hostels, a member of the International Youth Hostel Federation, has provided educational and recreational travel experiences for youth and adults for more than 50 years. Our dynamic travel programs are backed by more than five decades of experience and provide you with the opportunity to discover the world, both near and far.

AYH Discovery Tours are planned both as vacation adventures and as enriching learning experiences. You will find yourself face to face with new people, cultures and environments. Join us and discover the spirit of hostelling and the excitement of travel.

For A Free Catalog
Contact the AYH council nearest you or call the AYH Travel Department at 202-783-6161.

Colorado

Antonito

Conejos River AYH-Hostel

Enjoy the great outdoors of southern Colorado and northern New Mexico while staying in a homey cabin next to the scenic Conejos River. Watch hummingbirds as you eat the home-cooked breakfast included in your overnight fee. Fish for trout or walk along the river, 50 feet from the hostel's front gate. The river canyon is full of trails for hiking, mountain biking, backpacking, and four-wheel-drives. The adjacent Rio Grande National Forest and nearby San Juan Mountains also attract outdoor enthusiasts.

See beautiful and remote areas while riding the Cumbres and Toltec Scenic Railroad, the highest narrow-gauge steam train in North America, which runs daily between Antonito and Chama, New Mexico. If train reservations are made and prepaid through the hostel, your overnight price will be discounted $2 per person.

3591 County Road E.2, Antonito, CO 81120.

Mail (✉): same.
Phone (☎): 719-376-2518.
Price (●): $8 U.S. + tax.
Closed (X): October 18–May 26.
Office Hours: 7–9 a.m., 5–9 p.m.
Grade: Hostel.
Beds (🛏): 10, sleeping bags are permitted.
Facilities: fireplace, wood stove, kitchen, linen rental, on-site parking, gas grill, picnic tables, telescope, **MSA**.
Meals (🍴): free breakfast.
Family rooms (👪): reservations required.
Groups (🏠): reservations required.
Reservations: not essential.

Credit cards: not accepted.
Manager: Sandy Davis.
Directions: 10 miles west of Antonito on Colorado Highway 17, turn south (left) on Broyles Bridge at FDR 103/County Road E.2, hostel is immediately after the bridge.

Colorado

Breckenridge
Fireside Inn

The Fireside Inn, located in a national historic district, is a ski lodge during the winter, with non-hostel rates (see below). Enjoy hiking, biking, rafting, and sailing in the summer. The inn is on free bus routes to four ski areas. Walk to 60 restaurants.

114 North French Street.
Mail (✉): P.O. Box 2252, Breckenridge, CO 80424.
Phone (☎): 303-453-6456,
FAX: (303) 453-6456.
Price (💲): $13 U.S. + tax, May 1–November 13; discount rates at ski lodge for members in winter season.
Closed (X): May 1–Friday before Memorial Day.
Office Hours: 7–10 a.m.; check in after 2 p.m.; check out prior to 10 a.m.
Beds(🛏): 12. **Grade: (SA)**.
Facilities: hot tub, color TV with HBO, bicycle storage, ski storage, information desk, on-site parking.

Meals (🍴): breakfast.
Groups (🎪): welcome.
Reservations essential (🔔e): November 17–April 30. **By phone:** 303-453-6456.
Credit cards: for reservations only.
Managers: Mary and Mike Keeling, Jack and Jean Wells.
Directions: take exit #203 off Interstate 70, go south on Colorado Highway 9 (9 miles) to Breckenridge, turn east (left) on Wellington 1 block before stoplight in town); 2 blocks to corner of French Street and Wellington.

Colorado Springs
Garden of the Gods Campground

These cozy cabins are surrounded by the Garden of the Gods Campground. Pike's Peak is the area's premier attraction. Conquer this mountain by foot or go on the guided tour given by hostel management. Take a horseback ride through Garden of the Gods Park to see ancient sandstone formations.

3704 West Colorado Avenue, Colorado Springs, CO 80904.
Mail (✉): same.
Phone (☎): 719-475-9450.
Price (💲): $10 U.S. + tax.
Closed (X): October 16–April 30.
Office Hours: 10 a.m.–8 p.m.
Grade: (SA).
Beds (🛏): 48.
Facilities (mixed use): 6 cabins, pool, hot tub, equipment storage area, information desk, laundry facilities, lockers/baggage storage, on-site parking, **MSA**.
Family rooms (👶): available.
Groups (🎪): welcome.

Reservations essential (🔔e): June–September; May–September for groups. **Reservations advisable (🔔a):** always. **By phone:** accepted with 24-hour notice. **By FAX:** 719-633-9643 with credit card confirmation.
Credit cards: MasterCard, Visa.
Manager: Mary Lou Murphy.
Directions: west on Colorado Avenue to 37th Street entrance to Garden of the Gods Campground.
Bus: take city bus #1 to campground entrance.

Colorado

Denver

Melbourne International AYH-Hostel

The Melbourne International AYH-Hostel is in the heart of downtown. The capitol building, complete with a gold dome, was built during the city's gold rush era. It's now the U.S. Mint that makes the money, not the prospectors.

Visit the Denver Art Museum and the Black American West Museum and Heritage Center to learn more about the contributions Native and African Americans have made to the West. Other superb museums include the Museum of Western Art, the Colorado History Museum, and the Denver Museum of Natural History. Enjoy performance art at the spectacular Red Rock Amphitheater, carved into the mountains on Denver's west side.

The city has several parks and a great zoo. Skiing, hiking, climbing, rafting, swimming, and horseback riding are available in the nearby mountains, lakes, and national forests.

607 22nd Street,
Denver, CO 80205.
Mail (✉): same.
Phone (☎): 303-292-6386.
Price (◕): $8 U.S. + tax.
Closed (X): never.
Office Hours: 7 a.m.–midnight.
Grade: Hostel.
Beds (⊨): 38.
Facilities: courtyard, equipment storage area, information desk, kitchen, laundry facilities, linen rental, parking, **MSA**.
Reservations advisable (☎): June–October. **By phone:** accepted with 24-hour advance notice.
Credit cards: not accepted.
Managers: Gary White, Hilda Dossman.

Directions: 1/2 mile northeast of downtown off Broadway between Welton and California. **Airport (✈):** RTD bus #28, #38 and #32 all stop 2 blocks from the hostel.

Colorado

Dolores/Cortez
Mountain View

Located midway between Dolores and Cortez, near the famous Four-Corners area and Mesa Verde National Park, Mountain View features 22 secluded acres with a creek and hiking trails. The Anasazi Heritage Center Museum, two miles west of Dolores, includes exhibits on this mysterious ancient tribe.

28050 County Road P,
Dolores, CO 81323.
Mail (✉): same.
Phone (☎): 303-882-7861.
Price (💲): $10 U.S. + tax.
Closed (X): December–February.
Office Hours: 8–10 a.m., 4–8 p.m.
Beds (🛏): 11. **Grade: (SA)**.
Facilities: baggage storage area, laundry facilities, linen rental, on-site parking, showers, wheelchair accessible (♿).
Meals (🍴): breakfast.

Family rooms (👪): available.
Groups (🎪): welcome.
Reservations advisable (📞): always. **By phone:** accepted with credit card confirmation and 1-day advance notice.
Credit cards: MasterCard, Visa.
Directions: 6 miles from Cortez, take Colorado Highway 145 north 4-1/2 miles to County Road P. Go east 1 mile, turn on the gravel road, and follow the signs. The hostel is the second house.

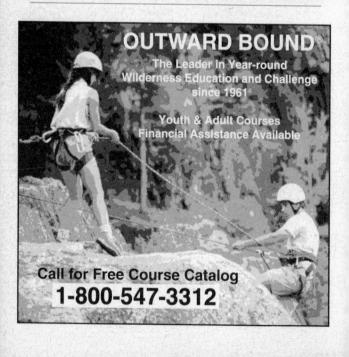

Colorado

Estes Park

H-Bar-G Ranch AYH-Hostel

This former dude ranch in Roosevelt National Forest is close to Rocky Mountain National Park. At an altitude of 8,200 feet, the hostel offers the best view of the entire Front Range in the park. Manager Lou Livingston shuttles hostel guests to and from town. There are more than 350 miles of diverse trails in the park. Experienced hikers can get to the top of Long's Peak during a six-week period from mid-July through August. Other hikes start from Bear Lake. Cyclists can ride on one of three bike trails or follow the Bikecentennial Great Parks South Bicycle Route.

3500 H-Bar-G Road.
Mail (⊠): P.O. Box 1260, Estes Park, CO 80517.
Phone (☎): 303-586-3688.
Price (☺): hostel members only, $7.50 U.S. + tax.
Closed (X): September 13–May 21.
Office Hours: 8 a.m.–9 p.m.
Grade: Hostel.
Beds (⊨): 100.
Facilities: kitchen, linen rental, rental cars available, **MSA**.
Family rooms (⚲): available.
Groups (⛺): welcome; reservations required.
Reservations essential (☎): July–August; for groups June 22–September 12. **By phone:** accepted with credit card confirmation and 24-hour notice.
Credit cards: MasterCard, Visa.
Managers: Anne and Lou Livingston.

Directions: From Denver, take Charles Limo (1-800-950-3274) or check with the local hostel for shuttle to Estes Park. From Estes Park, take U.S. Highway 34 east 1-1/2 miles from town, turn on Dry Gulch Road (Sombrero Stables), and follow signs to H-Bar-G. Call for free pick-up from Estes Park Tourist Information Center (daily at 5 p.m.).

Colorado

Glenwood Springs
Glenwood Springs Hostel

Along the Greyhound and Amtrak routes lies Glenwood Springs, on the western slope of the Rocky Mountains. The hostel is a large Victorian building featuring a full kitchen, communal areas, and a huge record collection. The hot springs, Indian Vapor Caves, rafting, biking, wilderness hiking, and cave exploration are near the hostel. Skiing at Sunlight, Aspen, and Snowmass are also close by.

1021 Grand Avenue,
Glenwood Springs, CO 81601.
Mail (✉): same.
Phone (☎): 303-945-8545.
Price (⬤): $9.50 U.S. + tax.
Closed (X): never.
Office Hours: 8–10 a.m., 4–10 p.m.
Beds (🛏): 25. **Grade: (SA).**
Facilities: laundry facilities, free linens, storage, on-site parking, private rooms.
Reservations advisable (☏a): always.
Credit cards: not accepted.
Manager: Gary Grillo.
Directions: 5 blocks off Interstate 70, take Glenwood Springs exit, follow signs to Highway 82.

Grand Junction
Hotel Melrose

The historic Hotel Melrose offers old-fashioned charm in scenic Grand Junction. The town is in a valley at the junction of the Colorado and Gunnison Rivers, near the Colorado National Monument. High rock canyons and desert area are to the west.

337 Colorado Avenue,
Grand Junction, CO 81501.
Mail (✉): same.
Phone (☎): 303-242-9636.
Price (⬤): $10.50 U.S. + tax.
Closed (X): never.
Office Hours: 24 hours.
Grade: (SA).
Beds (🛏): 10.
Facilities (mixed use): private rooms, linen rental, on-site parking.
Family rooms (⚏): available.
Groups (⚎): welcome.
Reservations not essential (☏e): for groups of 10 or more. **By phone:** accepted.
Credit cards: not accepted.
Managers: Maricaye C. Daniels, M. Elizabeth Davis.

Directions: from Interstate 70 east-bound, take exit 26, 5 miles south on I-70 Business, 2-1/2 blocks east (left) on Colorado Avenue; westbound take exit 37, 7-7/10 miles west on I-70 Business, 1 block north (right) on Colordao Highway 50W (Fifth Street), 2-1/2 blocks west (left) on Colorado Avenue. **Airport (✈):** 5-8/10 miles west on Horizon Drive, 2 miles south (left) on Seventh Street, 3-1/2 blocks west (right) on Colorado Avenue. **Bus:** 1/2 block north on Fifth Steet, 1-1/2 blocks west on Colorado Avenue. **Train:** 2 blocks north on Second Street, 1-1/2 blocks east on Colorado Avenue.

Colorado

Grand Lake

Shadowcliff AYH-Hostel

Perched on a cliff overlooking Grand Lake Village and the Colorado Great Lakes area, Shadowcliff AYH-Hostel is adjacent to Rocky Mountain National Park and next to the roaring North Inlet Stream. The area's many lakes and streams provide abundant places for fishing, sailing, and canoeing. Grand Lake and Granby Reservoir are popular summer spots.

Cyclists spend their days on the Bikecentennial Trail. Hikers can head to the national park or trek to Never Summer Wilderness Area which is accessible only on foot. Golfers can play 18 holes at the local golf course. Theater fans can attend the Grand Lake Theatre Association summer repertory performances.

405 Summerland Park Road.
Mail (✉): P.O. Box 658, Grand Lake, CO.80447.
Phone (☎): 303-627-9220.
Price (⊜): $7.50 U.S.
Closed (✗): September 27–May 31.
Office Hours: 8–10 a.m., 5–9 p.m.
Grade: Hostel.
Beds (⊨): 14.
Facilities: kitchen, linen rental, on-site parking.
Meals (✎): breakfast, lunch, dinner (by reservation).
Family rooms (👪): available (extra charge).
Groups (⊪): welcome.
Reservations advisable (📞a): always. **By phone:** accepted.
Off-season: call 303-355-1012.

Credit cards: not accepted.
Managers: Patt and Warren Rempel.
Directions: entering town off U.S. Highway 34 take left fork (West Portal Road) 2/3 mile, turn left at Shadowcliff sign.

Colorado

Pitkin
Pitkin Hotel and Hostelling International

A century ago, Pitkin was a booming gold-mining town, and the Pitkin Hotel and Hostel counted the leading political figures of the day among its guests. Today, the 47 or so residents of Pitkin put on an old-fashioned melodrama performance every summer. Enjoy hiking, climbing, skiing, and bicycling. Visit old mine sights and the first tunnel through the Continental Divide.

329 Main Street.
Mail (✉): P.O. Box 164, Pitkin, CO 81241.
Phone (☎): 303-641-2757.
Price (●): $10 U.S. + tax = $10.91.
Closed (X): never.
Office Hours: 8 a.m.–8 p.m.
Beds (🛏): 6. **Grade: (SA).**
Facilities (mixed use): 3 bunk rooms, unisex dorm, equipment storage area, information desk, shared kitchen, laundry facilities, linen rentals, on-site parking.

Meals (🍴): breakfast, lunch, dinner.
Family rooms (👪): available.
Reservations advisable (📞a): always. **By phone:** accepted.
Credit cards: not accepted.
Manager: JoAn Bannister.
Directions: 16 miles north of Parlin on U.S. Highway 50, go 12 miles east from Gunnison, turn north on County Road 76 at Parlin, go 16 miles.

Silverthorne
Alpen Hütte

The Alpen Hütte (pronounced Alpen HOO-ta) Lodge is modeled after the alpine huts of Europe. A busy ski lodge in the winter with non-hostel rates (see below), Alpen Hütte is located within 15 miles of four world-class ski areas and numerous trails for hiking, mountain biking, and cross-country skiing.

471 Rainbow Drive.
Mail (→): Box 919, Silverthorne, CO 80498.
Phone (☎): 303-468-6336.
Price (●): $10 U.S., May 1–November 21; $19 U.S., November 22–April 30; higher rates December 20–January 4 and March.
Closed (X): never.
Office Hours: 7 a.m.–noon, 4–11 p.m.
Beds (🛏): 64. **Grade: (SA).**
Facilities: bicycle rentals, kitchen (available May 1–November 21 only), lockers, on-site parking, **MSA.**

Meals (🍴): breakfast, lunch, dinner.
Family rooms (👪): available.
Groups (🎫): welcome.
Reservations advisable (📞a): November 22–April 30. **By phone:** accepted with credit card confirmation.
Credit cards: MasterCard, Visa., Discover.
Managers: Fran and Dave Colson.
Directions: 65 miles west of Denver on Interstate 70, take exit #205, north on Tanglewood Lane East 1/2 block, north on Rainbow Drive 4 blocks to hostel. **Bus:** Greyhound bus goes directly to Alpen Hostel.

DON'T JUST
GET A JOB...
PURSUE A LIFESTYLE—

HOSTELLING INTERNATIONAL offers training opportunities that cover:

- The philosophy and spirit of hostelling
- Hostel guest services and activities
- Organizational structure and opportunities
- Practical operational activities, and more

Courses Available:

April 19–22, 1993	Gardners, PA
July 19–22	Anchorage, AK
October 26–29	San Diego, CA
February 1994	To be announced

Course Fee:

$250 (includes all meals, accommodation, and course materials; HI membership required)

HOSTELLING
INTERNATIONAL
American Youth Hostels

For more information, ☎ or ✎:
**Hostelling International
American Youth Hostels**
Hostel Services
733 15th Street, NW, Suite 840
Washington, DC 20005
Phone: 202-783-6161
Fax: 202-783-6171

Colorado

Winter Park

Winter Park AYH-Hostel

Winter Park is best known for the Winter Park Mary Jane Ski Area, with 106 trails and 19 chair lifts. The hostel (at 9,000 feet) nestles in the pines next to Arapahoe National Forest. Right out the back door are 800 kilometers of mountain biking trails, 100 kilometers of groomed cross-country ski trails, extensive hiking, rafting, horses, and fishing. Saturday night rodeos are held in July and August. A 3,000-foot alpine slide and winter inner tubing (with a rope tow for the uphill trip) are fun extras. The hostel has many double rooms and is open during the day. Walk to most services (free shuttle service to all others). Greyhound stops one block away and Amtrak two miles away (free shuttle). There is a daily van service to/from Denver's Stapleton International Airport.

Mail (✉): P.O. Box 3323, Winter Park, CO 80482.
Phone (☎): 303-726-5356.
Price (💲): $7.50 U.S. (summer), $11 U.S. (winter); children are full price during peak seasons.
Closed (X): April 15–June 15.
Office Hours: 8 a.m.–noon, 4–8 p.m., unless arranged.
Grade: Hostel.
Beds (🛏): 32.
Facilities: equipment storage area, information desk, 4 kitchens, linen rental, lockers/baggage storage, on-site parking, **MSA**.
Family rooms (👪): available.
Reservations essential (✆): November 15–April 15. Mail full payment for 1-night stay or 50% for multiple nights.
Credit cards: not accepted.

Managers: Bill and Polly Cullen, and Mary Struzik.
Directions: 1/2 block east of U.S. Highway 40, behind Le Ski Lab, and Deno's in downtown Winter Park.

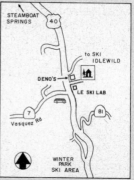

Connecticut

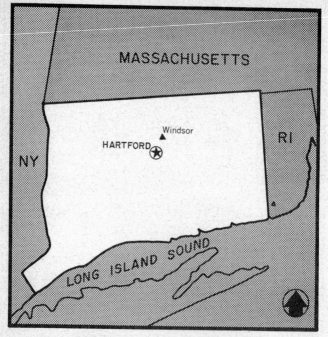

Helpful Organizations

AYH Council Office

Yankee Council
118 Oak Street
Hartford, CT 06106
Phone (☎): 203-247-6356

State Tourism Office

Connecticut Tourism Development
865 Brook Street
Rocky Hill, CT 06067
Phone (☎): 800-CT-BOUND,

Connecticut

Windsor
Windsor Home Hostel

Spend a day or two at this cozy home hostel in Windsor, Connecticut's oldest town. The town's history is on display at several 350-year-old historic buildings. Windsor's nearby Northwest Park offers hiking trails, a Braille Trail, an interpretive nature center, and a scenic reservoir. Catch Windsor's Shad Derby Festival in May, its Country Fair in September, or Hartford's exciting Fourth of July festivities. Visit Mark Twain's home in Hartford.

Call for reservations.
Phone (☎): 203-683-2847.
Price (◖): $11 U.S.
Closed (X): never.
Grade: home hostel (🏠).
Beds (🛏): 4.
Facilities: equipment storage area, laundry facilities, linen rental, on-site parking, **MSA**.

Reservations essential (🔑e): always. **By phone:** accepted.
Credit cards: not accepted.
Manager: Lois Macomber.
Directions: available upon reservation confirmation.

District of Columbia

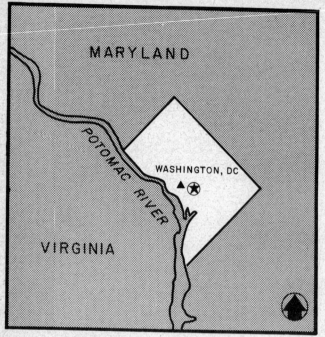

Helpful Organizations

AYH Council Office

Potomac Area Council
7420 Baltimore Avenue
College Park, MD 20740
Phone (☎): 301-209-8544

District Tourism Office

**Washington Convention and
Visitors Association**
1212 New York Avenue, Northwest
#600
Washington, DC 20005
Phone (☎): 202-789-7000

District of Columbia

Washington, D.C.

Washington International AYH-Hostel

The Washington International AYH-Hostel is centrally located near the Smithsonian Museums, the White House, and other attractions in the nation's capital. This newly renovated eight-story hostel offers tours, movies, and other special programs throughout the year. There's plenty to do in Washington...and it's free! Visit the National Air and Space Museum, the Museum of American History, and the National Gallery of Art. Tour the Capitol Building, Supreme Court, and Library of Congress. Climb to the top of the Washington Monument. Visit the Lincoln, Jefferson, and Vietnam War Memorials, and the National Zoo.

1009 11th Street NW, Washington, DC 20001.
Mail (✉): same.
Phone (☎): 202-737-2333.
Price (●): $15 U.S.
Closed (X): never.
Office Hours: 24 hours.
Grade: Hostel.
Beds (🛏): 250.
Facilities: couples rooms, day use, information desk, kitchen, laundry facilities, linen rental, lockers/baggage storage area, meeting rooms, hostel-based programs, travel store, vending machines, wheelchair accessible (♿), **MSA**.
Family rooms (👪): available for 4 or more.
Groups (IIII): welcome; reservations required.
Reservations essential (☎●): groups. **By phone:** accepted with credit card confirmation and 24-hour advance notice.
Credit cards: MasterCard, Visa, JCB.

Manager: Terry Hubbard.
Directions: downtown at 11th and K Streets NW. **Airport (✈):** from National Airport, take Metro train (blue line) to Metro Center stop, walk 3 blocks north on 11th; from Dulles or BWI, take Washington Flyer bus to Capital Hilton, walk 5 blocks east on K. **Bus or train:** take Metro train (red line) from Union Station to Metro Center stop, walk 3 blocks north on 11th.

Florida

Helpful Organizations

AYH Council Office

Florida Council
P.O. Box 533097
Orlando, FL 32853-3097
Phone (☎): 407-894-5872

State Tourism Office

Florida Division of Tourism
126 West Van Buren Street
Tallahassee, FL 32399
Phone (☎): 904-487-1462

Discounts

Present a valid hostel membership card at the time of purchase and receive the following discounts:

Orlando

Anne Cafeteria - 10% off each meal - Orange Ave., 3 blocks from hostel.
Budget Rent a Car - 15% off - AYH Hostel front desk, 407-843-8888.
Domino's Pizza - 50% off regular price - Call from AYH Hostel front desk, 407-843-8888.
InterAmerican Rent a Car - 15% off - AYH Hostel front desk, 407-843-8888.
Sea World - $3 off each ticket - AYH Hostel front desk, 407-843-8888.
Universal Studios - $3 off each ticket - AYH Hostel front desk, 407-843-8888.
Wet & Wild (water park) - $3 off each ticket - AYH Hostel front desk, 407-843-8888.

Florida

Miami Beach

Miami Beach International AYH-Hostel

The Miami Beach International AYH-Hostel is in the heart of the Old Miami Beach Art Deco District, which is listed on the National Register of Historic Places. In its early days, the building was a hangout for Al Capone's legendary gambling syndicate.

The hostel is only two blocks from the beach and within easy walking distance of ethnic restaurants, nightclubs, and boutiques that give Miami Beach a Latin sizzle.

1438 Washington Avenue,
Miami Beach, FL 33139.
Mail (✉): same.
Phone (☎): 305-534-2988.
Price (◔): $10 U.S. + tax (summer), $11 U.S. + tax (winter: December 15–April 15).
Closed (X): never.
Office Hours: 24 hours.
Grade: Hostel.
Beds (⊨): 200.
Facilities: equipment storage area, information desk, kitchen, laundry facilities, linen rental, lockers/baggage storage, restaurant (open 24 hrs.), **MSA.**
Meals (✎): breakfast, lunch, dinner.
Family rooms (⚥): available.
Groups (⊪): welcome.
Reservations essential (⚷e): December 15–April 15, July–September. Mail one night's payment for deposit 1 week in advance. **By phone:** accepted with credit card confirmation and 48-hour advance notice. **By FAX:** 305-673-0346 with credit card confirmation.

Credit cards: MasterCard, Visa, JCB.
Manager: Linda Polansky.
Directions: 2 blocks from the beach on Washington Avenue between 14th and 15th Streets. **Airport (✈):** take J bus to 41st Street, C bus to Washington Avenue and 15th Street. **Train:** take L bus to Lincoln Road and Washington. **Bus:** take C bus from Miami station to Washington.

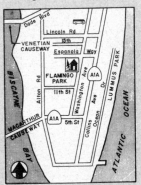

Florida

Orlando (Disney World)

Orlando International AYH-Hostel at Plantation Manor

The Orlando International AYH-Hostel at Plantation Manor overlooks beautiful Lake Eola. Those staying in the lovely Spanish-style hostel, located in downtown Orlando, can swim, jog and play basketball at the nearby YMCA or go on hostel-sponsored van trips. And what would a trip to Orlando be without a visit to Disney World? The hostel is just minutes from the Magic Kingdom, Epcot Center and Disney-MGM Studios. Transportation to area attractions is available from the hostel.

227 North Eola Drive,
Orlando, FL 32801.

Mail (✉): same.

Phone (☎): 407-843-8888.

Price (⊖): $11.50 U.S. + tax.

Closed (X): never.

Office Hours: 7 a.m.–midnight.

Grade: Hostel.

Beds (🛏): 90.

Facilities: information desk, kitchen, laundry facilities, linen rental, lockers/baggage storage, on-site parking, **MSA**, transportation to Disney World, Universal Studios, and Sea World.

Meals (🍴): breakfast.

Reservations essential (👥e): for groups, May–October.

Reservations advisable (👥a): June–September. Mail first-night deposit 1 month in advance. **By phone:** accepted with credit card confirmation. **By FAX:** 407-841-8867 with credit card confirmation.

Credit cards: MasterCard, Visa.

Manager: Milad Bassil.

Directions: downtown on North Eola Drive at East Robinson, on the east shore of Lake Eola.

Airport (✈): Take bus #11 to city terminal, transfer to bus #4 east to Hostel. **Train:** take bus #34 or 40 to city terminal, transfer to bus #4 east to hostel.

Greyhound: take bus #28 or 29 to city terminal, transfer to bus #4 east to hostel.

Florida

Orlando (Women's)
Women's Residential & Counseling Center, Inc.

The Women's Residential & Counseling Center offers a safe haven for women seeing the sights of Orlando. Many visitors trek off to see Mickey and the gang. Those looking for real animals should visit Sea World, home of dolphins and killer whales. See beautiful flora at Cyprus Gardens. Cape Canaveral and the Kennedy Space Center are a must for all future astronauts.

107 East Hillcrest Street, Orlando, FL 32801.
Mail (✉): same.
Phone (☎): 407-425-2502.
Price (◐): $12 U.S.
Closed (X): never.
Office Hours: 7 a.m.–midnight.
Beds (⊨): 6. **Grade: (SA).**
Facilities: accommodations for women ages 16 and up, swimming pool, exercise/music room, information desk, kitchen, laundry facilities, lockers/baggage storage, on-site parking, wheelchair accessible (♿).
Meals (🍴): breakfast, lunch, dinner.
Reservations: not accepted.
Manager: Judy Wilhelm.
Directions: 1 block south off Florida Highway 50 at Hillcrest between Magnolia and Highland.

Florida

St. Augustine

St. Augustine AYH-Hostel

The oldest permanent European settlement in the continental United States, St. Augustine is filled with reminders of its Spanish history. The St. Augustine AYH-Hostel is located in the old Spanish district. Walk down St. George Street past the restored houses and lush gardens to the old City Gates. Stop in at the Oldest Store Museum to see household remnants from America's early days. View some of the settlement's earliest buildings such as the Oldest Schoolhouse, the Old Jail and the Oldest House. Before returning to the hostel, one may wish to drink from the spring that was thought to be the Fountain of Youth—it couldn't hurt.

32 Treasury Street,
St. Augustine, FL 32084.
Mail (✉): same.
Phone (☎): 904-829-6163.
Price (⊖): $10 U.S.
Closed (X): never.
Office Hours: 5–10 p.m.
Grade: Hostel.
Beds: 24.
Facilities: roof garden, equipment storage area, information desk, kitchen, linen rental, lockers/baggage storage, on-site parking, **MSA**.
Family rooms: available.
Groups: welcome.
Reservations advisable: January–March. **By phone:** accepted.
Credit cards: not accepted.
Manager: Susan Bradley.
Directions: 5 blocks east off U.S. Highway 1, near historic Spanish Quarter.

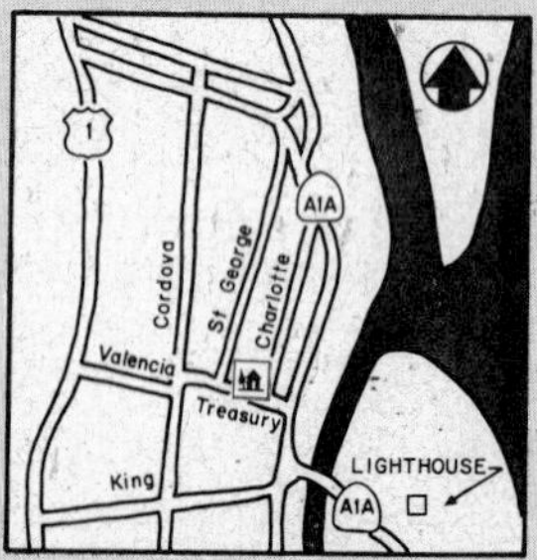

Georgia

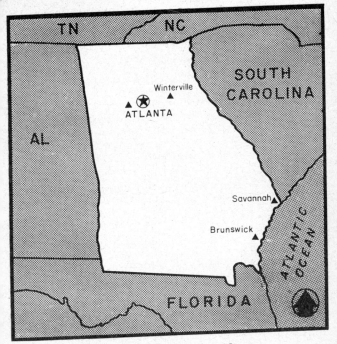

Helpful Organizations

AYH Council Office

Georgia Council
223 Ponce De Leon Avenue
Atlanta, GA 30308
Phone (☎): 404-872-8844

State Tourism Office

Georgia Tourist Division
P.O. Box 1776
Atlanta, GA 30301
Phone (☎): 404-656-3590

Georgia

HOME HOSTEL

Athens (Winterville)
Durhams Home Hostel

Experience old-fashioned Southern hospitality in a quiet country setting at Phyllis and Ray Durham's organic farm. This home hostel is just six miles from Athens, home of the University of Georgia. Stroll down Prince Street to see the dignified mansions that give the city a stately look. The Founders Memorial Museum and the State Botanical Garden of Georgia are beautifully landscaped areas full of colorful flora.

Call for reservations.
Phone (☎): 706-742-7803.
Price (☗): $12 U.S.
Closed (X): various times.
Grade: home hostel (🏠).
Beds (🛏): 3.
Facilities: linen rental, on-site parking, wheelchair accessible (♿), smoke-free environment.

Reservations essential (✆e): always; 50% deposit required. **By phone:** call for information.
Credit cards: not accepted.
Managers: Phyllis and Ray Durham.
Directions: available upon reservation confirmation.

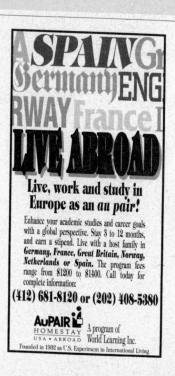

Georgia

Atlanta

Woodruff AYH-Hostel

A beautiful Victorian house built in 1915, the hostel is located in the heart of midtown Atlanta and close to many attractions and restaurants featuring fine Southern cuisine.

Host of the 1996 Summer Olympic Games, Atlanta is the home of the elaborately restored Fox Theatre and the popular World of Coca Cola Pavilion. The Carter Presidential Center and the Martin Luther King, Jr. Center for Nonviolent Social Change honor two of Georgia's favorite sons.

Spend an evening eating, dancing, and listening to music in Underground Atlanta, a huge complex of restaurants and shops, or relax in Atlanta's Piedmont Park.

223 Ponce de Leon Avenue, Atlanta, GA 30308.
Mail (✉): same.
Phone (☎): 404-875-2882.
Price (⬤): $12.50 U.S. + tax.
Closed (X): daily, noon-5 p.m.
Office Hours: 8–10 a.m., 5–11 p.m.
Grade: Hostel.
Beds (🛏): 20.
Facilities: kitchen, linen rental, on-site parking, free coffee and dough-nuts, **MSA**.
Family rooms (👪): available.
Groups (🏠): welcome.
Reservations advisable (📞a): always. **By phone:** accepted with credit card confirmation.
Credit cards: American Express, MasterCard, Visa.

Managers: Douglas and Joan Jones, Shauna Shuchaf
Directions: 1 mile east of Interstate 75 at the corner of Myrtle Street and Ponce de Leon Avenue. Free pick up from Marta.

Georgia

Brunswick

Hostel in the Forest, an AYH-Hostel

Located halfway between Savannah, Georgia, and Jacksonville, Florida, the Hostel in the Forest is one of America's most unique and photogenic facilities. Spend the night in geodesic domes and treehouses. Shuttle service from the bus station to the hostel is available for $3 daily from 8:30 a.m. to 10 p.m.

Nearby is the Cumberland Island National Seashore with its wealth of marshes, dunes and pristine beaches, and the more developed St. Simons and Jekyll Islands. Visit the famous Okefenokee Swamp and National Wildlife Refuge.

The biggest festival in the area, "Blessing of the Fleet," is held each April in Darien, Georgia, just a few miles north of the hostel.

Call for information.
Mail (✉): P.O. Box 1496, Brunswick, GA 31521.
Phone (☎): 912-264-9738, 912-261-0784, 912-265-0220, 912-638-2623.
Price (☻): $8 U.S.
Closed (X): never.
Office Hours: 8 a.m.–11 p.m.
Beds (🛏): 40. **Grade:** Hostel.
Facilities: 2 geodesic domes plus treehouses, swimming pool, fish pond, equipment storage area, kitchen, laundry facilities, linen rental, on-site parking, **MSA**.
Family rooms (👪): available.
Groups (🏠): welcome.
Reservations: not accepted.

Credit cards: not accepted.
Directions: 2 miles west of Interstate 95 (exit #6) on U.S. Highway 82. Daily pick-up from the bus station ($3), from 8:30 a.m. to 10 p.m.

Georgia

Savannah

Savannah International AYH-Hostel

Historic Savannah, a classic "old South" city where cotton once was king, abounds with restored stately 18th- and 19th-century homes. The hostel occupies an 1884 Victorian home in the city's historic district, complete with 13-foot ceilings and slate fireplaces. Famous Riverfront Plaza, only a few blocks away, has pubs, shops, restaurants, and music housed in old cotton warehouses along cobblestone streets. Visit the Juliette Gordon Low Girl Scout National Center for its collection of Girl Scout memorabilia. A variety of tours of Savannah are available, ranging from carriage tours and historic home tours to the Black Heritage tour. Experience a city that has kept its past alive. There are three Civil War forts in the surrounding area. Forsyth Park is filled with Spanish moss and monuments, just two blocks from the hostel.

304 East Hall Street
Savannah, GA 31401.
Mail (✉): same.
Phone (☎): 912-236-7744.
Price (●): $11 U.S.
Closed (X): never.
Office Hours: 7–10 a.m., 5–11 p.m.
Grade: Hostel.
Beds (🛏): 15.
Facilities: baggage storage area, laundry, kitchen, linen rental, on-site parking, showers, **MSA**.
Reservations (✉☎): not needed.
Credit cards: not accepted.
Manager: Brian Sherman.

Directions: Take I-95, exit Savannah Historic District, north on Abercom Street, east on Hall Street.

Hawaii

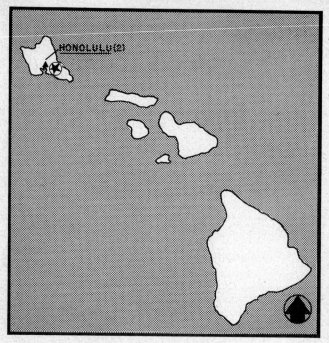

Helpful Organizations

AYH Council Office

Inquires about Hawaii
c/o AYH National Office
PO Box 37616
Washington, DC 20013-7613
Phone (☎): 202-783-6161

State Tourism Office

Hawaii Visitors Bureau
2270 Kalakaua Avenue #801
Honolulu, HI 96815
Phone (☎): 808-923-1811

Discounts

Present a valid hostel membership card at the time of purchase and receive the
following discounts:

Honolulu

Consolidated Theatres - $4.00 movie coupons ($5.50 value) sold at hostel office.
2323A Seaview Avenue, 808-946-0591.
Marcella Besser - 10% discount on dives (go to the Waianae Coast). 6 people per
dive limit. Mention this booklet. 4614 Kilauea Avenue, #322, 808-373-3590.
Mark Imhoof - 25% discount on snorkeling and scuba diving in Hanauma Bay,
808-226-9814.
Rhonda Copeland of Kaneohe Bay Cruises - $7.50 for a 1 1/2 hour snorkling tour
on a glass bottom boat. P.O. Box 1604, Kaneohe, HI 96744, 808-235-2888.

Hawaii

Honolulu (University)

Honolulu International AYH-Hostel

Watch the sun rise over the ridge of the beautiful Manoa Valley from this home-like hostel in a quiet residential area near the University of Hawaii. Hike through the tropical foliage in this valley to the gorgeous Manoa Falls or take the other available trails for breathtaking views of Honolulu. Nearby Mo'ili'ili is a great area for the college crowd with pubs, ethnic restaurants, and health food stores. Once the home of Hawaii's King Kalakaua and Queen Liliuokalani, the Iolani Palace in downtown Honolulu is now a fascinating museum filled with Hawaiian and European artifacts. Join in the hostel's hiking trips, video nights, and excursions to local attractions. Join in the barbecues to meet the local people.

2323A Seaview Avenue, Honolulu, HI 96822.

Mail (✉): same.
Phone (☎): 808-946-0591.
Price (◔): $12 U.S. including tax.
Closed (✗): never.
Office Hours: 7 a.m.–noon, 4:30 p.m.–midnight.
Grade: Hostel.
Beds (⊨): 40.
Facilities: patio under coconut trees, day use, TV room, tours and activities, kitchen, laundry facilities, linen rental, lockers/baggage storage, on-site parking, **MSA**.
Groups (🏠): small groups welcome.
Reservations advisable (✆): always. Write early and include first-night deposit. **By phone:** accepted with credit card confirmation. **By FAX:** 808-946-5904 with credit card confirmation and 7-day advance notice.

Credit cards: MasterCard, Visa, JCB.
Manager: Susan Akau.
Directions: Airport (✈): By car: H-1 east to exit 24B, 3 blocks north on University Avenue. By bus: take bus #19 or #20, then transfer to bus #6 or #18. By shuttle: EM tours, phone: 836-0210.

Hawaii

Honolulu (Waikiki)

Hale Aloha AYH-Hostel

The Hale (pronounced HAH-LAY) Aloha AYH-Hostel is two blocks from Oahu's fabulous Waikiki beach. This former playground of the Hawaiian monarchy attracts sun worshippers and surfers from around the world. Nights are filled with luaus, hula shows, visits to dance clubs, and dinner cruises. Nearby are great beach spots: Ala Moana, Sandy, Kailua, and Hanauma Bay with snorkeling around coral reefs to view the colorful tropical fish. Not to be missed is the famous monument in Pearl Harbor, dedicated to the men who died during an air raid that began America's involvement in World War II. Video nights and beach and nature walks are available or just sit back and enjoy this peaceful retreat in the heart of Waikiki.

2417 Prince Edward Street, Honolulu, HI 96815.
Mail (✉): same.
Phone (☎): 808-926-8313.
Price (●): $15 U.S. including tax.
Closed (X): never.
Office Hours: 8 a.m.–midnight.
Beds (🛏): 50. **Grade:** Hostel.
Facilities: kitchen, patio, TV room, laundry facilities, linen rental, on-site parking, tours and activities, double rooms available.
Groups (卌): small groups welcome.
Reservations essential (☎e): always. Write early and include first-night deposit. **By phone:** accepted with credit card confirmation.
Credit cards: MasterCard, Visa, JCB.
Manager: Joanna Akau.
Directions: 2 blocks from Waikiki Beach, east of Kaiulani on Prince Edward Street. **Airport (✈):** By car: east on H-1, south (right) on Punahou Street, west (right) on Beretania Street, south (left) on Kalakaua Avenue, north (left) on Liliuokalani, west (left) on Prince Edward Street. **By bus:** take bus #19 or #20, or take airport shuttle from ground level ($6). **By taxi:** $20 U.S.

Idaho

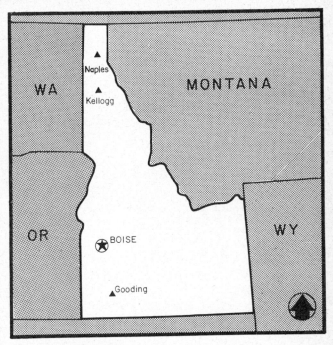

Helpful Organizations

AYH Council Office

Oregon Council
American Youth Hostels
1520 S.E. 37th Avenue
Portland, OR 97214
Phone (☎): 503-235-9493

State Tourism Office

Idaho Division of Travel Promotion
700 West State Street
State House Mail
Boise, ID 83720
Phone (☎): 208-334-2470

Discounts

Present a valid hostel membership card at the time of purchase and receive the following discounts:

Kellogg

The Alpine House - 10% discount on all merchandise except consignment and collectibles. 114 McKinley Ave., 208-786-3231.

Excelsior Cycle - $5 off any regular mountain bike rental. 10 W. Portland Ave., 208-786-3751.

Fred's Restaurant and Lounge - 10% discount on all food items. 113 McKinley Ave., 208-784-7055.

Ratskeller's McKinley Lounge - One free drink per person. 114 McKinley Ave., 208-783-3901.

Silver Tees, Textiles, and Gifts - 20% discount on anything in the store. Must be staying at hostel and must have hostel identification. 402 Main St., 208-783-1194.

Idaho

Gooding
Gooding Hotel

The Gooding Hotel is the place to stay in Gooding. Enjoy skiing at Soldier Mountain or exploring the unique geological surroundings. Visit the Hagerman Fossil Beds and Malad Gorge with its 250-foot canyon. See the plunging Shoshone Falls, known as the "Niagara of the West." Go spelunking in Shoshone Ice Cave, a lava tube filled with ice forms.

112 Main Street,
Gooding, ID 83330.
Mail (✉): same.
Phone (☎): 208-934-4374.
Price (◒): $9 U.S. + tax.
Closed (X): never.
Office Hours: 8–10 a.m., 5 p.m.– midnight.
Beds (🛏): 8. **Grade: (SA)**.
Facilities (mixed use): TV, equipment storage area, information desk, kitchen, laundry facilities, linen rental, on-site parking, **MSA**.

Meals (✎): breakfast.
Family rooms (👪): available.
Reservations: not essential. **By phone:** accepted with 24-hour notice.
Credit cards: MasterCard, Visa.
Manager: Elsa Freeman.
Directions: 1 mile north of U.S. Highway 26 on Idaho Highway 46. I-84: exit at Wendell or Bliss.

Idaho

Kellogg

Kellogg International AYH-Hostel

Kellogg, a historic mining community, is near Silver Mountain, a new world-class ski resort which also has a variety of summer activities such as mountain biking on 59 miles of trails. It has the world's longest gondola (1 block from the hostel), stretching 3.1 miles from the valley floor to the upper terminal. Tour historic silver mines or take in a concert at the Summer Amphitheater. Housed in a historic 80-year-old building, the hostel also has free "you-fix" pancake breakfasts and discount packages for bikes and skiing.

834 West McKinley Ave.
Kellogg, ID 83837
Mail (✉): same.
Phone (☎): 208-783-4171.
Price (💲): $10 U.S. + tax., $12 ski season.
Closed (X): May 1–15.
Office Hours: 8–10 a.m., 3–10 p.m.
Grade: Hostel.
Beds (🛏): 36.
Facilities: baggage storage area, kitchen, laundry, linen rental, lockers, showers, on-site parking, wheelchair accessible (&), **MSA**.
Family rooms (⚲): available.
Meals (✎): fix your own breakfast.
Reservations advisable: November–April, ski season.
By phone: accepted, written (1 day notice).

Credit cards: not accepted.
Manager: Tom Parmenter.
Directions: Eastbound I-90, exit 50 (Hill Street), go south 1/4 mile, west on McKinley, 1/4 mile to hostel.

Idaho

Naples

Naples AYH-Hostel

Naples is a farming and logging community set in a tranquil valley 35 miles south of the U.S.–Canadian border. The area is teeming with wildlife, streams, and lakes. The Naples AYH-Hostel blends in with this fabulous wilderness setting. Built as a dance hall 50 years ago, the hostel even has its own old-fashioned general store and laundromat.

The Kootenia Wildlife Refuge, a 3,000-acre wilderness, is filled with bears, moose, coyotes, deer, and birds. Hike on its well-maintained foot trails along a river that provides breeding areas for migratory birds. Take a drive on the Big Moyie Canyon Bridge, high over the Moyie River Canyon and its scenic waterfalls. Ski the powdery slopes at Schweitzer in the Selkirk Mountains. Sail, windsurf, and fish at Pend Oreille and Lake Coeur d'Alene.

Idaho Highway 2,
Naples, ID 83847.
Mail (✉): same.
Phone (☎): 208-267-2947.
Price (●): $7.50 U.S. + tax.
Closed (X): never.
Office Hours: 7 a.m.–7 p.m., except Sunday 7 a.m.–6 p.m.
Grade: Hostel.
Beds (🛏): 23.
Facilities: general store, equipment storage area, kitchen, laundry facilities, linen rental, lockers/baggage storage, on-site parking, **MSA**, half-court basketball, piano.
Family rooms (👪): available.
Groups (🏫): welcome.
Reservations: not essential.
By phone: accepted.
Credit cards: not accepted.
Managers: Earl and Linda Berwick.

Directions: downtown at the junction of U.S. Highway 95 and Idaho Highway 2, in Kootenia Wildlife Refuge, 35 miles south of Canada–U.S. border.

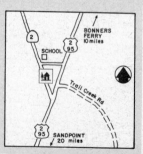

Illinois

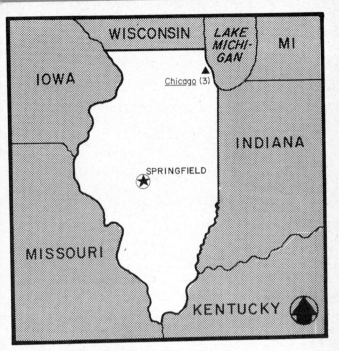

Helpful Organizations

AYH Council Offices

Metropolitan Chicago Council
3036 North Ashland Avenue
Chicago, IL 60657
Phone (☎): 312-327-8114
FAX: 312-327-4287

Ozark Area Council
7187 Manchester Road
St. Louis, MO 63143
Phone (☎): 314-644-4660

State Tourism Office

Illinois Bureau of Tourism
310 South Michigan Avenue #108
Chicago, IL 60604
Phone (☎): 800-223-0121
(brochure requests only) or
312-793-2094

Discounts

Present a valid hostel membership card at the time of purchase to receive the
following discounts:

Chicago
City Garden Home Hostel - 10% discount on CTA tokens, good for all local CTA
buses and trains - 312-925-0447.

A new hostel to open June 1993. . .

Come and visit the Windy City and let it blow you away with all there is to see and do! The city on the shores of Lake Michigan is where blues music was born and is still thriving along with various festivals almost every summer weekend. Chicago is a sports enthusiast's dream, being home to the world champion Chicago Bulls as well as America's favorite baseball team, the Chicago Cubs. Chicago is home to the world's tallest building and first-class museums.

For more information, write/call:
Metropolitan Chicago Council of AYH
3036 North Ashland Avenue
Chicago, IL 60657
Phone (☎): 312-327-5350

Illinois

HOME HOSTEL

Chicago (Southwest)
City Garden Home Hostel

Mary Gorney and John Uram invite hostellers to discover the vibrant neighborhoods of southwest Chicago. Play checkers, croquet, and watch free films. Beat the host at chess and win a free meal. Head downtown and shop on Michigan Avenue or ride to the top of the Sears Tower. Enjoy Chicago's cultural heritage.

Call for reservations.
Phone (☎): 312-925-0447.
Price (☻): $8.50 U.S.
Closed (X): never.
Grade: home hostel (🏠).
Beds (🛏): 2.
Facilities: baggage storage area, kitchen, laundry facilities, street parking.

Reservations essential (🔑e): always. **By phone:** accepted.
Credit cards: not accepted
Managers: Mary C. Gorney, John R. Uram.
Directions: Available upon reservation confirmation.

Illinois

Chicago (University)
International House of Chicago

When visiting Chicago, stay at International House with its single-room accommodations on the University of Chicago campus in historic Hyde Park. Neighborhood sights include Frank Lloyd Wright's architectural masterpiece, Robie House, as well as local museums. Especially notable is the Museum of Science and Industry with over 2,000 exhibits and the five-story-screen Omnimax Theater.

1414 East 59th Street, Chicago, IL 60637.
Mail (✉): same.
Phone (☎): 312-753-2270.
Price (●): $16 U.S.
Closed (X): August 29–January 2.
Office Hours: 24 hours.
Grade: (SA).
Beds (▭): 30.
Facilities (mixed use): tennis courts, game room, exercise/ weight room, cafeteria, laundry facilities, linens included.
Meals (🍴): at cafeteria.
Groups (IIII): welcome.
Reservations essential (📞e): always. **By phone:** accepted.

By FAX: 312-753-1227.
Credit cards: MasterCard, Visa.
Managers: Joyce Penner, C. Lester Stermer.
Directions: take commuter train - Metra Electric from downtown to 59th Street and walk 1 block west.
Bus: take #6 Jeffery Express from downtown to 59th Street and walk 2 blocks west. **Airport (✈):** From O'Hare, C.W. Airport, Service goes to International House; or take O'-Hare train downtown, get off at Washington, walk 1 block to State Street, and take #6 Jeffery Express to 59th Street, walk 2 blocks west. Call for alternate directions.

International House of Chicago
1414 East 59th Street, Chicago, IL 60637
(312) 753-2270

Enjoy Chicago's multiple tourist and cultural attractions. Explore the world-famous Museum of Science and Industry nearby International House. More than just a hostel, we are part of the University of Chicago community.

✔TV lounge   ✔recreation room   ✔exercise/ weight room   ✔tennis courts   ✔laundry room

Indiana

Helpful Organizations

AYH Council

Indiana Council
P.O. Box 30048
Indianapolis, IN 46230
Phone (☎): 317-844-5320

Northwest Indiana Council
8231 Lake Shore Drive
Gary, IN 46403
Phone (☎): 219-962-5396

State Tourism Office

Tourism Division
One North Capitol, Suite 700
Indianapolis, IN 46204
Phone (☎): 800-292-6337 (out of state) or 317-232-8860

Iowa

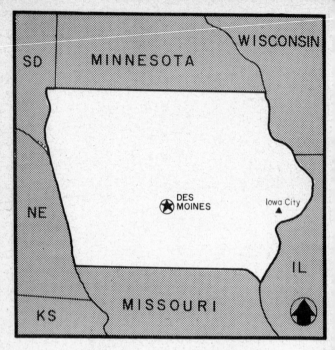

Helpful Organizations

AYH Council Office

Northeast Iowa Council
P.O. Box 10
Postville, IA 52162
Phone (☎): 319-864-3923

State Tourism Office

Iowa Bureau of Tourism
200 East Grand Avenue
Des Moines, IA 50309
Phone (☎): 800-345-4692,
515-242-4705

Iowa

Iowa City

Wesley House AYH-Hostel

Just six blocks from the Greyhound bus station, the Wesley House AYH-Hostel is the place to stay while checking out the University of Iowa. Cheer on the Hawkeye basketball and football teams against powerful Big Ten opponents. Enjoy plays and concerts in the Hancher Auditorium. View jade and African artifacts and student artwork in the Museum of Art. Grab the *Daily Iowan* and relax in the gardens at Memorial Union.

Tour the Greek revival Old Capitol Building or walk through the Museum of Natural History's exhibits on ecology, native culture, and the Marquette–Joliet expedition. Go hiking, swimming, and boating at the Coraville Lake Complex north of the city. Visit the city during the Regina Fall Fun Festival, riverfest, and the Iowa City Hospice Races.

120 North Dubuque.
Iowa City, IA 52245.
Mail (⌂): same.
Phone (☎): 319-338-1179.
Price (◗): $10 U.S.
Closed (X): November 24–27, December 17–January 3.
Office Hours: 8–10 a.m., 7–9 p.m.
Grade: Hostel.
Beds (⊨): 7.
Facilities: unisex dorms, equipment storage area, information desk, kitchen, linen rentals, lockers/baggage storage, **MSA**.
Reservation advisable (⛵a): June–August. **By phone:** not accepted.
Credit cards: not accepted.
Managers: David Schuldt, Kristine Stark.

Directions: 2 miles south of Interstate 80 at Dubuque and Jefferson.

Kentucky

Helpful Organizations

AYH Council Office

Tri-State Council
P.O. Box 141015
Cincinnati, OH 45250-1015
Phone (☎): 513-651-1294

State Tourism Office

Kentucky Travel Development
500 Mero Street
Capitol Plaza Tower, 22nd floor
Frankfort, KY 40601
Phone (☎): 800-225-8747,
502-564-4930

Kentucky

Pippa Passes
Pippa Passes Home Hostel

The Daniel Boone National Forest is just minutes away from this comfortable eastern Kentucky home. The 250-mile-long forest offers scenic waterfalls, caves, stone arches, and sandstone cliffs. Hikers, cyclists, and nature lovers are sure to enjoy the rugged beauty of the area. In September and October, the Appalachian Music Festival is a great place to hear real mountain music.

Call for reservations.
Phone (☎): 606-368-2753.
Price (⊜): $7.25 U.S.
Closed (X): never.
Grade: home hostel (🏠).
Beds (🛏): 8.
Facilities: kitchen, linen rental, on-site parking.
Family rooms (👪): available.

Groups (𝍠): welcome.
Reservations essential (✆e): always. **By phone:** accepted.
Credit cards: not accepted.
Managers: Charlotte and Ed Madden.
Directions: available upon reservation confirmation.

Louisiana

Helpful Organizations

AYH Council Office

Inquiries about Louisiana
c/o AYH National Office
P.O. Box 37613
Washington, DC 20013-7613
Phone (☎): 202-783-6161

State Tourism Office

Louisiana Office of Tourism
P.O. Box 94291
Baton Rouge, LA 70804
Phone (☎): 800-33-GUMBO,
504-342-8119

Louisiana

New Orleans

Marquette House
New Orleans International AYH-Hostel

An antebellum house near the Garden District, the Marquette House is just minutes away by streetcar from the lively French Quarter. Free tours explaining the rich history of the area are provided by the Jean Lafitte National Historical Park. Be sure to book a room well in advance for Mardi Gras and the Jazz Festival.

2253 Carondelet Street,
New Orleans, LA 70130.
Mail (✉): same.
Phone (☎): 504-523-3014.
Price (☻): $10.81 U.S. + tax, $13.96 U.S. + tax during Mardi Gras and Jazz Fest.
Closed (X): never.
Office Hours: 7:30 a.m.–1 p.m., 3–11 p.m., after 11 p.m. with advance notice.
Grade: Hostel.
Beds (🛏): 162.
Facilities: patio-garden area, day use, private rooms, equipment storage area, information desk, kitchen, laundry facilities, linen rental, lockers/baggage storage, on-site parking, **MSA**.
Family rooms (👪): available.
Groups (⛺): welcome.
Reservations essential (☎): February 4–15 (Mardi Gras), April 23–May 2 (Jazz Festival). Mail full payment 30 days in advance; include self-addressed, stamped reply envelope. **Reservations advisable (☎):** July 1–September 15. **By phone:** accepted with

credit card confirmation. **By FAX:** 504-529-5933 with credit card confirmation.
Credit cards: MasterCard, Visa, JCB.
Managers: Jon Conway, Alma and Steve Cross.
Directions: downtown, 1 mile west off Interstate 10. From Greyhound and Amtrak stations or airport bus stop downtown, walk 5 blocks south toward the river to St. Charles, take streetcar to Jackson Avenue, walk 1 block north to Carondelet Street.

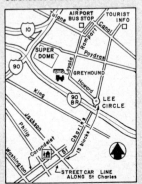

Maine

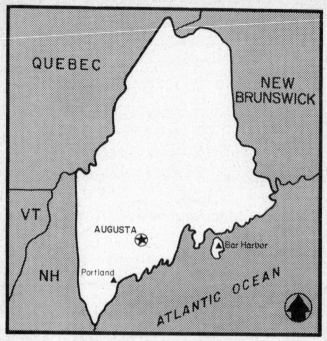

Helpful Organizations

AYH Council Office

Greater Boston Council
1020 Commonwealth Avenue
Boston, MA 02215
Phone (☎): 617-731-6692 (12–6 p.m.
M–F)
Activities hotline: 617-730-8-AYH
Worldwide Info-Line: 617-731-5430
FAX: 617-734-7614

State Tourism Office

Maine Tourist Division
P.O. Box 2300
Hallowell, ME 04347
Phone (☎): 207-582-9300

Discounts

Present a valid hostel membership card at the time of purchase to receive the following discounts:

Bar Harbor

Arcady Music Festival - IYHF members admitted at children's ticket rate - 18 Bridge Street, 207-288-3151.
Bar Harbor Festival - IYHF members admitted at student rate - 59 Cottage Street, 207-288-5744.
Bar Harbor Photo - 10% discount for IYHF members - 65 Main, 207-288-2290.
Museum of Natural History, College of the Atlantic - 10% discount on admission - 105 Eden Street.
Ryan's Pizza Restaurant - 15% discount for IYHF members - 131 Cottage Street, 207-288-9797.

Discounts

Bar Harbor (continued)
Subway Salad & Sandwich - 15% discount for IYHF members - 11 Rodick Place, 207-288-9377.

Maine

Bar Harbor

Mount Desert Island AYH-Hostel

The Mount Desert Island AYH-Hostel is located in the town of Bar Harbor, known for its many shops and restaurants, Natural History Museum, and a world-class music festival in July and August. Whale-watching tours and excursions on working lobster boats leave from the wharf. The Bluenose Ferry also leaves from here on its way to Nova Scotia.

The rocky coastline, rugged cliffs, and mountainous interior inspired Henry Van Dyke to call Mount Desert Island "the most beautiful island in the world." Explore Acadia National Park along the island's 57 miles of carriage paths, perfect for hiking, biking, horseback riding, and cross-country skiing. Climb Cadillac Mountain for views of the coast and Maine's mountainous interior.

27 Kennebec Street.
Mail (✉): Box 32, Bar Harbor, ME 04609.
Phone (☎): 207-288-5587.
Price (●): $8 U.S.
Closed (X): August 31–June 14.
Office Hours: 7–9 a.m., 4:30–8:30 p.m.
Grade: Hostel.
Beds (🛏): 20.
Facilities: 2 dorm rooms, kitchen, on-site parking, **MSA**.
Groups (🏠): welcome.
Reservations advisable (✋a): always. **By phone:** not accepted.
Credit cards: not accepted.
Directions: From Ellsworth, take Maine Highway 3 east (23 miles), pass the Marine Atlantic ferry terminal in Bar Harbor, turn east onto Cottage Street (1-1/2 miles from the ferry), continue to post office (north side of Cottage), turn south on Kennebec Street until 90-degree turn, hostel is in Parish Hall of St. Saviour's Church.

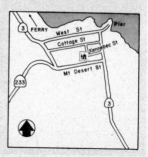

Maine

To open in June 1993...
near the Portland scenic coast

Portland Summer AYH-Hostel

Portland, Maine, is a city with a rich maritime history and an exciting mix of Victorian and modern architecture. Portland Summer AYH-Hostel is located in the University of Southern Maine's Portland Hall, downtown Portland.

You'll enjoy touring Portland Harbor's islands, visiting the Old Port, Victoria Mansion, Portland Observatory, and the Portland Museum of Art, and attending several summer festivals. For great shopping, take a short ride to Freeport, Maine, home of L.L. Bean and many other clothing manufacturers' outlet stores.

645 Congress Street
(in Portland Hall).
Mail (✉): to below address
Attn: Portland Summer Hostel
c/o AYH
1020 Commonwealth Avenue
Boston, MA 02215.
Phone (☎): 617-731-8096.
Price (💰): $14 U.S.
Closed (X): August 15–June 1.
Office Hours: 7–10 a.m., 5 p.m.–midnight.
Grade: (SA).
Beds (🛏): 48.
Facilities: baggage storage area, laundry, linen rental, showers, vending machines, cafeteria, **MSA**.
Family rooms (🏠): available.
Groups (🏨): welcome.
Meals (🍴): breakfast.

Reservations advisable (☎a): always. **By phone:** accepted with 1 day's notice.
Credit cards: MasterCard, Visa, JCB.
Directions: Take I-295 to Congress Street exit. Go northeast 1-1/4 miles to top of hill. Portland Hall is on left.

Maryland

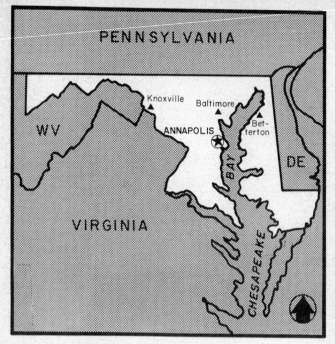

Helpful Organizations

AYH Council Office

Potomac Area Council
7420 Baltimore Avenue
College Park, MD 20740
Phone (☎): 301-209-8544

State Tourism Office

Maryland Office of Tourism
217 East Redwood Street
Baltimore, MD 21202
Phone (☎): 800-543-1036 (out of state), or 410-333-6611

Maryland

Baltimore

Baltimore International AYH-Hostel

An elegant three-story townhouse, the Baltimore International AYH-Hostel is within walking distance of Inner Harbor and Camden Yards, the new home of Major League Baseball's Baltimore Orioles. Inner Harbor features more than 100 restaurants and shops, plus the historic frigate USS Constellation. Be sure to visit the renowned National Aquarium and the Maryland Science Center. Nearby Fort McHenry is where Francis Scott Key witnessed "the rocket's red glare" during the War of 1812, which inspired him to write "The Star-Spangled Banner."

17 West Mulberry Street, Baltimore, MD 21201.
Mail (✉): same.
Phone (☎): 410-576-8880.
Price (●): $10 U.S.
Closed (X): December 24–January 2.
Office Hours: 8–10 a.m., 5–10 p.m.
Grade: Hostel.
Beds (🛏): 40.
Facilities: outdoor courtyard, piano, kitchen, library, information desk, laundry facilities, linen rental, lockers/baggage storage, travel shop, **MSA**.
Groups (🏠): welcome.
Reservations advisable (📷a): groups. **By phone:** not accepted.
Credit cards: not accepted.

Manager: Joelle Porter.
Directions: downtown at Cathedral and Mulberry, near Inner Harbor.

Maryland

Betterton
Lantern Inn

Built in 1904, the Lantern Inn is two blocks from Betterton Beach, the only public beach on Chesapeake Bay's Eastern Shore. Facilities for boating, fishing, and windsurfing are nearby. Away from the beach are tennis courts, nature trails to hike, country roads ideal for cycling, and three wildlife refuges to explore.

115 Ericsson Avenue.
Mail (✉): P.O. Box 29, Betterton, MD 21610.
Phone (☎): 410-348-5809.
Price (◗): $15 U.S.
Closed (X): mid December–mid January.
Office Hours: noon–10 p.m.
Beds (⊨): 10. **Grade: (SA).**
Facilities (mixed use): no kitchen restaurant one block, linen rental, on-site parking.

Family rooms (⚲): available for children age 10 or older.
Groups (⦀): welcome.
Reservations essential (⦁●): always.
By phone: accepted 8 a.m.–10 p.m.
Credit cards: MasterCard, Visa.
Managers: Ann and Ken Washburn.
Directions: 12 miles northeast of Chestertown on Maryland Highway 292, 1 block west of Main Street between Howell Point Road and Idlewhile.

Maryland

Knoxville

Harpers Ferry AYH-Hostel

Standing high on a bluff, this recently restored lodge overlooks the Potomac and Shenandoah rivers. Hike the nearby Appalachian Trail. Cycle or hike along the C&O Canal Towpath. Enjoy a game of volleyball in the hostel's yard. In the evening, relax in front of the fireplace or take the Guest Tour of Harpers Ferry.

Visit the Harpers Ferry National Historic Park, site of John Brown's famous raid. Experience life in the 1860s at the historic village shops and exhibits. Ride down the Shenandoah River on an inner tube, raft, or canoe.

19123 Sandy Hooks Rd, Knoxville, MD 21758.
Mail (✉): same.
Phone (☎): 301-834-7652.
Price (⬤): $9 U.S.
Office Hours: 7–9:30 a.m., 5–9 p.m.
Grade: Hostel.
Beds (🛏): 36.
Facilities: stone fireplace, interpretive materials, hostel-based programs, kitchen, laundry facilities, linen rental, on-site parking, wheelchair accessible (♿), **MSA**.
Family rooms (👪): available.
Groups (🏠): welcome.
Reservations advisable (📞a): for groups. **By phone:** accepted with deposit.
Credit cards: not accepted.
Manager: Jeanne and Harry Thomas.

Directions: 16 miles west of Frederick off U.S. Highway 340, across Potomac River from Harpers Ferry National Historic Park.

Massachusetts

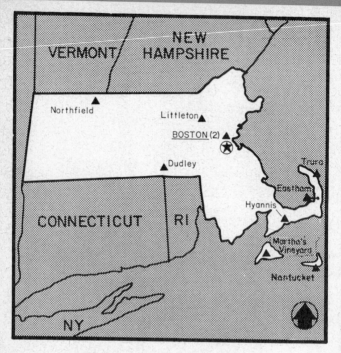

Helpful Organizations

AYH Council Offices

Greater Boston Council
1020 Commonwealth Avenue
Boston, MA 02215
Phone (☎): 617-731-6692 (12–6 p.m.
M–F)
Activities hotline: 617-730-8-AYH
Worldwide Info-Line: 617-731-5430
FAX: 617-734-7614

Yankee Council
118 Oak Street
Hartford, CT 06106
Phone (☎): 203-247-6356

State Tourism Office

**Massachusetts Office of Travel and
Tourism**
100 Cambridge Street, 13th floor
Boston, MA 02202
Phone (☎): 800-447-6277 (guide
book requests only), 617-727-3201

Discounts

Present a valid hostel membership card at the time of purchase to receive the
following discounts:

Boston

A.C. Cruiser Line, Inc. - 10% discount on price of whale watch, cruise, and
Gloucester excursions. 25 Northern Ave., 617-426-8419.
Avenue Victor Hugo Bookshop - 10% discount with AYH-Hostel receipt. 339
Newbury St., 617-266-7746.

Discounts

Boston (continued)

Back Bay Bicycles - 15% discount and $15.00 daily bike rental. 333 Newbury St., 617-247-2336.

Back Bay Pharmacy - 10% discount on all merchandise except cigarettes and food; 20% discount on prescriptions. 1130 Boylston St., 617-267-5331.

Bangkok Cuisine Restaurant - 10% discount with AYH-Hostel receipt. 177A Mass Ave., 617-262-5377.

Boston Chicken - 10% discount on food and beverages with AYH-Hostel receipt. 241 Mass Ave., 617-247-1230.

Boston Museum of Fine Arts - $1.00 off entrance fee with AYH-Hostel receipt. 465 Huntington Ave., 617-227-9300.

Cafe Bouquet - 10% discount with AYH-Hostel receipt, 20% discount with a group of more than three people. 151 Mass Ave., 617-266-7738.

Cafe Jaffa - 10% discount on all food. 48 Gloucester St., 617-536-0230.

Cafe Rasmus - 10% discount with AYH-Hostel receipt. 175 Mass Ave., 617-266-2928.

The Children's Museum - $1.00 off price of Museum Admission with presentation of AYH-Hostel receipt. Not valid on holidays. 300 Congress St., 617-426-6500.

City Sports - 10% discount on all merchandise with coupon from the Boston AYH-Hostel. Coupon available at the Boston Hostel. 168 Mass Ave., 617-236-2222.

The Computer Museum - $1.00 off regular admission with AYH-Hostel receipt. 300 Congress St., 617-426-2800 Ext. 396.

Counter Point Cafe - 20% discount on all food with AYH-Hostel receipt. 1124 Boylston St., 617-424-1789.

Crossroads - 10% discount on all food with AYH-Hostel receipt. 495 Beacon St., 617-262-7371.

Dunkin Donuts - 10% discount with AYH-Hostel receipt. 153 Mass Ave., 617-247-3861.

Dixie Kitchen - 15% discount with AYH-Hostel receipt. 182 Mass Ave., 617-536-3068.

Earth Bikes Bicycle Rentals - 25% discount on all rentals. Urban Cruiser Day rental-$7.00 (available Monday-Friday only). 35 Huntington Ave. & Copley Square, 617-267-4733.

Institute of Contemporary Art - $1.00 of entrance fee to Art Gallery and Theatre with AYH-Hostel receipt. Boylston St.

Kenmore Army and Navy Store - 10% discount on all purchases with AYH-Hostel receipt. 508 Commonwealth Ave., 617-267-2504.

Newbury's Steak House - 20% discount on all food. 94 Mass Ave., 617-536-0184.

SBI Sales - 5% discount on film and processing except special sale dates. 34 Gloucester St., 617-266-9797.

Steve's Greek Restaurant - 10% discount on food for a $10.00 or more purchase for dining only. 316 Newbury St., 617-267-1817.

Steve's Ice Cream - 10% discount with AYH-Hostel receipt. 95 Mass Ave., 617-247-9401.

Supreme Pizza - 10% discount with AYH-Hostel receipt. 177 B Mass Ave., 617-247-8252.

Trident Booksellers and Cafe -10% discount on cafe items. 338 Newbury St., 617-267-8688,

YMCA - $3.00 per person per day for use of fitness facility, aerobics classes included. 316 Huntington Ave., 617-536-7800.

Cambridge

Charles River Boat Company - $2.00 off boat tour on the Charles River with AYH-Hostel receipt. 100 Cambridge Side Place #320, 617-742-4282.

Discounts

Cambridge (continued)

Timeless Tours - 30% discount on daily rate (includes boat lodging, 3 meals a day, and a guided tour of Southern Belize, Central America, by sailboat. 2304 Mass Ave., 1-800-370-0142 in U.S.

Hyannis

Hy-Line Cruises - $2.50 off one-way ticket from Hyannis to Martha's Vineyard. $1.75 off one-way ticket from Hyannis to Nantucket; coupon required - available at all Cape Island Hostels. Pier 1, Ocean St. Dock, 508-778-2600.

Whale Watch - Dolphin Fleet - $3.00 discount coupon for the whale & dolphin watch for hostellers. Chamber of Commerce Building, The Pier, Provincetown, Cape Cod, 1-800-826-9300.

Martha's Vineyard

Bunch of Grapes Bookstore, Inc. - 15% discount on all travel books. Main St., 508-693-2291.

Chilmark Chocolates - One free piece of chocolate (limit one per day). State Road, 508-645-3013.

CJ Cafe - $1.00 off any pizza. State Road, West Tisbury, 508-693-7875.

Cronig's Markets - 10% discount on all groceries for members staying overnight at the Manter Memorial AYH Hostel. AYH-Hostel receipt is required. 109 State Rd., West Tisbury, 508-693-6272.

Cycle Works - 10% discount on parts used for repair for Manter Memorial hostellers. 105 State Rd., 508-693-6966.

Healthy Gourmet Natural Food Markets - 10% discount on all non-sale items. 125 State Rd., 508-693-4818/627-7171.

Island Transport, Inc. - $1.00 off one-way trip or $2.00 off round-trip from Tisbury to West Tisbury on VP-Island Shuttle Bus during operating hours. Circuit Ave. Ext, Oak Bluffs, 508-693-0058.

Marlene's Taxi - $2.00 off return trip - Washington Ave. Ext., Oak Bluffs, 508-693-0037.

Morning Glory Farm - 10% discount on all purchases. RFD #39, Edgartown-West Tisbury Rd., 508-627-9003.

Mosher Photo - 10% discount on 3-hour processing of color prints film (35mm, 110 sizes). 10% discount on all film. 63 Main St., 508-693-9430.

MV Scooter and Bike - $5.00 off on overnight rentals for Manter Memorial hostellers. Union St., 508-693-0782.

Tesoro Charters - 30% discount on sailing excursions. Sailing three times daily out of Edgartown. 3 South Water St., 508-627-7245.

Northfield

Northfield Creamie - 10% discount on any ice cream concoction for Smith Hostel guests only. 60 Main St., 413-498-5304.

Springfield

Peter Pan Bus Lines - 2–4 week unlimited travel for AYH-Hostel members. Pass sold only in AYH-Hostels and AYH-Council offices.

Massachusetts

Boston (International)

Boston International AYH-Hostel

A four-story building, the Boston International AYH-Hostel is located downtown in the Fenway, which includes some of the best museums and night spots in the city. Guests can enjoy one of the special "Evening at the Hostel" programs, lectures, films, and workshops. A walk along the famous Freedom Trail is the best way to see the sights that played a part in the American Revolution.

12 Hemenway Street,
Boston, MA 02115.
Mail (✉): same.
Phone (☎): 617-536-9455.
Price (●): $14 U.S.
Closed (X): never.
Office Hours: 7 a.m.–2 a.m.
Grade: Hostel.
Beds (🛏): 190 (summer), 110 (winter).
Facilities: equipment storage area, information desk, laundry facilities, kitchen, linen rental, lockers/baggage storage, wheelchair accessible (♿), **MSA**.
Family rooms (👪): available.
Groups (🏚): welcome.
Reservations advisable (📞a): always; should be made at least 3 weeks prior to arrival. Mail 1-night deposit with self-addressed, stamped envelope. **By phone:** accepted with credit card confirmation. **By FAX:** 617-424-6558 with credit card confirmation. IBN global reservation system available.
Credit cards: MasterCard, Visa, JCB.
Manager: Merrilee Zellner.

Directions: 1 block west of Massachusetts Highway 2A (Massachusetts Avenue) at Boylston and Hemenway Street. **Airport (✈):** take free shuttle service to Airport T subway station. Take blue line train downtown to Government Center station and transfer to green line. Take westbound B, C, or D train to Hynes Convention Center stop. Walk 1/2 block on Massachusetts Avenue to Boylston Street. Turn right and walk to Hemenway. Turn left and walk 1/2 block to the hostel.

Massachusetts

Boston (Summer)

Back Bay Summer AYH-Hostel

There's so much to see and do in Boston! Walk the Freedom Trail to see part of historic Boston. Stroll around Boston Common to see the various monuments. Take in a Boston Pops concert at the Hatch Shell or Symphony Hall. Snack your way through Quincy Market and Faneuil Hall with their food stalls and restaurants. In the summer, free outdoor concerts take place at the marketplace. Hostellers staying at the Back Bay Summer AYH-Hostel may also participate in the many activities, tours, and events hosted by the Boston International AYH-Hostel.

519 Beacon Street, Boston, MA
Mail (✉): to below address:
Attn: Back Bay Summer Hostel
c/o AYH
1020 Commonwealth Ave.
Boston, MA 02215.
Phone (☎): 617-731-8096.
Price (●): $15 U.S. (single), $14 U.S. (double or triple).
Closed (X): August 8–June 15.
Office Hours: 7–10 a.m., 5 p.m.–2 a.m.
Grade: Hostel.
Beds (🛏): 63.
Facilities: baggage storage area, laundry, linen rental, showers, vending machines, **MSA**.
Family rooms (🏠): available.
Groups (🎪): welcome.

Meals (🍴): breakfast.
Reservations by phone: accepted with 1 day notice.
Credit cards: MasterCard, Visa, JCB.
Directions: Take Mass. Turnpike, exit at Copley Square Boston—inbound exit, turn left at Dartmouth Street (corner of Copley Place), follow to Beacon Street, turn left at Beacon Street. **Airport (✈):** Take free shuttle service to Airport T subway station. Take Blue Line train downtown to Government Center station and transfer to Green Line. Take outbound B, C, or D train to Kenmore station. Walk 1/4 mile east on Beacon Street to the hostel.

Massachusetts

HOME HOSTEL

Dudley
Dudley Home Hostel

Chet and Ann Kulisa's home is a traditional working New England dairy farm conveniently located on the Bikecenntenial East Coast Bike Trail, 55 miles west of Boston. The comfortable old farmhouse, which dates from 1834, overlooks the hills of south central Massachusetts. The Old Sturbridge Village, just a few miles away, provides a more detailed look at 18th-century life in New England farming communities.

Call for reservations.
Phone (☎): 508-943-6520.
Price (●): $10 U.S.
Closed (X): December 1–March 31.
Grade: home hostel (🏠).
Beds (⊨): 7.
Facilities: equipment storage area, kitchen, laundry facilities, linen rental, on-site parking.

Reservations advisable (⊨🏠a): always. **By phone:** accepted.
Credit cards: not accepted.
Managers: Ann and Chet Kulisa.
Directions: available upon reservation confirmation.

IBN INTERNATIONAL BOOKING NETWORK

Massachusetts

Eastham

Mid-Cape AYH-Hostel

Surrounded by three acres of wooded land in a quiet rural area, the cozy cabins of the Mid-Cape AYH-Hostel are only a short distance from the wide, white ocean beaches or the Bay of Cape Cod. Sailing instruction and sunfish and windsurfer rentals are available to hostellers at the beach.

Located roughly halfway between the Hyland AYH-Hostel in Hyannis and the Little America AYH-Hostel in Truro, Mid-Cape makes for a fun and relaxing stopping point for those working their way up the Cape. The nearby Salt Pond National Seashore Visitor's Center provides hiking and biking maps of the Cape Cod National Seashore, general information on the park, and ranger-led tours of the area. The beautiful Cape Cod Rail Trail for bikers runs 14 miles from Eastham to Dennis.

75 Goody Hallet Drive, Eastham, MA 02642.
Mail (✉): same.
Phone (☎): 508-255-2785.
Price (⬤): $10 U.S.
Closed (X): September 16–May 14.
Office Hours: 7:30–9:30 a.m., 5–10:30 p.m.
Beds (🛏): 50. **Grade:** Hostel.
Facilities: cabins, bicycle rental, equipment storage area, information desk, kitchen, linen rental, on-site parking, barbecue and volleyball, **MSA**.
Family rooms (👪): 2 cabins (surcharge). **Groups (🏠):** welcome.
Reservations essential (📞): July–August; off-season, mail to 465 Falmouth Road, Hyannis, MA 02601, or call 508-775-2970. **By phone:** accepted with credit card confirmation.
Credit cards: MasterCard, Visa, JCB.

Directions: 1/2 mile west off U.S. Highway 6 downtown. From traffic rotary (north of Orleans Center), left on Rock Harbor Road 1/4 mile, right on Bridge Road 1/4 mile, right onto Goody Hallet Drive. The hostel driveway is 100 yards on left.

Massachusetts

Hyannis

Hyland AYH-Hostel

The Hyland AYH-Hostel, surrounded by acres of pines and evergreens, is the perfect base for exploring the Cape, Nantucket, and Martha's Vineyard. Charter fishing boats, whale-watching tours, and ferries for the islands leave from the nearby town wharf. Swim, windsurf, or rent a sailboat at the Atlantic beaches, located a few minutes from the hostel by car. After a day at the water, wander around the shops of Hyannis and play a round of mini-golf. Be sure to check local listings for excellent summer theater.

A good time to stay at the hostel is in the fall or early spring when the harbor towns are quiet and visitors have the windswept marshes and cranberry bogs to themselves.

465 Falmouth Road,
Hyannis, MA 02601.
Mail (✉): same.
Phone (☎): 508-775-2970.
Price (●): $10 U.S.
Closed (X): December–February.
Office Hours: 7:30–9:30 a.m., 5–10:30 p.m.
Grade: Hostel.
Beds (🛏): 40 (summer), 16 (winter).
Facilities: bike rental, equipment storage area, kitchen, linen rental, on-site parking, wheelchair accessible (♿), **MSA**.
Groups (ⅢⅢ): welcome.
Reservations essential (↳e): July–August **By phone:** accepted with credit card confirmation.
Credit cards: MasterCard, Visa, JCB.
Managers: David Matthews.

Directions: on small hill 300 yards from junction of Bearses Way and Massachusetts Highway 28. **Bus:** direct service from Boston and New York year-round.

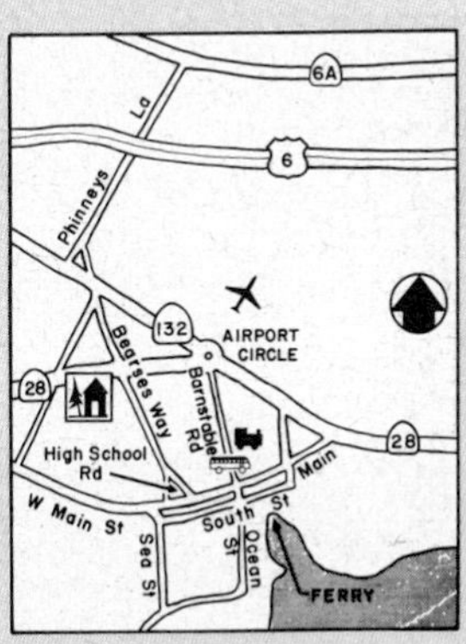

Massachusetts

Littleton

Friendly Crossways AYH-Hostel

Located in a quiet farm area, this spacious and friendly hostel is only 25 miles from Boston by train or car. The White Mountains of New Hampshire, the seacoast from Portland, Maine, to Cape Cod are all within a two-hour drive. Nearer, Thoreau's Walden Pond, and National Parks in Concord or Lowell are 15 miles away. The town of Harvard is home to the Fruitlands Museums and a Shaker Village. Bare Hill Pond provides swimming or ice skating. Hiking trails are spectacular during the fall foliage season.

Whitcomb Avenue.
Mail (✉): P.O. Box 2266, Littleton, MA 01460-3266.
Phone (☎): 508-456-3649.
Price (◖): $10 U.S.
Closed (X): never.
Office Hours: 8–10 a.m., 4–9 p.m.
Grade: Hostel.
Beds (🛏): 50.
Facilities: equipment storage area, information desk, kitchen, linen rental, on-site parking, wheelchair accessible (&), **MSA**.
Meals (🍴): for groups.
Family rooms (👪): available.
Groups (🛏🛏): welcome; reservations always required.
Reservations advisable (📇☎a): By phone: 508-456-3649 or 508-456-9386.
Credit cards: not accepted.
Managers: Anne and Martin Vesenka.
Directions: 2 miles south of Massachusetts Highway 2 and west of Interstate 495 in Harvard. From Interstate 495, take Route 2 west to Taylor Street (Littleton/Boxborough exit). Turn left on Taylor Street. Just beyond the highway fence, make second left onto Porter Road and bear left onto Whitcomb (Whitcomb becomes Littleton County Road). The hostel is 1/2 mile past the red barn, on the right, opposite the pond.

Massachusetts

Martha's Vineyard (West Tisbury)

Manter Memorial AYH-Hostel

The Island of Martha's Vineyard has long been a favorite destination for exploration and recreation. Famous for its beauty and diverse geographical landscape, visitors to The Vineyard quickly become enchanted by "the land beyond the sea beyond the land."

Scenic beaches, biking trails, art galleries, and a variety of preservation lands are among the island's many attractions. Favorite destinations include The Gay Head Clay Cliffs, Chappaquiddick Island, Menemsha Fishing Village, and the Oak Bluffs "Ginger Bread" cottages.

The Manter Memorial AYH-Hostel is centrally located on the island in the town of West Tisbury. Constructed in 1955, this traditional cedar-shake saltbox homestead was the first purpose built youth hostel in the United States. The hostel is situated at the edge of a state forest and along a bike path.

Edgartown-West Tisbury Road.
Mail (✉): Box 158, West Tisbury, MA 02575.
Phone (☎): 508-693-2665.
Price (⬤): $10 U.S.
Closed (X): November 15–March 31.
Office Hours: 7:30–9:30 a,m, 5–10:30 p.m.
Grade: Hostel.
Beds (🛏): 78.
Facilities: equipment and bike storage area, information desk, kitchen, linen rental, on-site parking, displays and programs, **MSA**.
Groups (🏠): welcome.
Reservations essential (📞): always. **By phone:** accepted with credit card confirmation and 24-hour notice. **Off-season reservations:** mail to 465 Falmouth Rd., Hyannis, MA 02601 or call 508-775-2970.

Credit cards: MasterCard, Visa, JCB.
Manager: Mark Gesner.
Directions: 7 miles south of Vineyard Haven ferry terminal (bicycle available at ferry). Right on State Rd., left on Old County Rd., left on Edgar Town Rd.

Massachusetts

Nantucket

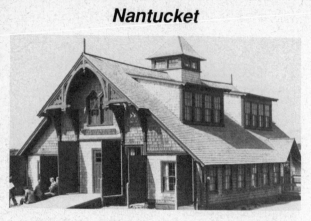

Robert B. Johnson Memorial AYH-Hostel

The Robert B. Johnson Memorial AYH-Hostel, named after a former executive director of American Youth Hostels, was built in 1873 as a life-saving station. One of the few remaining stations in the U.S., it's listed on the National Register of Historic Places. Located three miles from the village of Nantucket, the hostel is across the road from the beautiful Surfside Beach and can be reached by a paved bicycle path.

Like its neighbor, Martha's Vineyard, Nantucket has beautiful sand beaches for swimming, sunning, sailing, and windsurfing. The village offers historic buildings, art galleries, and quaint shops. The Whaling Museum displays artifacts from the days when men hunted the giant mammals with hand-held harpoons from wooden long boats.

Surfside, Nantucket, MA 02554.
Mail (✉): same.
Phone (☎): 508-228-0433.
Price (💰): $10 U.S.
Closed (✗): October 12–April 30.
Office Hours: 7:30–9:30 a.m., 5–10:30 p.m.
Grade: Hostel.
Beds (🛏): 49.
Facilities: kitchen, linen rental, **MSA**.
Groups (🏠): welcome.
Reservations essential (📞): always. **By phone:** accepted with credit card confirmation. **Off-season reservations:** mail to 465 Falmouth Rd, Hyannis, MA 02601 or call 508-775-2970.
Credit cards: MasterCard, Visa, JCB.

Manager: Greg Lockhart.
Directions: 3-1/2 miles from Nantucket ferry wharf on south side of island. Take Surfside bike path to Surfside Beach then 1/4 mile West to Hostel. Year-round ferry from Hyannis only.

Massachusetts

Northfield

Monroe and Isabel Smith AYH-Hostel

Come to the town where hostelling in the USA began! Monroe and Isabel Smith, founders of American Youth Hostels, started a hostel in Northfield in 1934. The current hostel, which opened in 1981, is a beautiful Victorian house with a large yard for croquet, volleyball, and summer barbecues. Tennis courts, an outdoor swimming pool, a nine-hole golf course, hiking trails, and the Connecticut River are all just minutes away. Tour the Northfield Mount Herman campus, the largest private secondary school in the U.S. The hostel is near Old Deerfield Village, Northfield Mountain Nature Center, and river boat rides.

51 Highland Avenue.
Mail (✉): Box 2602, Northfield, MA 01360.
Phone (☎): 413-498-3502.
Price (◖): $12 U.S., in season only.
Closed (X): September–mid-June.
Office Hours: 8–10 a.m., 4:30 p.m.–9:30 p.m.
Grade: Hostel.
Beds (🛏): 13.
Facilities: equipment storage area, information desk, kitchen, large lawn, linen rentals, on-site parking, picnic tables, **MSA**, smoke-free environment.
Family rooms (👪): available.
Groups (🎏): welcome.
Reservations essential (📞): June 21–July 3 and weekends through August 30; for groups, June 21–August 30. **By phone:** accepted.
Credit cards: not accepted.
Manager: Marilyn Barrett.

Directions: 1 block east off Massachusetts Highway 63 (Main Street) in Northfield. Northbound on Highway 63, turn right on Pine Street and go 1 block to Highland. Southbound on Highway 63, turn left on Moody Street, then turn right on Highland Avenue. The hostel is on the northeast corner of Pine and Highland.

Massachusetts

Truro

Little America AYH-Hostel

Originally a Coast Guard station, the Little America AYH-Hostel is the furthest hostel out on the "arm" of the Cape. Located in the Cape Cod National Seashore, the hostel is just a seven-minute walk from the beach. Large picture windows provide a breathtaking view from the spacious kitchen and dining area.

Explore the marshes, dunes, and cranberry bogs. Bird watchers will want to visit the National Audubon Bird Sanctuary a few miles away. Provincetown is 10 miles away and easily acccessible by car or bike. On the way, stop and climb the Pilgrim Monument which commemorates the first landfall of the Pilgrims in 1620. Whale-watching expeditions leave from MacMillian Wharf. Browse in the many art galleries and shops in Provincetown.

North Pamet Road.
Mail (✉): P.O. Box 402, Truro, MA 02666.
Phone (☎): 508-349-3889.
Price (⬤): $10 U.S.
Closed (X): September 6–June 24.
Office Hours: 7:30–9:30 a.m., 5–10:30 p.m.
Beds (🛏): 42. **Grade:** Hostel.
Facilities: kitchen, linen rental, **MSA**.
Groups (🛏): welcome.
Reservations essential (☎): always. **By phone:** accepted with credit card confirmation.
Off-season reservations: mail to 465 Falmouth Rd., Hyannis, MA 02601, or call 508-775-2970.

Credit cards: MasterCard, Visa, JCB.
Directions: 1.5 mile east off U.S. Highway 6.

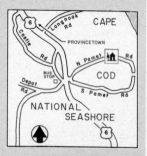

Michigan

Helpful Organizations

AYH Council Office

Michigan Council
3024 Coolidge
Berkley, MI 48072
Phone (☎): 313-545-0511

State Tourism Board

Michigan Travel Bureau
333 South Capitol, Suite F
Lansing, MI 48933
Phone (☎): 800-543-2937,
517-373-0670

Discounts

Present a valid hostel membership card at the time of purchase to receive the following discounts:

Flint
Crossroads Village - $1.00 off admissions. 313-736-7100.

Frankfort
Betsie Bay Furniture - 10% discount on any item in store, including sale items (great source of beach furniture). Main Street, 616-352-4202.

Michigan

HOME HOSTEL

Detroit (Country)
Country Grandma's Home Hostel

Located halfway between Detroit and Ann Arbor, or Chicago and Toronto, Betty and Carey Johnson's home is surrounded by three parks. Visit the Henry Ford Museum and Greenfield Village in Dearborn, the Motown Records Museum or the ethnic festivals held every weekend in summer. The University of Michigan and Tiger Stadium are nearby.

Call for information.
Phone (☎): 313-753-4901.
Price (●): $9 U.S.
Closed (X): never.
Grade: home hostel (🏠).
Beds (🛏): 6.
Facilities: kitchen, linen rental, on-site parking, camp sites, wheelchair accessible (♿), **MSA**.

Family rooms (👪): available.
Reservations essential (☎e): always. **By phone:** accepted.
Credit cards: not accepted.
Managers: Betty and Carey Johnson.
Directions: available upon reservation confirmation. **Note:** no public transportation available.

SUPPLEMENTAL ACCOMMODATION

Detroit (Downtown)
Park Avenue Hostel

Located in the heart of Detroit's theater district, Park Avenue Hostel is convenient to many Detroit-area attractions. These include Greenfield Village, downtown waterfront, cultural center, Greektown, Detroit Zoo, Belle Isle, and much more.

2305 Park Avenue
Detroit, MI 48230.
Mail (✉): same.
Phone (☎): 313-961-8310.
Price (●): $12 U.S.
Closed (X): never.
Check-in (🕐): 8 a.m.–10 p.m.
Grade: (SA).
Beds (🛏): 12.

Facilities: common room with kitchen, bike storage, laundry facilities, on-site parking, deli in lobby.
Groups (🎪): welcome.
Reservations essential (☎e): for groups and families.
Manager: Wilbur Harrington.
Directions: From I-75, take Grand River exit. Park Avenue is 1 block east. Located 1 block south of I-75.

Michigan

Flint

Mott Lake AYH-Hostel

Located on 4,400 acres of parks and recreation land, the Mott Lake AYH-Hostel is a welcome stop for hostellers on their way from Niagara Falls to Chicago and a great place for a weekend getaway. The surrounding Genesee County Park and Recreation Area provides a wealth of outdoor activities: hiking, biking, swimming, boating, windsurfing, sailing, ice skating, and cross-country skiing.

Across the lake, Crossroads Village and Huckleberry Railroad re-create an 1800s town. The Stepping Stone Falls underwater light show makes for a colorful evening. The Flint Cultural Center offers a cornucopia of culture, including an Art Center, Theater and Music Center, Planetarium, and the Sloan Museum.

G-6511 North Genesee Road, Flint, MI 48506.
Mail (✉): same.
Phone (☎): 313-736-5760.
Price (◗): $8 U.S.
Closed (X): never.
Office Hours: 8–10 a.m., 5:30–9 p.m.
Grade: Hostel.
Beds (🛏): 20.
Facilities: private dock, canoe rentals, fenced children's playground, baggage storage, kitchen, linen rental, on-site parking, **MSA**.
Family rooms (🛏): available.
Groups (🛏): welcome.
Reservations: not essential.
Credit cards: not accepted.
Manager: Margot Pfeiffer.

Directions: from Interstate 75, take Mount Morris Road exit, go east approximately 8 miles to Genesee Road, go south 1 mile to the hostel; from Interstate 69, take Belsay Road exit, go west on Stanley Road to Genesee Road. Hostel is at the intersection.

Michigan

Frankfort
Brookwood Home Hostel

Sit and relax on Marjorie Pearsall-Groenwald's wrap-around deck and admire the picturesque view of Crystal Lake below. The scenic country roads around the hostel are perfect for cycling.

Call for reservations.
Phone (☎): 616-352-4296.
Price (●): $7 U.S.
Closed (X): September 2–May 27.
Check-in (⌂): before 10 p.m.
Grade: home hostel (⌂).
Beds (►): 6 singles, 1 double.
Facilities: stone fireplace, trampoline, deck, equipment storage area, information desk, kitchen, laundry facilities, on-site parking; smoke-free environment.
Meals (✎): breakfast, lunch, dinner.

Family rooms (⌂): 1 double bed.
Groups (▥): welcome.
Reservations essential (⌂e): always. **By phone:** accepted with 24-hour notice. **Off-season reservations:** mail to 120 Southway, Severna Park, MD 22146, or call 410-544-4514.
Credit cards: not accepted.
Manager: Marjorie Pearsall-Groenwald.
Directions: available upon reservation confirmation.

Michigan

Grattan

Wabasis Lake North Country AYH-Hostel

Located in the former park rangers' residence, this three-bedroom cabin is on the banks of clear, spring-fed Lake Wabasis. Swimming, boating, and fishing are all great on the lake, as is the hiking around the park or on the nearby North Country Trail. The Wabasis Lake Kent County Park offers nature hikes and educational programs for children. Visit the Flat River Museum in Greenville, or the famous Red Flannel Factory in Cedar Springs. Just to the west, visit Rockford and its restored century-old buildings with artisans at work in their studios. Nearby Grand Rapids, known for the production of high-quality furniture, also has the Gerald R. Ford Museum and a variety of cultural offerings.

Wabasis Lake Kent County Park and Campground.
Mail (✉): 11277 Springhill Drive, Greenville, MI 48838.
Phone (☎): 616-691-7260.
Price (◐): $6 U.S.
Closed (X): September 16–May 14.
Office Hours: 8–10 a.m., 5–10 p.m.
Grade: Hostel.
Beds (►): 14.
Facilities: kitchen, laundry facilities, on-site parking, **MSA**.
Family rooms (⚥): available.
Reservations advisable (⚑): May 15–September 15. By phone: accepted. **Off-season reservations:** mail to 937 Fairmount, S.E., Grand Rapids, MI 49506, or call 616-454-8854.
Credit cards: not accepted.

Managers: Connie and Jim Winter-Troutwine.
Directions: 10 miles east off Interstate 131, take Rockford exit, east on 10 Mile Road (10 miles), north onto Wabasis Road (1-1/2 miles) to Wabasis Lake Kent County Park and Campground.

Michigan

Marquette
Northstar Home Hostel

Regis Walling's home comes with a fieldstone fireplace and two fat cats. It offers quiet beauty, an unobstructed view of Lake Superior, meteor showers, aurora borealis, and unsurpassed sunrises and sunsets. Nearby Presque Isle Park is great for hiking, picnicking, swimming, and rock hunting along the shore. Take the self-guided historical walking tour through the town of Marquette or visit its historical museums.

Call for reservations.
Phone (☎): 906-249-3085 (after 5 p.m. and weekends).
Price (◑): $8 U.S.
Closed (X): December 20—January 2.
Checkout: 7:30 p.m. (weekdays).
Grade home hostel (🏠).
Beds (🛏): 2.

Facilities: blueberry patch in front yard, equipment storage area, linen rental, on-site parking.
Reservations essential (📵e): always. **By phone:** accepted.
Credit cards: not accepted.
Manager: Regis Walling.
Directions: available upon reservation confirmation.

Milford
Heavner Home Hostel

Take advantage of all the great outdoor activities just an hour's drive from Detroit while staying at the Heavner home. Rent skis or a canoe and take on the Proud Lake Recreational Area. Hiking and skiing start right at the hostel door. Sailing, swimming, and biking is available at nearby Kensington Metropark. Alpine Valley Ski Area is open for downhillers December to March.

Call for reservations.
Phone (☎): 313-685-2379.
Price (◑): $10 U.S.
Closed (X): never.
Grade: home hostel (🏠).
Beds (🛏): 4.
Facilities: canoe and cross-country ski rentals next door.

Reservations essential (📵e): always. **By phone:** accepted.
Credit cards: not accepted.
Manager: Alan Heavner.
Directions: available upon reservation confirmation.

Michigan

White Cloud

NCTA Schoolhouse AYH-Hostel

Through efforts by American Youth Hostels and the North Country Trail Association, this century-old schoolhouse has been refurbished and is now open to members of both organizations.

Just a half-mile from the hostel, the North Country Trail, great for day hikes as well as backpacking, stretches from New York to the Lewis and Clark Trail in North Dakota. Manistee National Forest, Newago State Park, and Newago Country Parks offer a wealth of hiking and nature exploration in this popular mushrooming area of Michigan. The nearby Muskegon River is a fisherman's dream with steelhead, pike, bass, and a salmon run in the fall.

3962 North Felch,
White Cloud, MI 49349.
Mail (✉): same.
Phone (☎): 616-689-6876.
Price (💲): $5 U.S.
Closed (X): November 1–March 30.
Office Hours: 8–10 a.m., 6–10 p.m.
Grade: Hostel.
Beds (🛏): 6.
Facilities: equipment storage area, kitchen, on-site parking, **MSA**.
Groups (🏠): welcome.
Reservations essential (📞e): April–October. **By phone:** accepted with 24-hour advance notice.
Credit cards: not accepted.
Managers: Art and Virginia Wunsch.

Directions: 7 miles north of White Cloud, turn west (left) on 5 Mile Road, go 1 mile south to Felch.

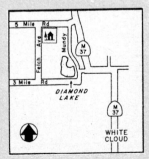

Minnesota

Helpful Organizations

AYH Council Office

Minnesota Council
795 Raymond Avenue
St. Paul, MN 55114-1522
Phone (☎): 612-659-0407

State Tourism Office

Minnesota Office of Tourism
100 Metro Square
121 7th Place East
St. Paul, MN 55101-2112
Phone (☎): 800-657-3700,
612-296-5029

Discounts

Present a valid hostel membership card at the time of purchase to receive the following discounts:

Grand Marais

The Book Station - 5% discount on books under $5 and 10% discount on books over $10. 12 First Ave., 218-387-2153.

Lake Superior Trading Post - 20% discount on purchases of $25 or more of regularly priced merchandise. On the Harbor, 218-387-2020.

Seagull Canoe Outfitters - 10% discount on completely outfitted canoe trips, partially outfitted canoe trips, or a stay in a housekeeping cabin. 920 Gunflint Trail, 218-388-2216.

Sven and Ole's - 10% discount on pizza, subs and croissant sandwiches, etc. 9 West Wisconsin St., 218-387-1713.

Way of the Wilderness Canoe Outfitters - 10% discount on any canoe outfitting service. 947 Gunflint Trail, 218-388-2212.

Minnesota

Grand Marais

Spirit of the Land AYH-Hostel

The call of the wild can still be heard in the Boundary Waters Canoe Area (BWCA) of northern Minnesota. Visitors to Spirit of the Land Island AYH-Hostel can hear that call first-hand.

The hostel is on an island in Seagull Lake and features naturalist programs and environmental study groups. Knowledgeable hostel staff encourages low-impact, environmentally sound travel and an appreciation of the delicate balance of nature in the BWCA. The hostel is only accessible by boat; phone from Grand Marais to arrange your round-trip boat ride ($3). On the way to the hostel, watch for moose, loons, and eagles along the Gunflint Trail.

Boundary Waters Canoe Area.
Mail (✉): 940 Gunflint Trail, Grand Marais, MN 55604.
Phone (☎): 218-388-2241.
Price (◐): $12.50 U.S.; minimum 4 people December–March.
Closed (X): April, October 21–December 26.
Office Hours: 7 a.m.–10 p.m.
Grade: Hostel.
Beds (🛏): 12.
Facilities: equipment storage area, kitchen, laundry facilities, linen rental, on-site parking, **MSA.**
Meals (✎): breakfast, lunch, dinner.
Groups (⛺): welcome; reservations always required.
Reservations essential (☎): December 27–March 31, May–August.
By phone: call 218-388-2241, 218-387-1443, or 612-522-6501.
Credit cards: MasterCard, Visa.
Manager: Jim Wiinanen.

Directions: 58 miles north of Grand Marais on County Road 12, in Boundary Waters Canoe Area of Superior National Forest. Call from Grand Marais for boat pick-up.

Minnesota

Lake Itasca (Itasca State Park)

Mississippi Headwaters AYH-Hostel

Located in Itasca State Park, just a short distance from the headwaters of the Mississippi River, the hostel is a beautifully restored log building. Constructed in 1923 as the park head-quarters, it is listed on the National Register of Historic Places.

Itasca State Park features Minnesota's last remaining virgin pine forest and offers unparalleled opportunities for outdoor recreation year-round. Enjoy over 25 miles of hiking and cross-country ski trails right from the hostel's doorstep. Bike and boat rentals and swimming beach are right across the road. Bike the 10-mile Wilderness Drive or the Headwaters 100 Bike Tour in late September. Visit prehistoric Indian sites; visitor centers offer naturalist programs and displays on Native American culture and explorers.

Itasca State Park.
Mail (✉): HC 05, Box 5A
Lake Itasca, MN 56460.
Phone (☎): 218-266-3415.
Price (⬤): $12 U.S. max.
Closed (X): never.
Office Hours: 8–10 a.m., 5–10 p.m.
Beds (🛏): 34. **Grade:** Hostel.
Facilities: baggage storage area, ultramodern kitchen, laundry facilities, linen rental, lockers, on-site parking, fireplaces, picnic area, showers, wheelchair accessible (♿), private rooms at additional cost, **MSA**.
Family rooms (👪): available.
Groups (🏠): welcome.
Reservations essential (📞e): all holidays and the last weekend in September. **Reservations advisable (📞a):** always. **By phone:** accepted.

Credit cards: MasterCard, Visa.
Manager: Tom Cooper.
Directions: 24 miles north of Park Rapids and 38 miles south of Bemidji on U.S. Highway 71. The hostel is on the main drive, directly across the service road from the main park headquarters. A $4 daily vehicle pass is required to enter Minnesota State Parks.

Minnesota

SUPPLEMENTAL ACCOMMODATION

St. Paul
The College of St. Catherine - Caecilian Hall

The College of St. Catherine offers its dormitories in Caecilian Hall to hostellers visiting the area in summer. The Twin Cities of Minneapolis and St. Paul offer a wealth of cultural and recreational opportunities.

Randolph Avenue.

Mail (✉): 2004 Randolph Avenue, St. Paul, MN 55105.

Phone (☎): 612-690-6604.

Price (⬤): $14 U.S.

Closed (X): August 16–May 31.

Office Hours: 24 hours.

Grade : (SA).

Beds (🛏): 103.

Facilities (mixed use): computer rooms, TV lounges, information desk, limited kitchen, laundry facilities, linen rental, on-site parking, wheelchair accessible (♿), **MSA**.

Meals (✎): breakfast, lunch, dinner.

Family rooms (👪): available.

Groups (🏛): welcome.

Reservations essential (☎): June 1–August 15. **By phone:** 612-690-6604 or 612-690-6617 (off-season).

Credit cards: not accepted.

Managers: Deb Miner, Curt Galloway.

Directions: Take Interstate 94 to Cretin/Vandalia exit, go south on Cretin to Randolph, go east on Randolph to college. **Airport ():** go east on Highway 5 to Edgecumbe exit, take Edgecumbe north to Fairview, take Fairview north to Randolph.

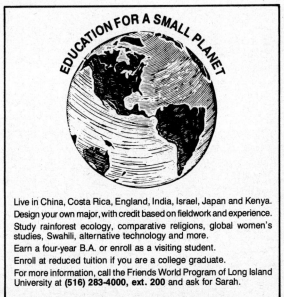

Missouri

Helpful Organizations

AYH Council Office

Ozark Area Council
7187 Manchester Road
St. Louis, MO 63143
Phone (☎): 314-644-4660

State Tourism Office

Missouri Division of Tourism
P.O. Box 1055
Jefferson City, MO 65102
Phone (☎): 314-751-4133

Discounts

Present a valid hostel membership card at the time of purchase to receive the following discounts:

St. Charles

Noah's Ark Restaurant - 5% discount (restaurant at the hostel).
The St Charles Landing Spirit Cafe - 10% discount.
Spirit of St. Charles River Cruises - 10% discount - 1500 South Fifth Street, contact Rose.

St. Louis

Cahokia Mounds World Heritage Site - free admission to interpretive slide presentation, details available at the hostel.
Domino's Pizza - 10% off all deliveries to the hostel - 1611 South Ninth Street.
Municipal Opera (open air theater at Forest Park) - free admission to all shows, details available at the hostel.
Subway Sandwiches & Salads - 10% off sandwiches, salads, and sodas with hostel discount card - 1628 South Broadway, 314-621-2252.

Missouri

St. Louis (Downtown)

Huckleberry Finn Youth Hostel, an AYH-Hostel

The hostel consists of three vintage brick buildings in the Soulard National Historic District. Also nearby are the Cahokia Mounds World Heritage Site and internationally acclaimed Missouri Botanical Garden. Don't miss the World Headquarters and Brewery of the King of Beers, Budweiser, a 15-minute walk south. The neighborhood gets its name from the Soulard Farmers Market, which is about six blocks from the hostel, open Fridays and Saturdays. Within 20 minutes by bus is the Jefferson Expansion Memorial Museum and 620-foot-high stainless steel Gateway Arch, designed by Eero Saarinen to commemorate the Louisiana purchase in 1804. Watch Cardinals baseball 20 minutes north at Busch Stadium all summer.

1904-08 South 12th Street (Tucker Boulevard), St. Louis, MO 63104.
Mail (✉): same.
Phone (☎): 314-241-0076.
Price (●): $12 U.S.
Closed (X): daily 10 a.m.–6 p.m.
Office Hours: 7:30–9:30 a.m., 6–10 p.m.
Beds (⊨): 28. **Grade:** Hostel.
Facilities: day lounge with TV, equipment storage area, kitchen, linen rental, lockers, off-street parking, vending machines, picnic tables, **MSA**.
Groups (⊪): welcome with advance booking and deposit.
Reservations advisable (⬛a): August–September. Reservations accepted by phone.
Credit cards: not accepted.
Managers: Sheela and Thomas Cochran.
Directions: from "Arch" take bus #73 (Carondelet) or bus #21 (Tower Grove) to 12th and Russell and walk 1-1/2 blocks north on 12th to hostel, or take bus #05 (Gravois) to Russell Boulevard and walk 2 blocks to hostel. **Airport (✈):** take bus #04 (Natural Bridge) to downtown, take bus #73 to Russell Street; on Sunday, take airport limo to downtown hotel, take bus #73, #21 or #05 to Russell Street. **Bike:** call for directions by bike. The Greyhound bus station is at 13th and Cass. Best to take taxi's from bus and train stations ($4 fare). Commons room open during the day.

Missouri

St. Louis (St. Charles)

Lewis and Clark International AYH-Hostel

The Lewis and Clark International AYH-Hostel at the Noah's Ark Motor Inn is on the Lewis and Clark Trail, where the famous explorers started their expedition into America's uncharted western wilderness. The Missouri River (KATY) Trailhead, which stretches 200 miles to the west, is adjacent to the hostel.

Missouri's first capital, historic St. Charles, has festivals throughout the year. The historic district is a scene from 19th-century America, with cobblestone streets and antique and craft stores housed in original settlers' buildings. Cruise the Missouri River on the Victorian-era paddle wheeler. The hostel is also convenient to St. Louis attractions—the Arch, Science Center, and many museums.

1500 South Fifth Street, St. Charles, MO 63303.
Mail (✉): P.O. Box 864, St. Charles, MO 63302.
Phone (☎): 314-946-1000.
Price (💰): $10 U.S.
Closed (X): never.
Office Hours: 24 hours.
Beds (🛏): 100. **Grade:** Hostel.
Facilities: 24-hour grocery and deli, equipment storage area, kitchen, common dining rooms, laundry facilities, linen rental, baggage storage, on-site parking, wheelchair accessible (♿), **MSA**.
Meals (🍴): breakfast, lunch, dinner.
Family rooms (👪): available.
Groups (🏠): welcome.
Reservations advisable (📅): June–September. **By phone:** By **FAX:** 314-946-7767.
Credit cards: American Express, MasterCard, Visa, Discover.

Managers: David B. Flavan, Susie Shaughnessy.
Directions: 5 miles west of St. Louis International Airport on Interstate 70 (exit 229A westbound, exit 229 eastbound), in Best Western Noah's Ark Motor Inn. **Bus:** Greyhound-Trailways bus lines 1-1/2 miles west at #3 Hawks Nest Plaza; Bi-state Transit at hostel entrance on Fifth Street Amtrak.

Youth Hostels — Your Base for Discovering Japan

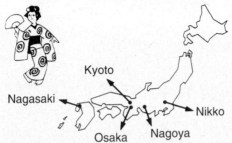

Nikko National Park — Resplendant temples set in an equally spectacular, volcanically-active landscape.

Nikko Youth Hostel
2854 Tokorono, Nikko-shi, Tochigi 321-14
Tel: (0288) 54-1013

Nagoya — The nation's fourth largest city and the gateway to central Japan.

Nagoya Youth Hostel
1-50 Kameiri, Tashiro-cho, Chikusa-ku, Nagoya-shi 464
Tel: (052) 781-9845 Fax: (052) 781-7023

Kyoto — A rich repository of the nation's cultural heritage, a living museum.

Kyoto-Utano Youth Hostel
29 Nakayama-cho, Uzumasa, Ukyo-ku, Kyoto-shi 616
Tel: (075) 462-2288 Fax: (075) 462-2289

Osaka — The nation's second largest metropolis and the hub of western Japan.

Osaka-Fu Hattori-ryokuchi Youth Hostel
1-3 Hattori-ryokuchi, Toyonaka-shi, Osaka-fu 560
Tel: (06) 862-0600 Fax: (06) 863-0561

Nagasaki — Beautiful harbor city with a complex and varied past, reflected in its Chinese temples, Western settlements, and atomic bomb center.

Nagasaki Youth Hostel
1-1-16 Tateyama-cho, Nagasaki-shi 850
Tel: (0958) 23-5032 Fax: (0958) 23-4321

Montana

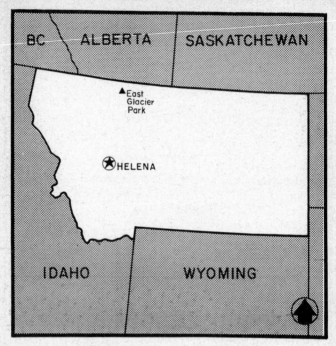

Helpful Organizations

AYH Council Office

Inquiries about Montana
c/o AYH National Office
P.O. Box 37613
Washington, DC 20013-7613
Phone (☎): 202-783-6161

State Tourism Office

Travel Montana
1424 Ninth Street
Helena, MT 59620
Phone (☎): 800-541-1447 (out of state), 406-444-2654

Montana

East Glacier Park

Brownie's Grocery and AYH-Hostel

Brownie's Grocery and AYH-Hostel in East Glacier Park is a gateway to spectacular Glacier National Park. The hostel is a pleasant, two-story log building near hiking and bicycling trails.

Living glaciers, rushing streams, 10,000-foot mountains, tumbling waterfalls, and abundant wildlife make Glacier National Park a unique wilderness and natural history experience. A wide variety of hiking trails, naturalist-guided hikes, boat tours, and horseback trips are available. Traverse the park's high country on the "Going-to-the-Sun Road," a wondrous 50-mile highway which crosses the Continental Divide at Logan Pass. The St. Mary's Visitor Center has exhibits on Indian crafts, geology, wildlife, and a slide presentation on the park.

1020 Montana Highway 49.
Mail (✉): Box 229, East Glacier Park, MT 59434.
Phone (☎): 406-226-4426.
Price (☺): $10 U.S. + tax for dorm, $15 for private room.
Closed (X): October 15–May 1.
Office Hours: 7:30 a.m.–10 p.m.
Beds (🛏): 31. **Grade:** Hostel.
Facilities: equipment storage, information desk, kitchen, laundry facilities, linens provided, baggage storage, on-site parking, **MSA**.
Family rooms (👪): available.
Groups (🏠): welcome; reservations required May–September.
Reservations essential (☎): July 4–August 15. **By phone:** 406-226-4426 or 4456.

Credit cards: accepted.
Managers: Linda and Denis Chase.
Directions: 1/4 miles north of U.S. Highway 2 on Montana Highway 49. Pickup from train station twice daily.

Nebraska

Helpful Organizations

AYH Council Offices

Nebraskaland Council
1237 R Street, Room 102
Lincoln, NE 68588
Phone (☎): 402-472-3265

State Tourism Board

Nebraska Travel and Tourism Division
P.O. Box 94666
Lincoln, NE 68509
Phone (☎): 800-228-4307 (out of state), 800-742-7595 (in state)

Nebraska

SUPPLEMENTAL ACCOMMODATION

Lincoln
Cornerstone

The Cornerstone is located on the University of Nebraska campus. See the huge collection of modern and fossil elephants at the University of Nebraska State Museum. Tour the beautiful state capitol building. See the sculpture of Lincoln and "The Sower." Visit Folsom Children's Zoo and gardens.

640 North 16th Street, Lincoln, NE 68508.
Mail (✉): same.
Phone (☎): 402-476-0355, 402-476-0926.
Price (●): $8 U.S.
Closed (X): periodically during Christmas vacation.
Office Hours: 7 a.m.–11 p.m.
Beds (🛏): 8. **Grade: (SA).**
Facilities (mixed use): equipment storage area, information desk, kitchen, laundry facilities, lockers/ baggage storage, on-site parking, shower.
Family rooms (👪): available.
Reservations advisable (📞a): always. **By phone:** accepted.
Credit cards: not accepted.
Managers: Vicki Burge, Kristin McCoig.
Directions: Take downtown or 9th Street exit, turn left on "O" Street, 6 blocks north of "O" Street on 16th Street.

Nevada

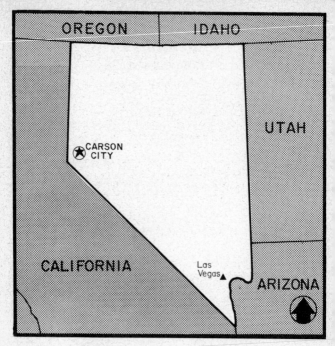

Helpful Organizations

AYH Council Office

Arizona-Southern Nevada Council
1046 East Lemon Street
Tempe, AZ 85281-3904
Phone (☎): 602-894-5128

State Tourism Board

Nevada Commission on Tourism
Capitol Complex
Carson City, NV 89710
Phone (☎): 800-NEVADA-8,
702-687-4322

Nevada

Las Vegas

Las Vegas International AYH-Hostel

Conveniently located on the fabulous Las Vegas Strip, this fun and friendly 24-hour hostel is less than one mile from the bus and train stations downtown. Downtown Las Vegas is also known as Glitter Gulch, named for the brilliant flashing casino lights. Get right in the gambling action—pick up coupons for free casino money, souvenirs, and outrageously cheap all-you-can-eat buffet dinners. Start your day right with free coffee or tea in the hostel kitchen. Many maps and brochures will help you plan self-guided or professional day trips to the Grand Canyon, Hoover Dam, Death Valley, Bryce Canyon, and Zion National Parks. Tired of the casinos? Spend your day hiking! Or, just relax in our beautiful patio garden. We will even help you plan your next destination at our new Travel Center, featuring books, maps, and accessories.

1236 South Las Vegas Boulevard, Las Vegas, NV 89104.
Mail (✉): same.
Phone (☎): 702-382-8119.
Price (●): $8.50 U.S. + tax; $11 U.S. +tax (Friday and Saturday evenings, May 1–September 30).
Closed (X): never.
Office Hours: 7–10 a.m., 4–10 p.m.
Grade: Hostel.
Beds (⊨): 85 (summer), 40 (winter).
Facilities: separate cabins, large garden courtyard, equipment storage area, kitchen, laundry facilities, linen rental, lockers/baggage storage, on-site parking, **MSA**.
Family rooms (⌂): available.
Groups (⫟): welcome.
Reservations essential (☎●): May–September. **By phone:** accepted.

Credit cards: MasterCard, Visa, JCB.
Directions: 8/10 of a mile south of downtown on Las Vegas Strip. **Bus:** take bus #6 south on Las Vegas Boulevard; to enter bus: be sure to carry backpacks like a suitcase. **Airport (✈):** take shuttle bus to hostel.

New Hampshire

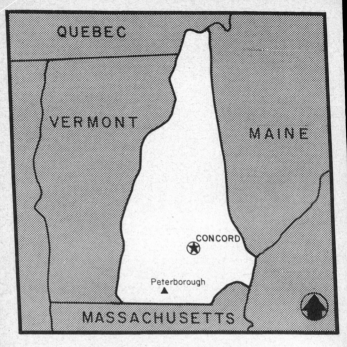

Helpful Organizations

AYH Council Office

Greater Boston Council
1020 Commonwealth Avenue
Boston, MA 02215
Phone (☎): 617-731-6692 (12–6 p.m.
M–F)
Activities hotline: 617-730-8-AYH
Worldwide Info-Line: 617-731-5430
FAX: 617-734-7614

State Tourism Office

**New Hampshire Office of
Vacation Travel**
P.O. Box 856
Concord, NH 03302-0856
Phone (☎): 800-678-5040 (brochure
requests only), or 603-271-2666

Discounts

Present a valid hostel membership card at the time of purchase to receive the
following discounts:

Peterborough

Silver Ranch Airpark - 10% discount for groups of 3 or more on scenic flights -
Jaffrey Airport, Jaffrey, NH, 603-532-8870.

New Hampshire

Peterborough

Peterborough AYH-Hostel

Located in a beautifully remodelled 1840s barn, the Peterborough AYH-Hostel overlooks the Contoocook River and the attractive "Yankee" town of Peterborough, which served as Thornton Wilder's model for "Our Town."

Long a favorite area for artists and writers, the Monadnock region wonderfully balances history and culture with natural beauty. The countryside has plenty of trails for hiking, biking, and cross-country skiing. Alpine skiing is available at Temple Mountain. Start the day by hiking Mount Monadnock, the second most climbed mountain in the world, and end it with a trip to town to hear world-class folk music at Folkways. Peterborough and nearby towns offer summer theater, folk and classical music concerts, the League of New Hampshire Craftsmen craft shop, and a historic train trip at Bellows Falls, Vermont.

52 Summer Street,
Peterborough, NH 03458-2340.
Mail (✉): same.
Phone (☎): 603-924-9832.
Price (💲): $11 U.S.
Closed (X): never.
Office Hours: 8–9 a.m, 5–10 p.m.
Grade: Hostel.
Beds (🛏): 26.
Facilities: day use, bike and equipment repair and storage room, kitchen, linen rental, on-site parking, **MSA**, smoke-free environment.
Family rooms (👪): available.
Groups (👫): welcome.
Reservations: not essential.
By phone: accepted.
Credit cards: not accepted.

Managers: Ann and Peter Harrison.
Directions: 1 mile north of U.S. Highway 202 and New Hampshire Highway 101.

New Jersey

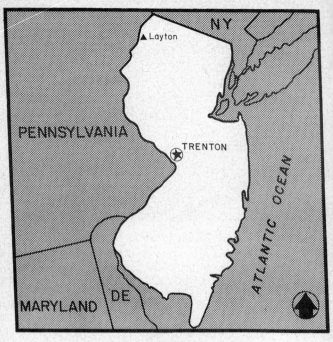

Helpful Organizations

AYH Council Office

Delaware Valley Council
624 South 3rd Street
Philadelphia, PA 19147
Phone (☎): 215-925-6004,
215-925-6005 (Activities Hotline)

State Tourism Office

New Jersey Division of Travel and Tourism
20 West State Street, CN826
Trenton, NJ 08625-0826
Phone (☎): 800-JERSEY-7,
609-292-2470

Discounts

Present a valid hostel membership card at the time of purchase to receive the following discounts:

Layton

Mata-port Bicycles - 15% discount on all parts and service, excluding credit card - 180 Pike Street, Port Jervis, NY, 914-856-4500.

New Jersey

Layton

Old Mine Road AYH-Hostel

The Old Mine Road AYH-Hostel is situated on the banks of the Delaware River in the Delaware Water Gap National Recreation Area. Less than two hours' drive from New York and Philadelphia, the park offers a quiet, relaxing getaway and plenty of outdoor activities, including swimming, canoeing, and rafting.

The hostel serves as a good base for cross-country skiing, snowshoeing, hiking, and biking. Nature study, slide shows, and interpretive programs can be arranged through the National Park Service. The Peters Valley Craft Village, three miles away, invites visitors to explore the studios of blacksmiths, weavers, and potters; one- to five-day courses are offered in the summer.

Old Mine Road.
Mail (✉): P.O. Box 172, Layton, NJ 07851.
Phone (☎): 201-948-6750.
Price (●): $8 U.S.
Closed (X): November 25, December 24–25.
Office Hours: 7–8:30 a.m., 5:30–10 p.m.
Grade: Hostel.
Beds (►): 12.
Facilities: equipment storage area, kitchen, linen rental, on-site parking, **MSA**.
Groups (⏍): welcome.
Reservations advisable (✆a): weekends. **By phone:** accepted.
Credit cards: not accepted.
Managers: Michael and Patrice Kealy.
Directions: take New Jersey Highway 206 north to New Jersey Highway 560 west (2-1/2 miles to Layton), turn right at Layton General Store, go 2-1/2 miles and make sharp right onto Old Mine Road, go 2 miles north to hostel. **From Milford, Pennsylvania:** take U.S. Highway 209 south, cross Milford Bridge into New Jersey, make first right turn onto Old Mine Road and go 4 miles south to the hostel.

New Mexico

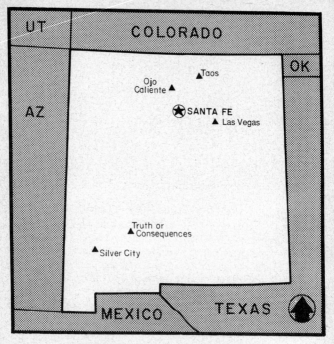

Helpful Organizations

AYH Council Office

New Mexico Council
P.O. Box 4177
Albuquerque, NM 87196
Phone (☎): 505-867-6596

State Tourism Office

New Mexico Tourism and Travel Division
491 Old Santa Fe Trail
Lamy Building
Santa Fe, NM 87503
Phone (☎): 800-545-2040 (out of state), or 505-827-7400

Discounts

Present a valid hostel membership card at the time of purchase to receive the following discounts:

Silver City

The Corner Cafe - 10% discount on food - 200 North Bullard Street, 505-388-2056.
Gila Hike & Bike - 10% discount on everything in the store - 103 E. College, 505-388-3222.
Pavlette Shephard - 10% discount on full body massage - 1702 N. Juniper Ave., 505-538-3108.
Schadels Bakery - 10% discount - 212 N. Bullard, 505-538-3031.
Silver City Museum Gift Shop - 10% discount - 312 W. Broadway, 505-538-5921.

Discounts

Truth or Consequences

The Bike Shoppe - 10% discount on bike rentals - 602 South Broadway.
El Rio Theater - $1.75 discount - 330 Broadway.
FR-C's Big-A-Burger - 10% discount - 719 Main.
Geronimo Springs Museum - $0.50 discount - 211 Main.
La Pinata Restaurant - 10% discount - 1990 South Broadway.
Pleasure Center Bowl - free game and $0.50 discount on a meal - 165 East Ninth.
Tortillas del Sol - 10% discount - 501 McAdoo.

AYH *AMERICAN YOUTH HOSTELS*

DISCOVERY TOURS

YOU HAVE TO SEE THE WORLD TO UNDERSTAND IT.

American Youth Hostels, a member of the International Youth Hostel Federation, has provided educational and recreational travel experiences for youth and adults for more than 50 years. Our dynamic travel programs are backed by more than five decades of experience and provide you with the opportunity to discover the world, both near and far.

AYH Discovery Tours are planned both as vacation adventures and as enriching learning experiences. You will find yourself face to face with new people, cultures and environments. Join us and discover the spirit of hostelling and the excitement of travel.

HOSTELLING INTERNATIONAL ®

For A Free Catalog
Contact the AYH council nearest you or call the AYH Travel Department at 202-783-6161.

New Mexico

Las Vegas
Hattle House Home Hostel

The former home of a Santa Fe Railroad baron and merchant, the hostel is located in a historic Wild West town (the Santa Fe Trail went right through the middle of downtown). Las Vegas is also the gateway to the Pecos Wilderness Area. Hostel owner Robert Hattle leads weekly treks up Hermit's Peak, the former home of an 18th-century hermit and mystic. Natural hot springs and The Armand Hammer United World College are five miles away.

Call for reservations.
Mail (✉): P.O. Box 2042, Las Vegas, NM 87701.
Phone (☎): 505-454-8855.
Price (●): $7.75 U.S. + tax.
Closed (X): never.
Grade: home hostel (🏠).
Beds (🛏): 8.

Facilities: baggage storage, natural hot spring, kitchen, laundry facilities, linen rental, on-site parking, showers, **MSA**.
Family rooms (🏠): available.
Reservations essential (☎): always. **By phone:** accepted.
Credit cards: not accepted.
Directions: available upon reservation confirmation.

New Mexico

Ojo Caliente

Hot Springs AYH-Hostel

The Hot Springs AYH-Hostel is located at the Inn at Ojo, just a short walk from the world-famous mineral hot springs of Ojo Caliente. Relax in the waters that Native Americans have enjoyed for 2,000 years, or relax in a hammock and enjoy the humming-birds.

Explore the rugged back country surrounding Ojo on horse-back, on mountain bike, or on foot, for a panoramic view of the Sangre de Cristo Mountain range. Or raft the nearby Rio Grande Gorge. View Native American dances at San Juan and other nearby Indian pueblos. Experience rural southwestern culture at the many picturesque Spanish villages that dot the area.

#11 New Mexico Highway 414.
Mail (✉): P.O. Box 215, Ojo Caliente, NM 87549.
Phone (☎): 505-583-2428.
Price (☻): $9.95 U.S. + tax.
Closed (X): November–February.
Office Hours: 8–10 a.m., 4–8 p.m.
Grade: Hostel.
Beds (⊨): 9.
Facilities: shaded courtyard, picnic tables, massage studio, meditation room, bike rental, equipment storage, information desk, kitchen, linen rental, on-site parking, **MSA**.
Meals (🍴): breakfast.
Groups (⑪): welcome.
Reservations essential (✆e): always. **By phone:** accepted with credit card confirmation.
Credit cards: American Express, Discover, MasterCard, Visa.
Managers: Rob Dorival and K.C. Kennedy.

Directions: 50 miles north of Santa Fe on U.S. Highway 285. In Ojo Caliente turn west onto New Mexico Highway 414, hostel is 100 yards ahead on right.

New Mexico

Silver City

The Carter House AYH-Hostel

The Carter House AYH-Hostel is a large home with a great front porch on the edge of Silver City's registered historic district. Located on section two of the Bike Centennial California-to-Florida Route, the hostel is a good stop for cross-country cyclists.

Silver City (6,000 feet elevation) is the gateway to the Gila Wilderness Area, the oldest designated wilderness area in the country. Experience wonderful hiking, biking, birdwatching, and rockhounding. The Wild West will come alive for you at local museums and nearby ghost towns. The Gila Cliff Dwellings National Monument offers you a close look at an ancient Southwest culture, world famous for its exquisite black and white pottery.

101 North Cooper Street,
Silver City, NM 88061.
Mail (✉): same.
Phone (☎): 505-388-5485.
Price (●): $11 U.S.
Closed (X): never.
Office Hours: 8–10 a.m., 4–9 p.m..
Grade: Hostel.
Beds (🛏): 22.
Facilities: equipment storage area, information desk, kitchen, laundry facilities, linen rental, baggage storage area, **MSA**.
Family rooms (👪): available (one).
Groups (🏛): welcome; reservations required.
Reservations essential (📞): for groups. **By phone:** accepted with credit-card confirmation.
Credit cards: MasterCard, Visa; minimum 2-night stay - if card used.

Managers: Lucy Dilworth.
Directions: 6 blocks west of New Mexico Highway 90, adjacent to Grant County Courthouse.

New Mexico

Taos (Arroyo Seco)

Taos/Indian Country AYH-Hostel

The Taos/Indian Country AYH-Hostel, located at the Abominable Snow Mansion Lodge, is an outdoor-oriented facility, featuring spectacular views of New Mexico sunsets, occasional evening coyote-choruses, and close contact with a small traditional Spanish community.

Right across from the hostel is the Taos Indian Pueblo's sacred land. A short drive away is the world-famous Taos Ski Valley and Carson National Forest. Hike, backpack, horseback ride, challenge the white water of the Rio Grande, or visit the 800-year-old adobe village at Taos Pueblo. Be sure to stop by the famous Taos artist colony and the 80 art galleries in the area.

Taos Ski-Valley Road, Arroyo Seco.
Mail (✉): P.O. Box 3271, Taos, NM 87571.
Phone (☎): 505-776-8298.
Price (●): $8.50–$12 U.S. + tax.
Closed (X): November–April
Office Hours: 8–10 a.m., 4–9 p.m.
Grade: Hostel.
Beds (▬): 76.
Facilities: tipis, bunkhouse dorm, equipment storage area, information desk, kitchen, meeting facilities, linen rental, baggage storage, on-site parking, **MSA**; on-site ski lodge operates during closed period (discount for hostellers).
Meals (✎): available for groups.
Family rooms (♠): available.
Groups (▥): welcome, reservations required.
Reservations advisable (☎a): always. **By phone:** accepted.
Credit cards: MasterCard, Visa.

Managers: Penny and Phil Kirk.
Directions: from Taos Plaza, go north 4 milesRt. 522 to blinking light, then east on Rt. 150 for 5 miles to Arroyo Seco. Hostel is first building on the left.

New Mexico

Truth or Consequences

Riverbend Hot Springs AYH-Hostel

Enjoy a FREE open-air hot mineral bath each evening at this homey hostel (with Apache tipi) situated on the banks of the Rio Grande. The year-round mild climate is enhanced by the icy river, hot springs, and gorgeous lakes and mountains surrounding this small, friendly Old West town. Favorite activities are rafting the river, hiking the Turtleback, jetskiing, fishing, and swimming at Elephant Butte Lake, or lounging on the hostel's riverside deck. Horseback riding treks are available, as well as one-day guided adventure tours (with transportation and campfire lunch included) to Mexican village, ghost towns, rockhound park, old forts, box canyon, and other historic sites. See prehistoric Mimbres pottery at the local museum. Other nearby attractions: Gila Forest, White Sands, Wildlife Refuge, Alamogordo Space Center, Ruidoso "Ski Apache", and "Billy the Kid" country, site of the Lincoln County wars.

100 Austin Avenue.
Mail (✉): 100 Austin Avenue, Truth or Consequences, NM 87901.
Phone (☎): 505-894-6183.
Price (⬤): $9.50 U.S. + tax.
Closed (X): never.
Office Hours: 8 a.m.–10 p.m.
Grade: Hostel.
Beds (🛏): 14.
Facilities: hot mineral baths, tipi, river deck, laundry, raft rental, small dorms, 2 kitchens, couples room, linen rental, on-site parking, **MSA**.
Family rooms (👪): available.
Groups (🏠): welcome.
Reservations advisable (📞): always. **By phone:** accepted.
Credit cards: not accepted.

Managers: Lee and Sylvia Foerstner.
Directions: downtown, 1 block south of Ralph Edwards City Park on river. **Bus:** Greyhound 9 blocks from hostel. Call for free pickup.

New York

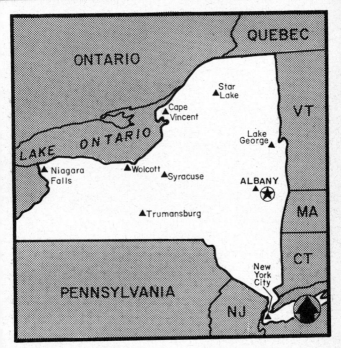

Helpful Organizations

AYH Council Offices

Hudson-Mohawk Council
P.O. Box 6343
Albany, NY 12206
Phone (☎): 518-437-9604

Niagara Frontier Council
P.O. Box 1110
Ellicott Station
Buffalo, NY 14203
Phone (☎): 716-852-5222

Syracuse Council
535 Oak Street
Syracuse, NY 13203
Phone (☎): 315-472-5788

For information on AYH in the
Metro New York Area
Phone (☎): 212-932-1860

State Tourism Office

New York Division of Tourism
One Commerce Plaza
Albany, NY 12245
Phone (☎): 800-225-5697

New York Division of Tourism
1515 Broadway
New York, NY 10036
Phone (☎): 212-827-6250

Discounts

Present a valid hostel membership card at the time of purchase to receive the
following discounts:

Buffalo

Shickluna Bike & Fitness - 10% discount on parts and accessories, 5% discount
on Bicycles & Fitness Equipment, 1233 Niagara Street, (716) 884-2670.

Discounts

Buffalo (continued)

Where The Wild Things Are - 10% discount on all merchandise, except sale items, 226 Lexington Avenue, (716) 882-3324.

Lake George

Flipflop Cycleshop - 10% discount on parts and rentals - 375 Canada St. (rear entrance), 518-668-2233.
F.R. Smith & Sons (canoe rental) - 10% discount at weekends, 15% discount weekdays - Sagamore Road, Bolton Landing, NY, 518-644-5181.
Inside Edge - 10% discount on bike rental - 630 Glen Street, Queensbury, NY, 793-5676.
Lake George Camping & Equipment Co. (canoe rental) - 10% weekends, 15% weekdays - Bolton Landing, NY, 518-644-9941.
Outdoor Sensations Bicycle Rental - 10% discount - 345 Canada Street.

New York City - Present a discount voucher available at the New York International AYH-Hostel's information desk.

AMH Deli - 15% discount on all sandwiches with hostel receipt - Amsterdam and 103rd Streets.
Atomic Wings (food service at various NYC pubs) - 10% off food charge for IYHF members.
Avalon Theatre - 2-for-1 admission ($5 per person) for New York Hostel guests with hostel receipt; discount valid for Thursday and Saturday evenings and Sunday afternoon shows - 2744 Broadway.
Birdland (jazz club) - free admission ($5 drink minimum) to Sunday–Thursday evening shows (call for reservations).
Broadway Cottage (Chinese food) - 10% discount for hostel guests with a hostel receipt - 103rd and Broadway.
Broadway Restaurant - 10% discount for check under $10; $15 discount if check is over $10; for New York Hostel guests with a hostel receipt - Broadway between 101st and 102nd.
Golden Plate (diner) - 15% discount for New York Hostel guests with a hostel receipt - Broadway between 102nd and 103rd.
Sounds of Brazil (salsa and reggae music club) - $5 discount on admission for IYHF members (call for reservations).
Stand Up NY (comedy club) - free admission (2-drink minimum) to Sunday–Thursday evening shows, 1/2 off cover charge for Friday night show (must make a reservation and arrive by 8:30 p.m.) - West 78th Street.
Theatresports (improv group) - half-price tickets for IYHF members (tickets must be picked up by 7:30 p.m.).
Tramps (blues and soul music club) - 1/2 off admission for IYHF members (call for reservations).
Wetlands (music/dance club) - 1/2 off admission for IYHF members.

Niagara Falls

Aquarium of Niagara Falls - $2.95 rate. Must have hostel coupon - 701 Whirlpool Street, 716-285-3575.
Maid of the Mist - $6.25 rate. Must have hostel coupon. Reduction is equal to group rate - 151 Buffalo Ave., 716-284-8897.

Syracuse

Syracuse Real Food Co-op Inc. - member prices with AYH/IYHF card - 618 Kensington Road, 315-472-1385.

Wolcott

Jim Berger - Massage Therapist - 10% discount for American Youth Hostel members - 5041 Galen Rd., 315-594-2750.

New York

Albany

Pine Haven AYH-Hostel

This Victorian-style house features antiques and a stained glass window. It's a three-hour drive to New York City, Boston, and Montreal. The Adirondack Mountains, the Catskill Mountains, Lake George, and Saratoga are all within a 45-minute drive from the hostel. In Albany, drop by the state capitol, city hall, and the Schuyler Mansion. The Albany Convention and Visitors Bureau runs daily walking tours and trolley tours.

531 Western Ave.,
Albany, NY 12203
Phone (☎): 518-482-1574.
Price (☻): $12 U.S. + tax.
Closed (X): never.
Office Hours: 8–10 a.m., 5–10 p.m.
Grade: Hostel.
Beds (🛏): 16.
Facilities: equipment storage area, kitchen, laundry facilities, linen rental, on-site parking, **MSA**.
Family rooms (👪): available.
Groups (🍽): welcome.
Reservations essential (📞e): always. **By phone:** accepted.
Credit cards: not accepted.
Manager: Janice Tricarico.
Directions: from I-87 (Thruway), Exit #24, follow I-90 East to Exit 5 (Everett Rd.). Go right off exit to Central Avenue (2 lights), go left for 2 more lights—go right onto North Allen Street. Go 10–12 blocks to Western Avenue. Go right onto Western—Pine Haven is first driveway on right. Parking lot is behind the house. (5 minutes from Everett Road exit).

New York

Cape Vincent

Tibbetts Point Lighthouse AYH-Hostel

The Tibbetts Point Lighthouse is located on the shores of the St. Lawrence Seaway. After the lighthouse became fully automated in 1976, the Victorian-era lightkeeper's quarters were leased by the Coast Guard to American Youth Hostels for use as a hostel. Take the ferry from Cape Vincent to Wolf Island and Kingston, Ontario.

R.R. 1, Box 330,
Cape Vincent, NY 13618.
Mail (⌧): same.
Phone (☎): 315-654-3450.
Price (●): $10 U.S.
Closed (X): October 25–May 14.
Office Hours: 7–9 a.m., 5–9 p.m.
Grade: Hostel.
Beds (🛏): 31.
Facilities: kitchen, linen rental, on-site parking, **MSA**.
Groups (🏠): welcome; reservations required.

Reservations essential (🔑e): September 1–October 24; always for groups. **By phone:** accepted. **Off-season reservations:** mail to 535 Oak Street, Syracuse, NY 13203, or call 315-472-5788.
Credit cards: not accepted.
Managers: George and Jean Cougler.
Directions: 25 miles west of Watertown. Take New York Highway 12E west to the stop sign in Cape Vincent, turn south (left) on Broadway (becomes Tibbetts Point Road), follow road to dead end at lighthouse. From Kingston, Ontario, take ferry to Wolfe Island and Cape Vincent, then east on James Street to Broadway.

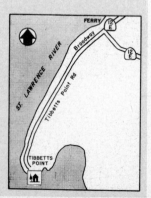

New York

Lake George

Lake George AYH-Hostel

If jet skiing, sailing, canoeing, windsurfing, swimming, and every other water activity imaginable sounds fun, head for Lake George. The hostel is just one block from the lake in the basement of St. James Episcopal Church Hall. Great Escape Amusement Park and several local waterslides are also in town.

The area features wonderful hikes through the Adirondack Mountains, the largest natural preserve in the East. Be sure to take advantage of the free weekly concerts on Wednesdays in Shepard Park and the numerous festivals and fairs held each summer in the village. Summer Fest, a music and arts and crafts festival, kicks off the season in June and the annual Jazz Festival rounds out the summer on the second weekend in September.

Montcalm Street.
Mail (✉): P.O. Box 176, Lake George, NY 12845.
Phone (☎): 518-668-2634.
Price (●): $10 U.S.
Closed (X): September 7–May 26.
Office Hours: 7–9 a.m., 5–10 p.m.
Grade: Hostel.
Beds (🛏): 16.
Facilities: kitchen, linen rental, wheelchair accessible (♿), **MSA**.
Groups (🍴): welcome.
Reservations advisable (☎): always for groups. **By phone:** accepted.
Off-season information: call 518-668-2001.
Credit cards: not accepted.

Directions: at the intersection of Montcalm and Ottawa Streets.

New York

New York City

New York International AYH-Hostel

From museums to theaters, from skyscrapers to historic neighborhoods, New York City has it all. The New York International AYH-Hostel is in a landmark Victorian Gothic-style building on the city's bustling Upper West Side. Near Central Park and Columbia University, the hostel offers a lively program of walking tours; a hospitality desk staffed by neighborhood volunteers; group outings to concerts and sporting evenings; and discount or free tickets to off-Broadway shows, comedy clubs, concerts, and other events.

891 Amsterdam Avenue,
New York, NY 10025.

Mail (✉): same.

Phone (☎): 212-932-2300.

Price (⊖): $20 U.S. October–May, $22 U.S. June–September.

Closed (X): never.

Office Hours: 24 hours.

Grade: Gateway.

Beds (🛏): 480.

Facilities: air-conditioned rooms, TV room, meeting rooms, equipment storage, game room, information desk, kitchen, laundry facilities, linen rental, lockers/baggage storage, hostel-based programs, **MSA**.

Meals (🍴): breakfast.

Family rooms (👪): available.

Groups (🏠): welcome, for reservations call 212-932-2300, extension 219.

Reservations essential (📅): June–October, December 25– January 2. **By phone:** accepted with credit card confirmation & 24-hour notice. **By FAX:** 212-932-2574 with credit card confirmation. IBN global reservation system available.

Credit cards: MasterCard, Visa, JCB.

Manager: Len Brown.

Directions: on Manhattan's Upper West Side at Amsterdam and 103rd, take subway train #1 or #9 (Broadway local) to 103rd Street stop, walk 1 block east on 103rd.

New York

Niagara Falls

Niagara Falls International AYH-Hostel

Just a few blocks from Niagara Falls, the hostel is a historic Georgian-style home with beautiful oak woodwork. Take a boat tour to best experience the power and majesty of the Falls. For a lesson on how the Falls came to be, visit Schoellkopf's Geological Museum. The history of the native inhabitants of the area is featured at "The Turtle," which has a large collection of Iroquois arts and crafts. More than 40 special events, including the Newfane Apple Blossom Festival, are held year-round.

1101 Ferry Avenue,
Niagara Falls, NY 14301.
Mail (✉): same.
Phone (☎): 716-282-3700.
Price (●): $11 U.S.
Closed (X): December 16–January 4.
Office Hours: 7:30–9:30 a.m., 5–11 p.m.
Grade: Hostel.
Beds (🛏): 44.
Facilities: equipment storage area, information desk, kitchen, laundry facilities, linen rental, on-site parking, **MSA.**
Groups (⊞): welcome; reservations required June–September.
Reservations advisable (🏠): always. **By phone:** accepted.
Credit cards: accepted for reservations only. Deposit is nonrefundable.
Managers: Bob and Nancy Sherry.

Directions: downtown on Ferry Avenue. **Buffalo Airport (✈):** take Metro bus #24 to Buffalo Transportation Center, transfer to bus #40 to Niagara Falls, walk east on Niagara St., turn left on Memorial Parkway, walk 1 block to hostel. **Train:** 3 miles from Niagara Falls Amtrak station. Call hostel to book shuttle transportation.

New York

Star Lake
Star Lake Campus, Potsdam College of SUNY

The Star Lake campus of Potsdam College is just a few steps from the beach on Star Lake. Visitors can check out bicycles, canoes, or other recreational equipment. The nearby Adirondack Mountains Park is the largest natural preserve in the East.

Star Lake Road.
Mail (✉): Route 1, Box 60, Star Lake, NY 13690.
Phone (☎): 315-848-3486.
Price (⬤): $10 U.S. + tax.
Closed (X): November 1–December 31.
Office Hours: 8:30 a.m.–4:30 p.m.
Beds (🛏): 180. **Grade: (SA).**
Facilities (mixed use): rec room, information desk, laundry facilities, lockers, baggage, and equipment storage area, swimming during summer, on-site parking, wheelchair accessible (♿).

Meals (🍴): breakfast, lunch, dinner.
Family rooms (👪): available.
Groups (🏠): welcome.
Reservations essential (📞): always. **By phone:** accepted.
Credit cards: not accepted.
Manager: David Falvo.
Directions: south off New York Highway 3 in Adirondack Park, from at CIBRO station, take fourth right, then second right to camp office in main lodge.

IBN INTERNATIONAL BOOKING NETWORK

New York

Syracuse

Downing International AYH-Hostel

The Downing International AYH-Hostel is an ideal base for exploring central New York. Built in 1895, this huge house features stained glass windows and an ornate staircase in the main lobby and a new kitchen. It's also centrally located to the area's many attractions: the Finger Lakes, Rochester and the famous Kodak Museum, and Oneida Lake.

Explore Syracuse's history at the Erie Canal and Salt Museums and the newly renovated French Fort. Syracuse is home of the great New York State Fair in late August. In September and October, see the beautiful fall foliage. In January, Winterfest livens up downtown. Downhill and cross-country skiing are terrific.

535 Oak Street,
Syracuse, NY 13203-1609.
Mail (⊠): same.
Phone (☎): 315-472-5788.
Price (●): $9 U.S.
Closed (X): never.
Office Hours: 7–9 a.m., 5–9 p.m.
Grade: Hostel.
Beds (▭): 31.
Facilities: equipment storage area, information desk, kitchen, laundry facilities, linen rental, **MSA**.
Family rooms (🛏): available.
Groups (⏗): welcome; reservations required.
Reservations essential (↓●): during State Fair (late August–Labor Day).
By phone: accepted.
Credit cards: not accepted.
Managers: Anita and Francis Waddington.

Directions: 1-1/2 miles northeast of downtown. From Clinton Square (Salina Street and Erie Boulevard) take James Street (New York Route 290) 10 blocks to Oak Street, left on Oak 1 block to Highland Avenue, hostel is on left at corner. Take exit #14 from Interstate 690 to Teall Avenue, go north 3/4 mile to James Street (New York Route 290), turn left and go 1 mile to Oak, turn right and go 1 block to hostel.

New York

Trumansburg
Podunk Home Hostel

An old Finnish homestead farm complete with a sauna, the Podunk Home Hostel stands between the two largest Finger Lakes, the Cayuga and the Seneca. The region is famous for its deep river gorges and spectacular waterfalls, including nearby 215-foot Taughannock Falls. Great cross-country skiing starts at the farm in the Podunk Cross Country Ski Center. In the summer, enjoy bicycle touring, hiking, swimming, and boating. Ten miles away is Ithaca, home of Cornell University.

Call for reservations.
Mail (✉): same.
Phone (☎): 607-387-9277.
Price (⬤): $5 U.S.
Closed (X): November–March.
Grade: home hostel (🏠).
Beds (🛏): 8.
Facilities: sauna, equipment storage area, linen rental, lockers/baggage storage, on-site parking, **MSA**.
Groups (⛺): welcome.

Reservations essential (🔒e): always. **By phone:** accepted.
Credit cards: not accepted.
Managers: Osmo Heila.
Directions: available upon reservation confirmation.

Wolcott
Rose Ridge Home Hostel

The Rose Ridge Home Hostel is a good place to stay while enjoying all that Lake Ontario has to offer. The beaches and picnic grounds of Fairhaven State Park are 10 miles away, as are the Chimney Bluffs—cliffs which look out onto the lake. Sailboats, canoes, and rowboats are available at Sodus Point. Be sure to see the nearby Drumlins; these odd-looking hills running north to south were created during the last Ice Age.

Call for reservations.
Phone (☎): 315-594-2750.
Price (⬤): $8 U.S.
Closed (X): never.
Grade: home hostel (🏠).
Beds (🛏): 3.
Facilities: kitchen (vegetarian only), linen rental, on-site parking, sauna, smoke-free environment.
Family rooms (👪): available.

Reservations essential (🔒e): always. **By phone:** accepted.
Credit cards: not accepted.
Manager: Jim Berger and Renee Regis.
Directions: available upon reservation confirmation.

Sweden

At our hostels...

- stay the young and old.
- it's easy to make friends.
- you're welcome in the kitchen.
- you hire a bed or a family room.
- members pay 60-93SEK.
- non-members pay an extra 36SEK.
- you can make an advance reservation.

You'll find us at around 280 sites all over Sweden. Buy the *European Guide to budget accommodation* **in the book shops or from your country's youth hostel federation.**

North Carolina

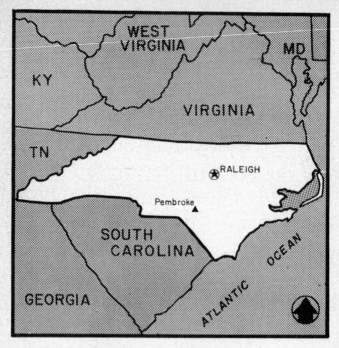

Helpful Organizations

AYH Council Offices

Piedmont Council
P.O. Box 10766
Winston-Salem, NC 27103
Phone (☎): 919-454-5027

**Research Triangle–
Coastal Carolina Council**
714 Ninth Street
Room 207
Durham, NC 27705
Phone (☎): 919-286-1477

State Tourism Office

North Carolina Travel & Tourism
430 North Salsbury Street
Raleigh, NC 27603
Phone (☎): 800-847-4862,
919-733-4171

North Carolina

SUPPLEMENTAL ACCOMMODATION

Pembroke
Baptist Student Union House

The Baptist Student Center is a clean, comfortable facility that provides floor mattresses for hostellers visiting this area. Adjacent to Pembroke State University, it's convenient to all campus activities. Pembroke, home of the Lumbee tribe, features the exciting outdoor drama "Strike at the Wind," July through August at the Lakeside Amphitheater and the PSU Native American Resource Center.

Odum Street.

Mail (✉): Baptist Student Center, Pembroke State University, Box 5025, Pembroke, NC 28372.
Phone (☎): 919-521-8777.
Price (●): $6 U.S.
Closed (X): never.
Office Hours: call ahead.
Beds (🛏): 12. **Grade: (SA)**.
Facilities (mixed use): floor mattresses, equipment storage area, kitchen, linen rental, lockers/baggage storage, on-site parking, wheelchair accessible (♿), **MSA**.

Family rooms (🛏): available.
Groups (🎪): welcome.
Reservations advisable (📞a): always. **By phone:** accepted.
Credit cards: not accepted.
Managers: Michael Cummings, Ron Sanders.
Directions: Interstate 95, exit #17 west to North Carolina Highway 711 to Pembroke, right at third stop light. Baptist Student Union House is 1/2 mile ahead on the right.

Ohio

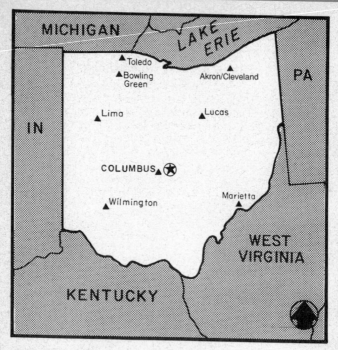

Helpful Organizations

AYH Council Offices

Columbus Council
P.O. Box 14384
Columbus, OH 43214
Phone (☎): 614-447-1006

Lima Council
P.O. Box 173
Lima, OH 45802
Phone (☎): 419-222-7301
FAX: 419-229-6960

Northeast Ohio Council
6093 Stanford Road
Peninsula, OH 44264
Phone (☎): 216-467-8711

Toledo Area Council
P.O Box 352736
Toledo, OH 43635-2736
Phone (☎): 419-841-4510

Tri-State Council
P.O. Box 141015
Cincinnati, OH 45250
Phone (☎): 513-651-1294

State Tourism Office

Ohio Division of Travel and Tourism
P.O. Box 1001
Columbus, OH 43266
Phone (☎): 800-BUCKEYE,
614-466-8844

Ohio

Akron/Cleveland

Stanford House AYH-Hostel

Located midway between Cleveland and Akron, the Stanford House AYH-Hostel sits in the scenic Cuyahoga Valley National Recreation Area. Built in 1843 by George Stanford, this Greek Revival farmhouse is on the National Register of Historic Places. Activities and programs are available year-round at the hostel and the recreation area.

Trails for biking, hiking, and cross-country skiing start just yards from the hostel's door. Downhill skiers have a one-mile trip to Boston Mills Ski Resort or a three-mile trip to Brandywine Ski Area. Also nearby are waterslides and Blossom Music Center, summer home of the Cleveland Orchestra. The Bikecentennial Maine-to-Iowa Bike Route is five miles away. Drive to Cleveland for a fun-filled evening in The Flats, or Akron to Quaker Square.

6093 Stanford Road,
Peninsula, OH 44264-9613.
Mail (✉): same.
Phone (☎): 216-467-8711.
Price (●): $10 U.S.
Closed (✗): never.
Office Hours: 7–9 a.m., 5–10 p.m.
Beds (⊨): 30. **Grade:** Hostel.
Facilities: kitchen, laundry facilities, linen rental, on-site parking, covered bicycle and motorcycle parking, ping pong table, **MSA**.
Family rooms (⌂): available. **Groups (⊞):** welcome; reservations required.
Reservations essential (⊞e): weekends.
Credit cards: not accepted.
Manager: Bob Utz.
Directions: 22 miles south of Cleveland. From Interstate 80, take exit #12, (Ohio Highway 8) south, take immediate right on Boston Mills Road, turn right on Stanford Road, hostel is 1/2 mile north on the right. From Interstate 271, take exit #12, east on Ohio Highway 303, turn north on Riverview Road, then east on Boston Mills Road, and north on Stanford Road.

Note: BMR is Boston Mills Rd

Ohio

Bowling Green

Wintergarden AYH-Hostel

The Wintergarden AYH-Hostel is the first and only U.S. hostel planned, designed, constructed, and financed by a city government, service organizations, and private contributions. Enjoy the area by bicycle along scenic, low-traffic roads or follow the two mapped bicycle routes (the Bikecentennial North Route and the Ohio "N" Route) which pass nearby. The great hiking trails and bridle paths in local parks double as cross-country ski trails. Canoeing and fishing are only 12 miles away on the Maumee River. Bowling Green is home to Bowling Green State University and has many shops and restaurants. Nearby Fort Meigs and the Battle of Fallen Timbers State Memorial commemorate the French and Indian War.

Wintergarden Road.
Mail (✉): 618 South Wintergarden Road, Bowling Green, OH 43402.
Phone (☎): 419-352-5953, 419-352-9806.
Price (💲): $4.75 U.S.
Closed (X): never.
Office Hours: 8 a.m.–9 p.m.
Beds (🛏): 32. **Grade:** Hostel.
Facilities: equipment storage area, information desk, kitchen, laundry facilities, lockers/baggage storage, on-site parking, wheelchair accessible (♿), **MSA**.
Groups (🏠): welcome.
Reservations essential (📞): always. **By phone:** 419-352-5953.
Credit cards: not accepted.
Managers: Bob and Deb Feehan.
Directions: 1 mile southwest of downtown off Wintergarden Road. Take exit #181 from Interstate 75, go west through town on Wooster Road, turn left (south) on Wintergarden Road, hostel is about 1/2 mile from the intersection on the left.

Ohio

Columbus

Heart of Ohio AYH-Hostel

The elegant Heart of Ohio AYH-Hostel is adjacent to Ohio State University. Take a trip to downtown Columbus to see the gorgeous state capitol and Capitol Square. Visit the Center for Science and Industry, a fascinating and fun "hands-on" museum of modern technology. And don't miss the Ohio Theater, a grand and glorious cinema of a bygone era, now the home of the Columbus Symphony Orchestra.

German Village is an old German settlement restored to its 18th-century grandeur. Be sure to take advantage of one of the hostel-sponsored hiking, cycling, or boating trips.

95 East 12th Avenue,
Columbus, OH 43201.
Mail (✉): same.
Phone (☎): 614-294-7157.
Price (⬤): $10 U.S.
Closed (X): December 24–25.
Office Hours: 7–9 a.m., 5–10 p.m.
Beds (🛏): 22. **Grade:** Hostel.
Facilities: equipment storage area, information desk, kitchen, laundry facilities, linen rental, lockers/baggage storage, on-site parking, **MSA.**
Groups (🎪): welcome; reservations required.
Family room (👪): available.
Reservations advisable (📅): May–September. **By phone:** accepted.
Credit cards: not accepted.

Managers: Richard and Megan.
Directions: Take Fifth Avenue exit west off Interstate 71 to High Street, north on High Street to 12th Avenue, hostel is less than a block east.

Ohio

Lima
Lima Home Hostel

Elton and Kitty Hammond's home is convenient to both north-south and east-west travel routes. Cyclists can enjoy excellent cycling on scenic backcountry roads. Fifteen miles south is the Neil Armstrong Space Museum, honoring the first man to walk on the moon, with exhibits about space exploration.

Call for reservations.
Mail (✉): P.O. Box 173, Lima, OH 45802.
Phone (☎): 419-222-7301.
Price (💰): $3.25 U.S.
Closed (X): March 21–April 10, July 1–9, December 16–January 10.
Grade: Hostel. **Beds (🛏):** 2.
Facilities: equipment storage area, information desk, laundry facilities, lockers/baggage storage, on-site parking, **MSA**.

Meals (🍴): breakfast, dinner.
Family rooms (🏠): available.
Reservations essential (📞): always. **By phone:** accepted with 24-hour notice.
Credit cards: not accepted.
Managers: Elton and Kitty Hammond.
Directions: available upon reservation confirmation.

Ohio

Malabar Farm State Park

Malabar Farm AYH-Hostel

Malabar is an ancient Asian word meaning "beautiful valley." Located on a 900-acre working farm in Malabar Farm State Park, the hostel—once the home of author/agriculturalist Louis Bromfield—lives up to its name.

Explore the rolling hills and valleys of this beautiful state park on foot, by bicycle, or on skis. Swim in or ice skate on nearby lakes. Visit the Amish community, only 10 miles away. Programs at Malabar Farm State Park include Heritage Days, Maple Sugaring Weekends, Draft Horse Workshops, and Christmas at Malabar.

3954 Bromfield Road.
Mail (✉): 3954 Bromfield Road, Lucas, OH 44843.
Phone (☎): 419-892-2055.
Price (☺): $8 U.S.
Closed (X): November 28, December 25, January 1.
Office Hours: 7–9 a.m., 5–9 p.m.
Grade: Hostel.
Beds (⊨): 26.
Facilities: information desk, kitchen, laundry facilities, on-site parking, **MSA**; bring a sheet sleeping sack, day use available by reservation, $1 per person.
Family room (⚲): available. **Groups (⛺):** welcome; reservations and deposit required.
Reservations advisable (☏a): always.
Credit cards: not accepted.
Manager: Florence Overholt.

Directions: off Interstate 71, take Ohio Route 13 north to first traffic light, turn right (Hanley Road), to 4-way stop at Pleasant Valley Road, turn right, go approximately 6 miles, turn right on Bromfield Road, hostel is first house on the right.

Ohio

HOME HOSTEL

Marietta
Marietta Home Hostel

Marietta, named after Marie Antoinette, is a quaint old city with brick streets and wonderful restored homes and buildings. The hostel is an old late-19th-century farmhouse near Wayne National Forest with numerous hiking trails. Visit Campus Martius and the Ohio River Museum or tour the Fenton Glass Factory. After a day of hiking or sightseeing, relax in the hostel's hot tub.

Call for reservations.
Mail (✉): Rt. 8, P.O. Box 229, Marietta, OH 45750.
Phone (☎): 614-373-8629.
Price (💰): $10 U.S.
Closed (X): never.
Grade: home hostel (🏠).
Beds (🛏): 4.
Amenities: hot tub, hiking trails, cycling.

Facilities: baggage storage area, laundry, linen rental, showers, kitchen, on-site parking, **MSA**.
Family rooms (🚼): available.
Reservations essential (📅e): write to mailing address or call.
Managers: Carl-Michal and Ruth Krawczyk.
Directions: available upon reservation confirmation.

Ohio

Toledo

Toledo AYH-Hostel

A warm welcome awaits hostellers at this cheerful, cozy hostel in a pleasant, quiet residential neighborhood. Take advantage of the hostel's interpretive brochures, articles, books, clippings, and personal tips about area historic sites, monuments, and displays. Visit the renowned Toledo Museum of Art, wave at the bears at the Toledo Zoo, or marvel at the flowers at the Toledo Botanical Gardens. View the Miami-Erie Canal system, once a vital link between the Great Lakes and the Atlantic Ocean. The Toledo Metropark system provides hiking and cycling opportunities.

4027 McGregor Lane,
Toledo, OH 43623.
Mail (✉): same.
Phone (☎): 419-474-1993, 419-474-2254.
Price (💲): $6 U.S.
Closed (X): November 1–March 31.
Office Hours: after 5 p.m until 10 a.m.
Grade: Hostel.
Beds (🛏): 38.
Facilities: air-conditioning, equipment storage area, information desk, kitchen, laundry facilities, linen rental, baggage storage, on-site parking, wheelchair accessible (♿), **MSA**.
Meals (🍴): breakfast.
Family rooms (👪): available.
Groups (🎏): welcome; reservations required.
Reservations essential (📞): for groups. **By phone:** accepted. **Off-season reservations:** mail to 4027 McGregor Lane, Toledo, OH 43623.
Credit cards: not accepted.
Managers: Carolyn and Floyd George.

Directions: north of Monroe Street, and Talmadge Rd., east on McGregor Lane. **From I-80/90** eastbound, exit 4, north on U.S. 20 to central, east to Talmadge Rd.; **From I-80/90 westbound**, exit 4a, north on I-75 to 475 and to exit 16, north on Talmadge.

Ohio

Wilmington

Caesar Creek AYH-Hostel

A century-old farm, the Caesar Creek AYH-Hostel is located in beautiful Caesar Creek State Park. Explore the park on foot, by bicycle, or by boat. The Caesar Creek Lake is perfect for boating, fishing, or swimming. In the winter, ice skating and cross-country skiing are the sports of choice. The area is great for fossil hunting.

For more urban pleasures, the hostel is a short drive from both Dayton and Cincinnati. Catch a Reds or Bengals game, visit the Cincinnati Zoo, see the Dayton Philharmonic, or just browse along either city's shopping districts. Also near the hostel is King's Island amusement park and the Air Force Museum.

8823 Center Road, Wilmington, OH 45177.
Mail (✉): same.
Phone (☎): 513-488-3755.
Price (💲): $7 U.S.
Closed (X): never.
Office Hours: 8–10 a.m., 6–9 p.m.
Grade: Hostel.
Beds (⊨): 16.
Facilities: baggage storage area, information desk, kitchen, linen rental, on-site parking, **MSA**.
Meals (🍴): groups by special arrangement.
Groups (⏍): welcome; reservations required.
Reservations essential (✆e): always for groups. **By phone:** accepted.
Credit cards: not accepted.

Manager: John Marmer.
Directions: take exit #45 off Interstate 71, east on Ohio Highway 73, north on Ohio Highway 380, west on Center Road.

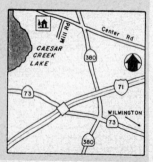

IBN INTERNATIONAL BOOKING NETWORK

HOSTELLING INTERNATIONAL

Reserve your bed up to 6 months in advance by visiting our reservation centers at hostels located in the following cities: Boston, Los Angeles (Santa Monica), Miami Beach, Montréal, New York City, Ottawa, San Francisco, Seattle, Toronto, Washington, D.C., and Vancouver.

Reserve for the following locations*

AUSTRALIA
- Brisbane City
- Melbourne—Queensberry Hill
- Sydney

AUSTRIA
- Salzburg Jugendgästehaus

BELGIUM
- Brugge—Europa
- Brussels—Jean Nihon

CANADA
- Banff International
- Montréal
- Ottawa International
- Vancouver International

ENGLAND & WALES
- London
- Stratford-upon-Avon

FRANCE
- Paris—Le d'Artagnan
- Rennes
- Strasbourg—René Cassin

GERMANY
- Düsseldorf
- Munchen—Neuhausen

REPUBLIC OF IRELAND
- Dublin International

NORTHERN IRELAND
- Ballygally
- Belfast International

NORTHERN IRELAND (continued)
- Castle Archdale
- Cushendall
- Newcastle
- Whitepark Bay

ITALY
- Venice

JAPAN
- Kyoto
- Nara—Nara-shi
- Tokyo—Yoyogi

LUXEMBOURG
- Luxembourg City—Mansfeld

NEW ZEALAND
- Auckland City

NETHERLANDS
- Amsterdam—Vondelpark

SCOTLAND
- Glasgow International
- Stirling

SWITZERLAND
- Zurich—Wollishofen

UNITED STATES OF AMERICA
- Boston International
- Los Angeles—Santa Monica
- New York International
- San Francisco International
- Seattle International
- Washington, DC, International

▲ You will receive confirmation while you wait.
▲ Booking fee is only US$2.00.
▲ Up to 9 people can be included in one booking.
▲ If you change your itinerary, get your money back less a small fee of US$1.00.

* *Additional hostels are being added to the system—ask your reservation agent for the most up-to-date list.*

For more information, contact any hostel listed above, or call or write to: Hostelling International/American Youth Hostels, 733 15th Street NW, Washington, DC 20005. Tel: 202-783-6161

Oregon

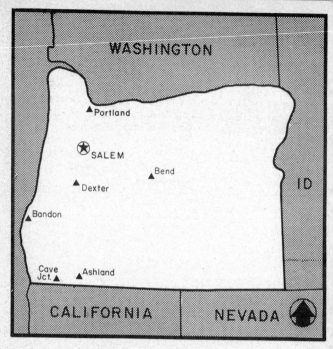

Helpful Organizations

AYH Council Office

Oregon Council
American Youth Hostels
1520 S.E. 37th Avenue
Portland, OR 97214
Phone (☎): 503-235-9493

State Tourism Office

Oregon Tourism Division
275 Summer Street, Northeast
Salem, OR 97310
Phone (☎): 800-547-7842 (out of state), 800-543-8838 (in state), or 503-378-3451

Discounts

Present a valid hostel membership card at the time of purchase to receive the following discounts:

Ashland

Rogue Brewery and Public House - 10% discount with cards available from the hostel.

Astoria

The Community Store - 5% discount given on all discountable purchases (milk, eggs, cheese, and a few other items excluded from discount). Must have IYHF membership card. 10% discount for two hours of volunteer work in store every week. 1389 Duane Street, 503-325-0027.

Cave Junction

Oregon Caves National Monument - $2.75 off the $6.75 admission price for American Youth Hostel members. Price is $4.00. 20000 Caves Hwy., 503-592-3400.

Oregon

Ashland

The Ashland AYH-Hostel

A drama-lover's paradise, Ashland is best known for its annual Shakespeare Festival, which runs from February to October. The Ashland AYH-Hostel is within walking distance of the town's three main theaters. If you hit culture overload after a few days, river rafting, canoeing, kayaking, and hiking are all great in the scenic surrounding hills and mountains. For serious hikers, the Pacific Crest Trail is 10 miles away. Reduced rate passes to Mount Ashland's challenging ski slopes are available at the hostel, as are directions for the best place for cross-country skiing.

150 North Main Street, Ashland, OR 97520.
Mail (✉): same.
Phone (☎): 503-482-9217.
Price (⬤): $11 U.S.
Closed (X): Thanksgiving day, Christmas Eve, and Christmas day.
Office Hours: 8–10 a.m., 5–11 p.m. for check-in.
Grade: Hostel.
Beds (🛏): 39.
Facilities: piano, recreation room, large outdoor porch, equipment storage area, information desk, kitchen, laundry facilities, linen rental, lockers/baggage storage, on-site parking, **MSA**.
Family rooms (⌂): available.
Groups (⛺): welcome.
Reservations essential (☎e): March–October. **By phone:** accepted.

Credit cards: not accepted.
Managers: Barbara and John Breneiser.
Directions: take exit #14 or #19 off Interstate 5 to downtown, 2 blocks north from Plaza on Main Street.

Oregon

Bandon

Sea Star AYH-Hostel

Located halfway between San Francisco and Seattle on the Oregon Coast Bicycle Route, Bandon features some of Oregon's most scenic coastline: dunes, cliffs, rock formations, and miles of white sandy beaches.

Open all day, the Sea Star AYH-Hostel is in the historic "Old Town Waterfront District" and features couple's rooms, skylights, exposed wood beams, a cozy wood-burning stove, and a deck with a gorgeous view of the harbor. There is also an international bistro in the hostel serving breakfast, lunch, and dinner.

Away from the beach, experience Bandon's art galleries, summer stock, and community theater groups. Visit one of the many studios of painters, potters, sculptors, and glass blowers.

375 Second Street,
Bandon, OR 97411.
Mail (✉): same.
Phone (☎): 503-347-9632.
Price (◐): $9 U.S.
Closed (X): never.
Office Hours: 8 a.m.–9 p.m.
Grade: Hostel.
Beds (🛏): 38.
Facilities: skylights, wood stove, deck and courtyard overlooking harbor, day use, equipment storage area, information desk, kitchen, laundry facilities, linen rental, **MSA**.
Meals (🍴): at bistro.
Family rooms (👪): available.
Groups (🎫): welcome.
Reservations advisable (☎): June–September. **By phone:** accepted with credit card confirmation.
Credit cards: American Express, MasterCard, Visa.

Managers: David and Monica Jennings.
Directions: just off U.S. Highway 101 in Old Town Waterfront District. **Bus:** from Bandon bus stop, north 3.5 blocks on left side Hwy 101, entrance to Old Town marked by arch, go under arch to 2nd Street, hostel and bistro is to the right, across from tourist info center.

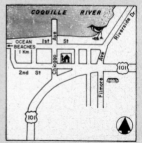

Oregon

Bend

Bend Alpine AYH-Hostel

Located near the Three Sisters Wilderness Area and the Newberry Volcanic National Monument, Bend provides a wealth of recreational opportunities such as white water rafting (discounts for hostellers), hiking, canoeing, mountain biking, and windsurfing. The hostel is just one block from the free ski shuttle to Mount Bachelor, one of the finest resorts for both cross-country and downhill skiing in the west.

19 S.W. Century Drive, Bend, OR 97707
Mail (✉): same.
Phone (☎): 503-389-3813 or 503-382-4430.
Price (◓): $ 14 U.S. + tax.
Closed (X): never.
Office Hours: 7–9:30 a.m., 5–11 p.m.
Grade: Hostel.
Beds (🛏): 40.
Facilities: baggage storage area, laundry, linen rental, lockers, kitchen, on-site parking, showers, wheelchair accessible (♿), **MSA**.
Meals (🍴): none.
Family rooms (👪): available.
Groups (🏠): available.
Reservations advisable (📅a): always, during Thanksgiving week, December 15–January 15, Easter/Spring Break. **By phone:** 503-389-3813. **By mail:** use mailing address.
Credit cards: MasterCard, Visa.
Managers: Dave and Pamela MacGurn.

Directions: Take US highway 97 to division street, go north (from south of bend) or go south (from north of bend), turn west on Colorado Ave., turn west on Simpson Ave., turn north on Century Drive. **Airport (✈):** take US 97 south. **Bus:** take highway 20 west to US 97 south. **Train:** shuttle available to hostel, call 1-800-955-8267 or 1-800-227-5244 for reservations.

Oregon

Cave Junction
Fordson Home Hostel

Set on 20 acres of woodlands with three streams and a lovely garden, the Fordson Home Hostel features large private rooms with fireplaces. Take the 40-minute historical and botanical tour, which includes the "Trees of Wonder", a working saw mill, "Big Foot", the world's tallest Douglas fir, plus 25 antique tractors and 100 toy tractors.

Call for reservations.
Phone (☎): 503-592-3203.
Price (●): $8 U.S.
Closed (X): never.
Grade: home hostel (🏠).
Beds (🛏): 5.
Facilities: solar shower, private rooms, private baths, free use of bicycles, camping, on-site parking.

Family rooms (👪): available; no small children.
Groups (👥): welcome.
Reservations essential (☎): always. **By phone:** accepted.
Credit cards: not accepted.
Manager: Jack Heald.
Directions: available upon reservation confirmation.

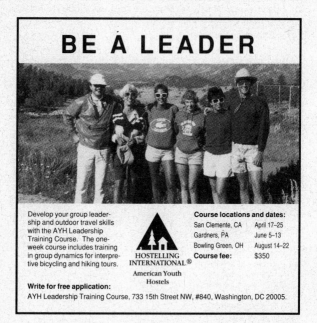

Oregon

Dexter

Lost Valley Center AYH-Hostel

The Lost Valley Center AYH-Hostel is located on the grounds of the Lost Valley Educational Center, a conference and retreat center which focuses on living in harmony with the land. Hostellers are welcome to take part in conferences and programs for an extra fee. Dinner ($6) is available most weekdays. The Center is surrounded by 90 acres of woodlands, streams, and forest hiking trails. The Eugene city bus #92 arrives at Dexter twice daily (Monday–Friday) and has a bike rack; call the hostel in advance for a pick-up from Dexter. Overflow accommodations usually available. Sleeping bags allowed.

81868 Lost Valley Lane,
Dexter, OR 97431.
Mail (✉): same.
Phone (☎): 503-937-3351.
Price (💲): $7 U.S.
Office Hours: 8 a.m.–9 p.m.
Closed (X): never.
Grade: Rustic.
Beds (🛏): 12.
Facilities: ecological retreat and conference center, kitchen, linen rental, **MSA.**
Meals (🍴): dinner, weekdays.
Family rooms (👪): available.
Reservations essential (📞): always. **By phone:** accepted.
Credit cards: not accepted.
Managers: Elizabeth Peele, Dianne Brause.

Directions: east of Interstate 5 on Oregon Highway 58, through Pleasant Hill to 8-mile marker, right 4 miles on Rattlesnake Creek Road, right 1 mile on Lost Valley Lane, look for Lost Valley Center sign on the right.

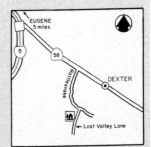

Oregon

Portland

Portland International AYH-Hostel

Whatever brings you to Oregon's largest city, the Portland International AYH-Hostel provides a comfortable home away from home. The hostel is two miles from downtown and sponsors daily van trips to Mount St. Helens and the Columbia River Gorge.

See the outstanding collection of Pacific Northwest Native American art at the Portland Art Museum or wander Old Town, where sailors used to frolic a century ago. Washington Park, one of three large parks in Portland, contains the Portland Zoo, Oregon Museum of Science and Industry (OMSI), the Japanese Garden, and the lovely International Rose Test Garden. In June, catch the Portland Rose Festival. August brings the world-class Mount Hood Jazz Festival to town.

3031 Hawthorne Boulevard, SE, Portland, OR 97214.
Mail (✉): same.
Phone (☎): 503-236-3380.
Price (⬤): $12 U.S.
Closed (X): never.
Office Hours: 7:30–10 a.m., 5–11 p.m.
Grade: Hostel.
Beds (🛏): 33 (winter), 47 (summer).
Facilities: equipment storage area, information desk, kitchen, linen rental, lockers/baggage storage, on-site parking, **MSA**.
Groups (|||||): welcome.
Reservations essential (📞): June–September. **By phone:** accepted with credit card confirmation and 24-hour notice.
Credit cards: MasterCard, Visa, JCB.
Manager: Bob Howell.

Directions: from Salem, take exit #299B off Interstate 405, right on Front Avenue (exit #1A), right across Hawthorne Bridge, straight 31 blocks to hostel; from Seattle, take exit #300B, left onto Belmont Street, right on 30th Street to Hawthorne, left 1 block. **Train or bus:** walk south to Fifth Avenue, take city bus #5 to 30th Street.

Pennsylvania

Helpful Organizations

AYH Council Offices

Delaware Valley Council
624 South 3rd Street
Philadelphia, PA 19147
Phone (☎): 215-925-6004

Pittsburgh Council
Wightman School Community Bldg.
5604 Solway Street, Room 204
Pittsburgh, PA 15217
Phone (☎): 412-422-2282

State Tourism Office

Pennsylvania Bureau of Travel
453 Forum Building
Harrisburg, PA 17120
Phone (☎): 800-847-4872,
717-783-5453

Discounts

Present a valid hostel membership card at the time of purchase to receive the following discounts:

Bowmansville

Horst's Bike Shop - discount on supplies - Kramer Mill Road, Denvep, PA, 215-267-3695.
Mennonite Information Center - admission discount - 2209 Millstream Road, Lancaster, PA.

Charleroi

YMCA - offers hostellers one free night at its facility. Taylor Run Road, 412-483-8077.

Discounts

La Anna

Alpine Ski Area - Special rates for skiers - individuals and groups with Hostelling International memberships. Route 447, Analomink, 717-421-7721.

Evergreen Park Golf Course - Special rates to Hostelling International members. Route 447, Analomink, 717-421-7721.

Litning Auto - 10% discount on auto leasing and auto parts. Newfoundland, PA 717-676-3366.

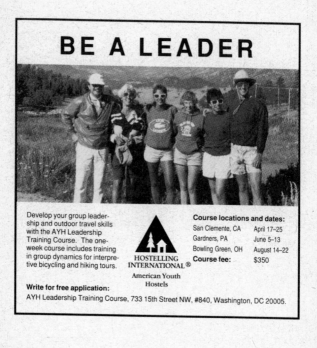

BE A LEADER

Develop your group leadership and outdoor travel skills with the AYH Leadership Training Course. The one-week course includes training in group dynamics for interpretive bicycling and hiking tours.

HOSTELLING INTERNATIONAL ®

American Youth Hostels

Course locations and dates:

San Clemente, CA	April 17–25
Gardners, PA	June 5–13
Bowling Green, OH	August 14–22
Course fee:	$350

Write for free application:

AYH Leadership Training Course, 733 15th Street NW, #840, Washington, DC 20005.

Pennsylvania

Charleroi
Rego's Hotel

While staying at the hotel, take a ride on the "Magic City Trolley." Near Rego's is a 15-acre community park with basketball courts and a fishing area.

Enjoy a FREE day at a fully equiped YMCA located one mile from Rego's, and two marinas with boat rentals two miles from Rego's.

601 McKean Avenue, Charleroi, PA 15022.

Mail (✉): same.

Phone (☎): 412-483-6200.

Price (●): $12 U.S. + tax.

Office Hours: 9 a.m.–10 p.m.

Closed (X): never.

Grade: (SA).

Beds (🛏): 4.

Facilities (mixed use): restaurant, equipment storage area, information desk, linen rental, lockers/baggage storage, on-site parking, wheelchair accessible (♿), **MSA**.

Meals (🍴): lunch, dinner.

Reservations essential (☎): always. **By phone:** accepted with credit card confirmation and 2-hour notice.

Credit cards: Discover, MasterCard, Visa.

Managers: Victoria Baxter, Nino Giorgi.

Directions: 30 miles south of Pittsburgh and 1 mile north of Interstate 70 (exit #17) on Pennsylvania Highway 88, at McKean and Sixth Street, across from post office.

Pennsylvania

Collegeville

Evansburg State Park AYH-Hostel

Acres of unspoiled wilderness in Evansburg State Park offer all sorts of outdoor activities within 30 minutes of Philadelphia. Hike, bike, ride horseback, canoe, or fish along Skippack or Perkiomen Creeks. In the winter, warm your feet at the fireplace after a day of cross-country or downhill skiing at Spring Mountain. Bird buffs can visit the Audubon Bird Sanctuary, while history buffs see where Washington and the Revolutionary Army spent the brutal winter of 1777–78 at Valley Forge National Historic Park. Golfers can use the 18-hole public golf course, and music lovers can enjoy the Valley Forge Music Fair and the annual Philadelphia folk festival.

837 Mayhall Road, Collegeville, PA 19426.
Mail (✉): same.
Phone (☎): 215-489-4326.
Price (⊖): $8 U.S.
Closed (X): never.
Office Hours: 7–9 a.m., 5–8 p.m.
Grade: Hostel.
Beds (⊨): 12.
Facilities: equipment storage area, kitchen, linen rental, on-site parking, **MSA**.
Family rooms (⚏): available.
Groups (⊞): welcome.
Reservations essential (⟟): September 15–May 15. **By phone:** accepted.
Credit cards: not accepted.
Manager: Beverly Levitsky.
Directions: east of Collegeville on Germantown Pike, north on Skippack Creek Road (intersection after Evansburg Road), west on Mill Road, turn right at park entrance, hostel is 1/2 mile north; park gate on Mill Road locked at dusk.

Pennsylvania

Downingtown

Marsh Creek State Park AYH-Hostel

Only an hour's drive from Philadelphia, this homey stone farmhouse looks down on a 500-acre lake, perfect for boating, windsurfing, fishing, and ice skating. Bicyclists can enjoy the backcountry roads nearby as well as the Struble Bike Trail. To the delight of hikers and cross-country skiers, the Brandywine Trail runs right by the hostel's front door. Great bird watching is anywhere you stand still for a moment. Amish farmlands, the beautiful Longwood Botanical Gardens, and the historic Brandywine Battlefield and Valley Forge National Park are all within driving distance. At night read a book or share the day's adventures around the fireplace in the common room.

East Reeds Road.
Mail (✉): P.O. Box 376, Lyndell, PA 19354.
Phone (☎): 215-458-5881.
Price (💲): $8 U.S.
Closed (X): never.
Office Hours: 7:30–9:30 a.m., 5–10 p.m.
Grade: Hostel.
Beds (🛏): 12.
Facilities: kitchen, linen rental, on-site parking, **MSA**.
Family rooms (👪): available.
Groups (🏛): welcome.
Reservations advisable (📞): always. **By phone:** accepted.
Credit cards: not accepted.
Managers: Barbara and Cecil Knutson.
Directions: 6 miles north northwest of Downingtown in Marsh Creek State Park, take Pennsylvania Highway 282 west for about 6 miles, right on Lyndell Road at the Lyndell Country Store, follow signs to Marsh Creek State Park and the hostel.

Pennsylvania

Geigertown

Shirey's AYH-Hostel

Shirey's AYH-Hostel is conveniently located for both hikers and bikers making their way across Pennsylvania. Both the Bikecentennial Maine-to-Virginia Bicycle Route and the Horseshoe Trail pass close by. No matter how you arrive, stay awhile to visit Pennsylvania Dutch Country. Glimpses of the past are also available at the 150-year-old Strasburg Railway and the National Wax Museum of Lancaster. Hostellers interested in nature can hike, canoe, or bike through the French Creek State Park, just a few steps from the hostel.

Box 49 Geigertown Road, Geigertown, PA 19523.

Mail (✉): same.

Phone (☎): 215-286-9537.

Price (☺): $8.25 U.S. (discount if no heat).

Closed (X): December–February.

Office Hours: 8–10 a.m., 5:30–9:30 p.m.

Grade: Hostel.

Beds (🛏): 20 (winter), 48 (summer).

Facilities: kitchen, linen rental, on-site parking, wheelchair accessible (♿), **MSA**.

Family rooms (👪): available.

Groups (👫): welcome; reservations required.

Reservations essential (✆e): always. **By phone:** accepted. **Off-season:** mail to Shirey's Store, Geigertown, PA 19523, or call 215-286-9835.

Credit cards: not accepted.

Manager: Millie Shirey.

Directions: Take exit #22 off Pennsylvania Turnpike and go south 1/2 mile to Morgantown, turn left on Pennsylvania Highway 23 to traffic light, turn left on Twin Valley Road north to Pennsylvania Route 82, take Route 82 north to Geigertown. After post office, first road right is Geigertown Road, 1/4 mile to Shirey's hostel, on left across from Shirey's Cash & Carry Store.

Pennsylvania

Gettysburg

Gettysburg International AYH-Hostel

Located in the center of the downtown historic district, the Gettysburg International AYH-Hostel is the oldest remaining hotel building in Gettysburg. The former City Hotel was used as a hospital during the Civil War. Today small rooms provide wonderful family or group accommodations.

The Gettysburg National Military Park, commemorating the historic battle and the site of President Lincoln's famous Gettysburg Address, is easily accessible from the hostel. Another popular attraction is the house and farm of President Eisenhower. Nearby is the Adams County Winery and Ski Liberty.

27 Chambersburg Street, Gettysburg, PA 17325.
Mail (✉): same.
Phone (☎): 717-334-1020.
Price (☺): $8 U.S.
Closed (X): never.
Office Hours: 7–9:30 a.m., 5–9 p.m.
Grade: Hostel.
Beds (🛏): 60.
Facilities: kitchen, laundry facilities, linen rental, on-site parking, **MSA**.
Family rooms (👪): available.
Groups (⛺): welcome.
Reservations advisable (📞): groups. **By phone:** accepted.
Credit cards: not accepted.
Manager: Mary Shank.

Directions: downtown, 1/2 block west of town square on U.S. Highway 30.

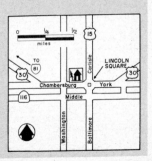

Pennsylvania

La Anna

Pocono AYH-Hostel

Only two hours from New York City, the Pocono AYH-Hostel is a charming rustic lodge set in the woods by a stream, between Tobyhanna State Park, Promised Land State Park, and Bruce Lake Natural Area. The recently renovated and expanded kitchen and dining areas plus friendly managers Roy and Mary Jane Walter make this rural escape worth the trip.

Bike or hike to one of the parks on beautiful secluded country roads. Cross-country skis and lessons are available nearby. Downhill skiers have the enviable choice of 10 nearby ski areas, including Mount Pocono, Alpine Mountain, and Camelback. The farming history of northeast Pennsylvania is re-created at the Quiet Valley Living Historical Farm. The Pocono Playhouse is also nearby for a fun evening.

La Anna Road.
Mail (✉): R.R. 2, Box 1026, Cresco, PA 18326.
Phone (☎): 717-676-9076.
Price (☻): $8 U.S.
Closed (X): December 24–January 2.
Office Hours: 7–9 a.m., 5–10 p.m.
Grade: Hostel.
Beds (🛏): 40.
Facilities: fireplace, wood stove, kitchen, linen rental, on-site parking, **MSA**.
Family rooms (👪): available.
Groups (🏛): welcome.
Reservations essential (☎): on weekends. **By phone:** accepted.
Credit cards: not accepted.

Managers: Mary Jane and Roy Walter.
Directions: 12 miles north of Cresco on Pennsylvania Highway 191, west on La Anna Road.

Pennsylvania

Newtown

Tyler State Park AYH-Hostel

A beautiful early Pennsylvania farmhouse, the Tyler State Park AYH-Hostel is a great place to stay while enjoying all the recreational activities of the surrounding 1,170-acre Tyler State Park. Bike and horse paths wind through the park. In the winter, these same paths and fields are great for cross-country skiing and sledding.

For a better idea of what life was like in early Pennsylvania, visit the Mercer Museum of pre-industrial tools. Then see the tools at work at Peddler's Village in Lahaska. Washington's Crossing Historic Park marks where George Washington made his famous Christmas-night crossing of the Delaware River to Trenton. Historic farms are also easily accessible.

Tyler State Park.
Mail (✉): P.O. Box 94, Newtown, PA 18940.
Phone (☎): 215-968-0927.
Price (●): $8 U.S.
Closed (X): December 25, January 1.
Office Hours: 8–10 a.m., 6–8 p.m.
Beds (🛏): 25. **Grade:** Hostel.
Facilities: kitchen, linen rental, **MSA**.
Family rooms (👪): available.
Groups (卌): welcome.
Reservations essential (📞): groups. **By phone:** accepted.
Credit cards: not accepted.
Managers: Susan Thompson, Jim Whitmoyer.
Directions: from Interstate 95, go 8 miles west on Pennsylvania Route 332, turn right on Pennsylvania Route 232 (Second Street Pike) and go north 1/2 mile to Twining Ford Road, turn right and continue into park on dirt road which makes a left turn. Go 300 feet after left turn and bear right on White Pine Trail, turn left at first intersection onto Covered Bridge Trail; hostel is at the end of Covered Bridge Trail.

Pennsylvania

Ohiopyle State Park

Ohiopyle State Park AYH-Hostel

Exciting white-water rafting and kayaking await visitors to the Ohiopyle State Park AYH-Hostel on the Youghiogheny River. This homey hostel has a vivid display of wildflowers in the spring, and is in the heart of the largest state park in Pennsylvania.

Cross-country ski or cycle along the former Western Maryland Railroad for breathtaking views of the gorges along the Yough. Tour guides and outfitters in town offer a wet, wild, and safe ride down the river. The Laurel Highlands Hiking Trail runs right across the road from the hostel. Downhill skiing is only 15 miles away at Seven Springs and Hidden Valley. Call ahead for reservations to tour Frank Lloyd Wright's famous "Fallingwater" house 3 1/2 miles north of the hostel.

Ferncliff Peninsula.
Mail (✉): P.O. Box 99, Ohiopyle, PA 15470.
Phone (☎): 412-329-4476.
Price (●): $8 U.S.
Closed (X): never.
Office Hours: 7–8 a.m. (Monday–Friday), 7–9 a.m. (Saturday and Sunday), 6–10 p.m. (daily).
Beds (🛏): 25. **Grade:** Hostel.
Facilities: equipment storage area, kitchen, linen rental, on-site parking, **MSA**.
Family rooms (🛏): available.
Groups (🎏): welcome.
Reservations advisable (📞): always. **By phone:** accepted.
Credit cards: not accepted.
Manager: Sue Moore.

Directions: 8 miles northeast of U.S. Highway 40 on Pennsylvania Highway 381, in southwest Pennsylvania's Laurel Highlands.

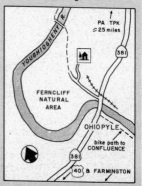

Pennsylvania

Philadelphia (Chamounix Mansion)

Chamounix Mansion AYH-Hostel

The elegant 19th-century Chamounix Mansion AYH-Hostel is located in Fairmount Park, near the renowned Philadelphia Zoo. Once a private country estate, Chamounix Mansion offers hostelers a quiet, relaxing retreat while visiting Philadelphia.

Philadelphia is known as America's birthplace and contains such popular historic attractions as Independence Hall, where the Declaration of Independence was signed, and the Liberty Bell. For more modern sights, visit the Franklin Museum of Science, Philadelphia Museum of Art, and the U.S. Mint.

Chamounix Drive, West Fairmount Park, Philadelphia, PA 19131.

Mail (✉): same.

Phone (☎): 215-878-3676.

Price (●): $10 U.S.

Closed (X): December 15–January 15; call for information.

Office Hours: 8–11 a.m., 4:30 p.m.–midnight.

Grade: Hostel.

Beds (►): 48.

Facilities: equipment storage area, information desk, kitchen, laundry facilities, linen rental, lockers/baggage storage, free parking, **MSA**.

Family rooms (⚥): available.

Groups (⫲): welcome; reservations required.

Reservations essential (✆): April–October for groups. **By phone:** accepted.

Credit cards: not accepted.

Managers: Nancy Khan, Val King.

Directions: 6-1/2 miles northwest of Center City (downtown) in West Fairmount Park, take exit #33 (City Avenue) off Interstate 76, south on City Avenue, left on Belmont, left on Ford Road, left on Chamounix Drive to dead end. **Bus:** take bus #38 from Market Street in Center City to corner of Ford and Cranston, walk 1 mile to hostel.

Pennsylvania

Pine Grove Furnace State Park

Ironmaster's Mansion AYH-Hostel

Located in beautiful Pine Grove Furnace State Park, Iron-master's Mansion AYH-Hostel was built in 1827 as the home of the ironmaster of the Pine Grove Furnace Ironworks. The iron-works manufactured cannonballs during the Revolutionary War, and the hostel was a stop on the Underground Railroad for sheltering runaway slaves.

The hostel has a hot tub and is on the Appalachian Trail. Pine Grove Furnace State Park is crisscrossed by bike trails for both mountain bikes and 10-speeds and has lakes and streams for fishing and swimming. In the winter, great cross-country skiing starts right at the hostel's front porch. Alpine skiing is also nearby.

Pine Grove Furnace State Park.
Mail (✉): R.D. 2, Box 397-B, Pine Grove Furnace State Park, Gardners, PA 17324.
Phone (☎): 717-486-7575.
Price (☺): $8 U.S.
Closed (X): December 24–January 2.
Office Hours: 7–9:30 a.m., 5–10:30 p.m.
Grade: Hostel.
Beds (🛏): 46.
Facilities: day use by arrangement, equipment storage, hot tub, kitchen, laundry facilities, linen rental, hot tub rental, on-site parking, wheelchair accessible (♿), **MSA.**
Groups (🎍): welcome.
Reservations advisable (📞a): families, groups. **By phone:** accepted.
Credit cards: not accepted.

Manager: Tom Martin.
Directions: 18 miles north of Gettysburg on Pennsylvania Highway 233, in Pine Grove Furnace State Park.

Pennsylvania

Quakertown

Weisel AYH-Hostel

The Weisel AYH-Hostel provides a beautiful country setting and fascinating glimpses at Pennsylvania's past. Reservations are a must at this popular hostel, surrounded by the Nockamixion State Park, featuring 1,450-acre Lake Nockamixion.

Quakertown, four miles away, is the gateway to historic Bucks County. The county, founded by William Penn in the 18th century, has many original churches, buildings, and farms. Visit the Burgess-Folke House and Liberty Hall, dating from 1812 and 1742, respectively. On weekends one may choose to stop by the Quakertown Farmers Market and taste wine at the Little Vineyard and Winery. And don't miss Rice's Sale and Country Market, which has been open every Tuesday for the past 100 years.

7347 Richlandtown Road, Quakertown, PA 18951.
Mail (✉): same.
Phone (☎): 215-536-8749.
Price (◔): $8 U.S.
Closed (X): December 25.
Office Hours: 8–10 a.m., 4–7 p.m.
Grade: Hostel.
Beds (⊨): 24.
Facilities: equipment storage area, kitchen, limited on-site parking, **MSA**.
Family rooms (⚭): available.
Groups (⏅): welcome.
Reservations essential (⚬): always. **By phone:** accepted.
Credit cards: not accepted.
Managers: Darlene and Stuart Davis.

Directions: 4 miles south of Quakertown on Pennsylvania Highway 313 east, left on Sternermill Rd. at Wagon Wheel Tavern, left on Clymer Rd. to stop sign, left on Richlandtown Rd.

Pennsylvania

Schellsburg

Living Waters AYH-Hostel

The sight of swans floating serenely on a spring-fed pond in front of a large white house and beautifully landscaped grounds greets visitors to the Living Waters AYH-Hostel. After setting your bags down, stroll through the magnificent hostel grounds. Shawnee State Park offers lake swimming, boating, fishing, or picnicking. Enjoy the self-guided nature trail or view 32-plus covered bridges in the area. Backpackers can hike the new "Lost Turkey Trail." Downhill skiers are only 20 miles from Blue Knob State Park Ski Area. The historic town of Bedford is 10 miles away. Fort Bedford, Old Bedford Village, and the Fall Foliage Festival make the trip worthwhile. After a busy day, relax by the fireplace in the common room.

Mail (✉): R.D. #1, Box 206, Schellsburg, PA 15559.
Phone (☎): 814-733-4212, 814-733-4607.
Price (●): $10 U.S.
Closed (X): never.
Office Hours: 8 a.m.–10 p.m.
Grade: Hostel.
Beds (🛏): 24.
Facilities: equipment storage area, information desk, kitchen, linen rental, on-site parking, **MSA**.
Family rooms (👫): available.
Groups (🏠): welcome; reservations required, mail to: Administrative Office, Living Waters, RD 1, Box 206, Schellsburg, PA 15559.
Reservations essential (📞): always. **By phone:** accepted.

Credit cards: not accepted.
Directions: 1 mile west of Pennsylvania Highway 96 off U.S. Highway 30.

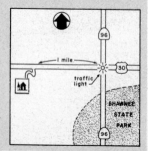

Pennsylvania

HOME HOSTEL

Tionesta
Little Hickory Home Hostel

The rugged beauty of the Allegheny National Forest is less than a mile away from the Little Hickory Home Hostel. Richard Schall's distinctive and comfortable log cabin is hidden in a secluded wooded setting with a trout stream 20 feet from the back door. Visit the Drake Well Historical Center and the Oil Creek Railroad for a fun change of pace.

Call for reservations.
Mail (✉): R2, Box 23, Tionesta, PA 16353.
Phone (☎): 814-755-4908 (hostel), 814-755-3317 (information).
Price (●): $8 U.S.
Closed (X): November 1–April 15.
Grade: home hostel (⌂).
Beds (🛏): 5.

Facilities: kitchen, on-site parking.
Family rooms (♙): available.
Reservations essential (✆e): always. **By phone:** accepted.
Credit cards: not accepted.
Manager: Richard Schall.
Directions: available upon reservation confirmation.

FOR $20 YOU CAN STAY HERE OR GET YOUR SHOES SHINED AT THE HOTEL DOWN THE STREET.

The New York International AYH-Hostel offers a clean, comfortable place to spend the night in New York City. Plus the opportunity to meet and share experiences with travelers from all over the world. And while you may have to do without a few of life's little luxuries, at this price we don't think you'll miss them. For reservations or more information, call (212) 932-2300.

HOSTELLING INTERNATIONAL

The new seal of approval of the International Youth Hostel Federation.

HOSTELLING INTERNATIONAL®

South Dakota

Helpful Organizations

AYH Council Office

Minnesota Council
795 Raymond Avenue
St. Paul, MN 55114-1522
Phone (☎): 612-659-0407

State Tourism Board

South Dakota Department of Tourism
Capitol Lake Plaza
711 Wells Avenue
Pierre, SD 57501
Phone (☎): 800-952-3625,
605-773-3301

South Dakota

Gary

Pleasant Valley AYH-Hostel

Located in the middle of Midwest farm country, Pleasant Valley AYH-Hostel is a great place to relax, unwind, and experience life in the heartland of America. Take a hostel-sponsored tour of the local farms and discover why agriculture is South Dakota's largest industry. Go for a swim at nearby Lake Cochrane or hike the trails that lead through this beautiful, wooded valley. Cobb Creek, which flows past the hostel, has a long history of Native American activities. Search for arrowheads and other Indian relics along the banks of the creek or just enjoy the view.

South Dakota Highway 22.
Mail (✉): R.R. 1, Box 256, Gary, SD 57237.
Phone (☎): 605-272-5614, 507-223-5492.
Price (☻): $10 U.S.
Closed (X): never.
Office Hours: 8–10 a.m.
Beds (⊨): 18. **Grade:** Hostel.
Facilities: linen rental, **MSA**.
Family rooms (⚥): available.
Groups (⌁): welcome.
Reservations advisable (☎): always for groups. **By phone:** accepted.
Credit cards: MasterCard, Visa.
Managers: Sharon and Steve Maas.

Directions: 3-1/2 miles south of Gary and 11 miles east of Clearlake on South Dakota Highway 22.

South Dakota

Rapid City
Rapid City YMCA

This YMCA makes a great base for hostellers to explore the Old West. The Badlands National Park offers spectacular scenery and the Oligocene fossil beds. Just minutes away is Mount Rushmore National Memorial. Devil's Tower, Crazy Horse Monument, and Wounded Knee are also nearby.

815 Kansas City Street, Rapid City, SD 57701.
Mail (✉): same.
Phone (☎): 605-342-8538.
Price (💲): $10 U.S.
Closed (X): August 21–June 6.
Office Hours: 6 a.m.–9 p.m.
Grade: (SA).
Beds (🛏): 14.
Facilities: unisex dorm, pool, gym, weight room, game room, running track, equipment storage area, information desk, lockers/baggage storage, on-site parking, wheelchair accessible (♿).
Reservations essential (☎): always. **By phone:** accepted with credit card confirmation and 24-hour notice.
Credit cards: MasterCard, Visa.
Manager: Roger Gallimore.
Directions: 1 block west of city center at Mount Rushmore Road and Kansas City Street.

DON'T JUST
GET A JOB...
PURSUE A LIFESTYLE—

HOSTELLING INTERNATIONAL offers training opportunities that cover:

- The philosophy and spirit of hostelling
- Hostel guest services and activities
- Organizational structure and opportunities
- Practical operational activities, and more

Courses Available:

April 19–22, 1993	Gardners, PA
July 19–22	Anchorage, AK
October 26–29	San Diego, CA
February 1994	To be announced

Course Fee:
$250 (includes all meals, accommodation, and course materials; HI membership required)

HOSTELLING
INTERNATIONAL
American Youth Hostels

For more information, ☎ or ✎:
**Hostelling International
American Youth Hostels**
Hostel Services
733 15th Street, NW, Suite 840
Washington, DC 20005
Phone: 202-783-6161
Fax: 202-783-6171

Texas

Helpful Organizations

AYH Council Office

Bluebonnet Council
2715 Bissonnet, #213
Houston, TX 77005
Phone (☎): 713-520-5332

North Texas Council
3530 Forest Lane, #127
Dallas, TX 75234
Phone (☎): 214-350-4294

Southwest Texas Council
2200 South Lakeshore Boulevard
Austin, TX 78741
Phone (☎): 512-444-2294

State Tourism Board

Texas Travel Division
State Department of Highways
P.O. Box 12728
Austin, TX 78711
Phone (☎): 800-888-8839 (brochure
requests only), or 512-483-3705

**Greater Houston Convention and
Visitors Bureau**
3300 Main Street
Houston, TX 77002
Phone (☎): 713-523-5050,
U.S. 800-231-7799

**Clear Lake/NASA Area Convention
and Visitors Bureau**
1201 Nasa Road I
Houston, TX 77058-3390
Phone (☎): 713-488-7676

Texas

Austin

Austin International AYH-Hostel

The Austin International AYH-Hostel, located on the south shore of Townlake, is the only hostel in the world with water beds (conventional beds, with brand-new extra-thick mattresses, are available also). Open 24 hours, this hostel serves as the base for Austin's famous Sixth Street music scene featuring everything from blues and jazz to new wave, funk, and folk. Barton Springs Pool, a natural spring-fed oasis, the University of Texas, the State Capitol, and our friendly staff make Austin a famous stop for road-worn travelers.

2200 South Lakeshore Boulevard, Austin, TX 78741.

Mail (✉): same.

Phone (☎): 512-444-2294.

Price (◒): $10 U.S.

Closed (X): never.

Office Hours: 8–10 a.m., 5–10 p.m.

Grade: Hostel.

Beds (🛏): 40.

Facilities: 24-hour common room, waterbeds, equipment storage area, information desk, kitchen, laundry facilities, linen rental, on-site parking, wheelchair accessible (♿), **MSA.**

Meals (🍴): breakfast and dinner (additional charge).

Family rooms (👪): available.

Groups (🎪): welcome.

Reservations advisable (📞): weekends. **By phone:** accepted with credit card confirmation and 24-hour notice.

Credit cards: MasterCard, Visa.

Directions: from Interstate 35, take exit #233 (Riverside Drive) and go east 4 blocks to Lakeshore Boulevard (a forked "Y" intersection), go 4 blocks to hostel in International Shores Park on south shore of Town Lake. **Bus:** take bus #26 or #27 from downtown (bus #7 from Greyhound station) to Riverside Drive and Tinnin Ford Road, walk 4 blocks north to hostel. **Train:** take taxi from Amtrak station.

Texas

El Paso

El Paso International AYH-Hostel

Located in the historic Gardner Hotel, the El Paso International AYH-Hostel is just a mile across the river from Juarez, Mexico, and provides long-term storage for those embarking on a southern journey. The hostel staff can provide information on Mexico and the local area.

El Paso's cultural heritage is a mix of Spanish, Indian, and American cowboy. Visit the Fort Bliss Replica Museum or stroll through downtown to see the colorful remains of El Paso's Wild West history. Outside of El Paso, visit Hueco Tanks State Historical Park for rock climbing and Indian pictographs. Carlsbad Caverns (New Mexico) and Guadalupe Mountains National Park are within easy driving distance.

311 East Franklin Avenue,
El Paso, TX 79901.
Mail (✉): same.
Phone (☎): 915-532-3661.
Price (●): $12 U.S.
Closed (X): never.
Office Hours: 24 hours.
Beds (⊨): 40. **Grade:** Hostel.
Facilities: private rooms, equipment storage area, information desk, kitchen, laundry facilities, linen rental, lockers/baggage storage,no chores, no curfew, **MSA**.
Private rooms: available.
Groups (⏅): welcome.
Reservations advisable (☎): always. **By phone:** accepted with credit card confirmation (1 day charge, no refunds).
Credit cards: MasterCard, Visa, JCB.

Manager: Joe Nebhan.
Directions: downtown, 1 mile from Juarez, Mexico. **Airport (✈):** take bus #33 to Plaza Park, walk 1 block north to Franklin.

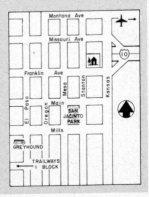

Texas

Friendswood (Houston/NASA)

Hostelling International–Space City AYH-Hostel

The hostel is just next door to the Space Center Houston/NASA (experience life in outer space!), Galveston Island (see one of America's greatest wildlife reserves and visit historical homes/shops), and Houston (a big city of international festivals and landmarks). Enjoy Astroworld, IMAX, Hermann Zoo, Burke Planetarium, four museums, and more. The hostel is warm, congenial, spacious, and lovely. Kind volunteers offer group tours of the city and neighboring towns.

2242 West Bay Area Blvd.
Friendswood, TX 77546
Mail (✉): same.
Phone (☎): 713-996-0323 or 713-482-9831.
Price (☻): $10.25 U.S.
Closed (X): never.
Office Hours: 7 a.m.–11 p.m.
Grade: Hostel.
Beds (🛏): 18.
Facilities: parking, tour guide, picnic/wooded area, kitchen, laundry, video/TV/stereo, indoor/outdoor games, lockers, storage area, linens, information desk, **MSA.**
Reservations: not essential.
Credit cards: MasterCard, Visa.
Managers: Carmen and Paul Eisler.
Directions: Airport (✈): from Intercontinental Airport–Houston, connect with Continental Airlines to Ellington AFB (other local airlines connect with Hobby Airport). **Bus:**
from IAH, bus 102 to downtown Milam Street, then Park & Ride 246 or 245 ($1.20–$2.90 one way) to Bay Area Park & Ride Station; call for pick-up. **Train:** Bus 40 to Milan Street, then Park & Ride 246 or 245 (same as above). **Greyhound Station:** Go to Milam Street, then Park & Ride 246 or 245 (same as above).

Texas

Houston

Houston International AYH-Hostel

A large house with a shaded front porch, the hostel is the perfect base for exploring NASA's Lyndon B. Johnson Space Center, the Astrodome, and other area attractions. Located in the Museum District, the hostel is just one-half mile from four museums, including the Menil and the Museum of Fine Arts. Free concerts and other performances occur all summer. Hermann Park, four blocks from the hostel, is the site of the Houston Museum of Natural Science, Burke Baker Planetarium, IMAX Theater, and the Houston Zoo.

5302 Crawford, Houston, TX 77004.
Mail (✉): same.
Phone (☎): 713-523-1009.
Price (●): $10.25 U.S.
Closed (X): never
Office Hours: 7–10 a.m., 5–11 p.m.
Grade: Hostel.
Beds (🛏): 30.
Facilities: veranda, gazebo, courtyard, piano, organ, bicycles, stereo, TV, equipment storage area, kitchen, laundry facilities, linen rental, lockers/baggage storage, on-site parking, **MSA**.
Family rooms (👪): available.
Groups (🎪): welcome.
Reservations advisable (✉a): always. **By phone:** accepted with 18-hour notice.
Credit cards: JCB.
Managers: Dawn Boone, Joy Boone.

Directions: U.S. Highway 59 to TX Highway 288 South, take Southmore exit then right 4 blocks to Crawford, then left. **Bus, train:** from Trailways bus station or Amtrak station, go to Main Street and take city bus #2, #4, #8, or #9 southbound on Main Street to Southmore, walk 6 blocks east to Crawford, 1 block south. **Airport (✈):** take airport shuttle to downtown Hyatt, then same as above, or Metro city bus (limited service 635-4000).

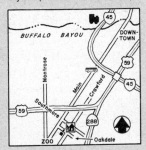

Texas

San Antonio

San Antonio International AYH-Hostel

The San Antonio International AYH-Hostel is a comfortable, ranch-style building with a swimming pool and day-accessible common area. Adjacent to historic Bullis House and Fort Sam Houston Military Reservation and Museums, the hostel provides a perfect base for exploring scenic San Antonio. The Alamo, where Davy Crockett and other heroes of the Texas Revolution died, is the city's best-known attraction. Stroll along the romantic River Walk with its outdoor cafes, boutiques, water taxis, and night life. Visit the historic Spanish Missions and Sea World Marine Park, or enjoy the rides, music, and entertainment at Fiesta Texas Theme Park.

621 Pierce Street.
Mail (✉): P.O. Box 8059, San Antonio, TX 78208.
Phone (☎): 210-223-9426.
Price (●): $12.62 U.S. + tax.
Closed (X): never.
Office Hours: 7:30 a.m.–11 p.m.
Grade: Hostel.
Beds (🛏): 38.
Facilities: swimming pool, information desk, kitchen, linen rental, lockers/baggage storage, on-site parking, **MSA**.
Meals (🍴): breakfast $4.
Family rooms (👪): available.
Groups (🛏🛏): welcome; reservations required.
Reservations advisable (📅): July–September. **By phone:** accepted with credit card confirmation. **By FAX:** 210-299-1479 with credit card confirmation.
Credit cards: MasterCard, Visa.

Managers: Alma and Steve Cross.
Directions: 2 miles north of downtown off Interstate 35. **Airport (✈):** take super van to hostel or airport express bus to downtown. **Bus:** take bus #11 or #15 from Navarro Street downtown. **Train:** take bus #516 from Hackberry to Grayson.

FOR $14 YOU CAN STAY HERE. OR GET YOUR SHOES SHINED AT THE HOTEL DOWN THE STREET.

The Santa Monica International AYH-Hostel offers a clean, comfortable place to spend the night in Southern California. Plus the opportunity to meet and share experiences with travelers from all over the world. And while you may have to do without a few of life's little luxuries, at this price we don't think you'll miss them. For reservations or more information, call (310) 393-9913.

Vermont

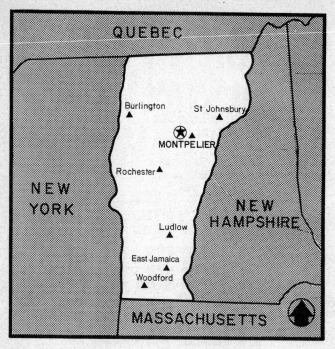

Helpful Organizations

AYH Council Office

Yankee Council
118 Oak Street
Hartford, CT 06106
Phone (☎): 203-247-6356

State Tourism Office

Vermont Travel Division
134 State Street
Montpelier, VT 05602
Phone (☎): 802-828-3236

Discounts

Present a valid hostel membership card at the time of purchase to receive the following discounts:

Ludlow

Trojan Horse AYH-Hostel - $1 off for groups of 10–14, $2 off for groups of 15–18. From November 1 to December 20 and during March there is a $2 discount for all groups.

Vermont

Burlington
Mrs. Farrell's Home Hostel

Nancy Farrell welcomes hostellers to her cozy home in Burlington, Vermont's largest city. Situated on the shore of Lake Champlain, Burlington boasts five universities and colleges and a thriving artistic community. The city's historic district features structures dating back to the 1700s. Enjoy the Reggae Festival, Vermont Mozart Festival, Festival of Fine Arts, and the Discover Jazz Festival. Skating, bicycle, canoe, sail boat, and surfboard rentals are nearby. Beaches are one mile away.

Call for reservations.
Phone (☎): 802-865-3730.
Price (◒): $15 U.S.
Grade: home hostel (🏠).
Beds (▬): 6.
Facilities: equipment storage area, kitchen, linen rental, on-site parking, **MSA**.
Reservations essential (⚓e): always. **By phone:** accepted with 24-hour notice; call before 8 p.m.

Credit cards: not accepted.
Manager: Nancy Farrell.
Directions: available upon reservation confirmation.
Note: In warm months one room is available to travelers in wheelchairs.

Vermont

East Jamaica

Vagabond AYH-Hostel

Managers Joe and Pat Miramontes have converted part of their ski lodge into a hostel. Located 25 miles north of Brattleboro, the hostel provides a large game room with three pool tables, TV, and a volleyball court. Breakfast and dinner can be arranged for groups of 20 or more. Boating and nature trails are available at Jamaica State Park and Townsend State Park. Visit the longest covered bridge in the state and Bromley Alpine Slide nearby.

Vermont Route 30, Box 224,
East Jamaica, VT 05343.
Mail (✉): same.
Phone (☎): 802-874-4096.
Price (💰): $12 U.S. + tax.
Closed (X): November 16–May 14.
Office Hours: 9 a.m.–9 p.m.
Grade: Hostel.
Beds (🛏): 20.
Facilities: game room, TV, kitchen, linen rental, on-site parking, showers, **MSA**.
Family rooms (👪): available.
Groups (🎏): welcome.
Meals (🍴): can be arranged for groups of 20 or more.
Reservations advisable (📞a): always. **By phone:** accepted with credit card confirmation and 24-hour notice.

Credit cards: MasterCard, Visa.
Directions: 25 miles north on Vermont Route 30 from Brattleboro, hostel is on the right.

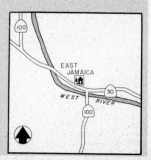

Vermont

Ludlow

Trojan Horse AYH-Hostel

Ludlow is in the Black River Valley of Vermont's scenic Green Mountains. After a day of skiing or exploring, relax by the wood stove at the Trojan Horse AYH-Hostel. The century-old carriage barn is furnished with bunk beds (six to a room), common baths, and a kitchenette. The hostel is close to Okemo Mountain Ski Area and within 25 miles of nine other ski areas, including Killington and Stratton Mountain. Cross-country ski trails radiate out from Ludlow. Cycle or hike in Green Mountain National Park. Canoe or swim in cool mountain streams and lakes; canoe rentals are available at the hostel. In early October, enjoy the brilliant colors of Vermont's famous fall foliage. Visit the birthplace of President Calvin Coolidge in nearby Plymouth.

Vermont Highway 100 South.
Mail (✉): 44 Andover Street, Ludlow, VT 05149.
Phone (☎): 802-228-5244.
Price (●): $10 U.S. + tax (May–November), $18 U.S. + tax (December–March).
Closed (X): April.
Office Hours: 8–10 a.m., 5–9 p.m.
Beds (🛏): 18. **Grade:** Hostel.
Facilities: canoe rentals, information desk, kitchen, linen rental, on-site parking, **MSA.**
Family rooms (👪): available; reservations required.
Groups (🏠): welcome; reservations required.
Reservations essential (📞●): December–March. **By phone:** accepted.

Credit cards: MasterCard, Visa.
Manager: Rich Gray.
Directions: 1/3 mile south of the village of Ludlow on Vermont Highway 100.

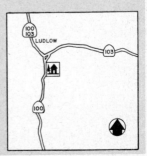

Vermont

HOME HOSTEL

Montpelier
Capitol Home Hostel

Situated on a hill, the hostel is Montpelier's first chalet, built in 1967. The historic state capitol is topped by a 14-karat gold-leaf dome and a statue of the goddess of agriculture. Vermont College hosts the T.W. Wood Art Gallery. Stop by the Morse Farm, a working maple syrup farm, and fruit and vegetable stands for a tour and samples. On another hill is a 100-acre park with views of the largest granite quarries in the world, the surrounding mountains, and the Long Trail.

Call for reservations.
Mail (✉): R.D. 1, Box 2750, Montpelier, VT 05602; include self-addressed stamped reply envelope.
Phone (☎): 802-223-2104, 802-223-2240; no calls after 9 p.m.
Price (💲): $10 U.S.
Closed (X): never.
Grade: home hostel (🏠).
Beds (🛏): 2.

Facilities: equipment storage, kitchen, linen rental, on-site parking.
Family rooms (👪): available.
Reservations essential (📞): always. **By phone:** accepted.
Credit cards: not accepted.
Directions: available upon reservation confirmation.

AYH DISCOVERY TOURS

AMERICAN YOUTH HOSTELS

Scheduled to open in 1993. . .

Schoolhouse AYH-Hostel
Rochester, VT

A former church, the hostel still shows much of its history with original stained glass windows and church pews. The setting on the eastern edge of Green Mountain National Forest is beautiful.

Rochester is the perfect location to enjoy almost any recreational activity, including mountain biking, hiking, and excellent alpine and cross-country skiing. Vermont Highway 100, a designated scenic highway, is wonderful for cycling.

Directions: from Interstate 89 (northbound) take exit #3 to Vermont Highway 107, north on Vermont Highway 100, (southbound) take exit #10, then Vermont Highway 100. From Interstate 87 (northbound) take exit #24 to Northway, take exit #20 to Vermont Highway 149, go east to Vermont Highway 4, go east to Vermont Highway 100.

For reservations, call:
Phone (☎): 617-731-6692

Vermont

HOME HOSTEL

St. Johnsbury
Sleeper's River Home Hostel

Pamela and Richard Smith welcome you to their 19th-century home. It is situated among flower, herb, fruit, and vegetable gardens along the Sleeper's River. The Athenaeum holds the oldest unaltered Victorian Art gallery in the USA. The elegant Fairbanks Museum features a planetarium and the finest natural history display in Northern New England. The Maple Grove Museum and Factory offers tours.

Call for reservations.
Mail (✉): same.
Phone (☎): 802-748-1575.
Price (●): $10 U.S.
Closed (X): December 23–31.
Grade: home hostel (🏠).
Beds (🛏): 6.
Facilities: equipment storage, information desk, kitchen, linen rental, on-site parking, **MSA**; smoke-free environment, no sleeping bags.

Family rooms (👪): available.
Groups (👥): welcome.
Reservations essential (📞): always. **By phone:** accepted 8 a.m. to 9 p.m.
Credit cards: not accepted.
Managers: Pamela and Richard Smith.
Directions: available upon reservation confirmation.

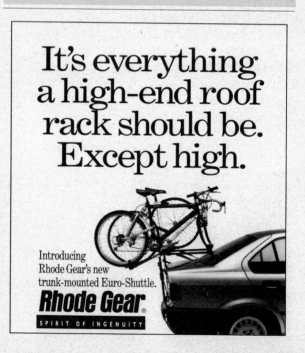

Vermont

Woodford
Greenwood Lodge

Swim, fish, boat, canoe, bike, and hike on 120 scenic acres, three miles from the Appalachian Trail. Cross-country ski at adjacent Prospect Mountain or alpine ski at Mount Snow, 23 miles away. Bennington, Vermont's first chartered town, is full of history.

Vermont Highway 9.
Mail (✉): P.O. Box 246, Bennington, VT 05201.
Phone (☎): 802-442-2547.
Price (●): $13 U.S. + tax, May 15–October 18.
Closed (X): October 19–May 14 for individuals.
Office Hours: 8–10 a.m., 5–10 p.m.
Beds (⊨): 40. **Grade: (SA)**.
Facilities (mixed use): piano, camping, game room, equipment storage area, kitchen, linen rental, on-site parking, clean sleeping bags allowed, **MSA**.

Meals (⚒): groups only.
Family rooms (⌂): available.
Groups (⊞): welcome.
Reservations advisable (⌂a): always. **By phone:** accepted.
Credit cards: not accepted.
Managers: Ann and Ed Shea.
Directions: 8 miles east of Bennington off Vermont Highway 9, entrance at Prospect Ski Mountain sign, go through parking lot, pass between logs, make immediate left turn, continue 1,000 feet to lodge.

Virginia

Helpful Organizations

AYH Council Office

Potomac Area Council
7420 Baltimore Avenue
College Park, MD 20740
Phone (☎): 301-209-8544

State Tourism Office

Virginia Division of Tourism
James Center
1021 East Cary Street
Richmond, VA 23219
Phone (☎): 800-VISITVA,
804-786-4484

Virginia

Bluemont

Bear's Den AYH-Hostel

Spend the night in this beautiful stone lodge in the Blue Ridge Mountains overlooking the Shenandoah River. Hike the Appalachian National Scenic Trail, just 150 yards away, or cycle the W&OD Trail, nine miles east. Self-guided interpretive trail walks are available from the hostel.

For rafting, canoeing, swimming, and fishing, head for the Shenandoah River, three miles west. Nearby Harpers Ferry, former site of the federal armory and arsenal and target of John Brown's infamous raid in 1859, offers guided tours and living history programs.

Spectacular panoramic views can be found along Skyline Drive in Shenandoah National Park, 35 miles southwest. Back at the hostel, enjoy gorgeous sunsets at Bear's Den Rock.

Virginia Highway 601.
Mail (✉): R.R. 1, Box 288, Bluemont, VA 22012.
Phone (☎): 703-554-8708.
Price (⬤): $9.
Closed (X): December 24–January 7.
Office Hours: 5–9 p.m.
Grade: Hostel.
Beds (⊨): 20.
Facilities: kitchen, interpretive information, laundry facilities, linen rental, on-site parking, **MSA**.
Family rooms (⌂): available.
Groups (⫫): welcome; reservations required.
Reservations advisable (⌂a): spring and fall weekends. **By phone:** accepted; call ahead for morning assistance.

Credit cards: not accepted.
Manager: John Vassar.
Directions: 1/2 mile south of Virginia Highway 7 on Virginia Highway 601, first driveway on the right, follow signs for 1/2 mile.

Virginia

Galax

Blue Ridge Country AYH-Hostel

Just minutes away from the Blue Ridge Parkway, the Blue Ridge Country AYH-Hostel provides a spectacular view and a variety of recreation and fun. Canoe, raft, or tube down the scenic New River. Try your hand at square dancing or "clogging" at the hostel's activity barn.

Bike along the beautiful parkway and through Virginia's winding backroads. Hike the Gully Creek Trail, go trout fishing, or just enjoy the view from the hostel deck. Don't miss hearing old-time mountain music every first and third Saturday of the month. In the summer, pick strawberries, blueberries, and peaches at nearby farms. Local celebrations include the Syrup Making Festival in March, The Ramp Festival in May, and the White Mountain Molasses Festival in the fall.

Blue Ridge Parkway.
Mail (✉): R.R. 2, Box 449, Galax, VA 24333.
Phone (☎): 703-236-4962.
Price (●): $10 U.S. + tax
Closed (X): never.
Office Hours: 5–8 p.m. (morning check-in by advance reservation only).
Beds (🛏): 22. **Grade:** Hostel.
Facilities: music room, piano, kitchen, linen rental, on-site parking, **MSA**, smoke-free environment.
Family rooms (👪): available.
Groups (🏛): welcome.
By phone: accepted, 7–9 a.m.
Credit cards: not accepted.
Managers: Alex and Lois Koji.

Directions: 7 miles south of Galax on Virginia Highway 89, north approximately 1 mile on Blue Ridge Parkway, halfway between mileposts 214 and 215 on right side, look for gray iron pipe gate and paved driveway; call for additional directions if arriving after dark.

Virginia

Urbanna

Sangraal By-The-Sea AYH-Hostel

Located on the Chesapeake Bay, this hostel offers visitors a friendly, rural setting on 18 acres of private land. Gain a better understanding of Chesapeake Bay and its wildlife by attending one of the hostel's environmental education programs. Take a walk down the nature trails that wind through the area near streams and bubbling springs.

For great fishing and crabbing, head for the nearby pier. Canoes and sailboats are available and are perfect for exploring the Bay. Take a day trip to historic Williamsburg, just 30 miles away, and experience life in colonial America amid an array of homes, shops, gardens, and taverns.

Mill Creek Landing Road, Wake, VA.
Mail (✉): P.O. Box 187, Urbanna, VA 23175.
Phone (☎): (804)776-6500.
Price (☉): $12 U.S. + tax.
Closed (X): never.
Office Hours: 5–10 p.m.
Grade: Hostel.
Beds (🛏): 40.
Facilities: equipment storage area, kitchen, information desk, laundry facilities, linen rental, lockers/baggage storage, on-site parking, wheelchair accessible (&), **MSA**.
Meals (🍴): breakfast, lunch, dinner.
Family rooms (👪): 3 cottages.
Groups (🏛): welcome; reservations required.
Reservations advisable (📅): May–September. **By phone:** accepted.
Credit cards: not accepted.
Managers: Linda Kay and William Wade Douglas.

Directions: take Virginia Route 33 east from Saluda 10 miles to Farm Road 626 and follow the signs to the hostel.

Virginia

Virginia Beach
Angie's Guest Cottage, Bed and Breakfast and AYH-Hostel

Just one block from the beach, with lots of activities and no curfew, Angie's Guest Cottage is a great summertime retreat. Enjoy swimming and sailing. Biking and hiking trails are nearby at Seashore State Park.

302 24th Street,
Virginia Beach, VA. 23451.
Mail (✉): same.
Phone (☎): 804-428-4690.
Price (◐): $7.55 U.S. + tax (April 1–May 20), September 6–30); $10.50 U.S. + tax (May 21–September 5).
Closed (X): October–March; open late March and early October with advance booking.
Office Hours: 10 a.m.–9 p.m.
Grade: (SA).
Beds (⊨): 42.
Facilities: bungalow-style beach house, barbecue and picnic area, camping area, exchange library, information desk, kitchen, laundry facilities, linen rental, lockers/baggage storage, **MSA**; private rooms available in guesthouse.
Groups (⊞): welcome; 2-night minimum stay.
Reservations advisable (☎a): June–September. **By phone:** accepted with credit card confirmation.
Credit cards: accepted (reservations only).
Manager: Barbara Yates.
Directions: east of Interstate 64 on Virginia Highway 44 to oceanfront area (25-cent toll), north on Arctic Avenue 3 blocks to 24th Street, east to top of block; call for pick-up from train and bus stations. Free on-street parking with permit ($20 refundable deposit).

Washington

Helpful Organizations

AYH Council Office

Washington State Council
419 Queen Anne Avenue North
#101
Seattle, WA 98109
Phone (☎): 206-281-7306

State Tourism Office

Washington Tourism Division
101 General Administration Bldg.
Olympia, WA 98504
Phone (☎): 206-586-2088

Discounts

Present a valid hostel membership card at the time of purchase to receive the following discounts:

Bellevue
Pioneer Maps - 10% discount on all purchases - 1645 140th Street, 206-746-3200.

Chinook
Bikes & Beyond - 10% off any goods in the store except bikes with IYHF membership card - 1335 Marine Drive, Astoria, OR, 503-325-2961.
The Community Store - 5% discount given on all discountable purchases (milk, eggs, cheese, and a few other items excluded from discount). Must have IYHF membership card. 10% discount for two hours of volunteer work in store every week. 1389 Duane St., Astoria, OR, 503-325-0027.

Discounts

Port Townsend

Guided Historical Sidewalk Tours - 25% off daily tours at 10 a.m. and 2 p.m. leaving from museum at Water and Madison Streets. 820 Tyler Street (mailing address), 206-385-1967.

Kayak Port Townsend - $5.00 off any day sea kayak wildlife tour. P.O. Box 1387, 206-385-6240.

Port Townsend Cyclery - 10% discount on rentals. 215 Taylor, 206-385-6470.

Sea Sport Charters - 10% discount for all IYHF members. P.O. Box 805, 206-385-3575.

Sport Townsend - 10% discount on outdoor equipment or books (does not apply to sale items) - 1044 Water Street, 206-379-9711.

Poulsbo

Olympic Outdoor Center - 10% discount off regular rafting and kayaking prices (not to be used in conjunction with any other special offers). No monetary returns are provided. 26469 Circle Northwest, 800-659-6095.

Seattle

Angle Lake Cyclery - 10% discount on all bicycle parts and accessories - 20840 Pacific Highway South, 206-878-7457.

AYH Travel Store - 10% discount on most travel books and related merchandise - 419 Queen Anne Avenue North, #101, 206-281-7306.

Center for Wooden Boats - 25% on use of museum boats and sailing instruction; free admission to museum - 1010 Valley Street, 206-382-2628.

Empty Space Theatre - half price on day-of-show tickets (1 ticket per membership card; not valid with other discounts; no phone reservations; subject to availability) - 107 Occidental Avenue South, 206-467-6000.

Grayline Water Sightseeing - Cruise from the waterfront through the locks into the freshwater Lake Union. 2-for-1 tickets for IYHF members. Pier 57 on the Seattle waterfront, 206-623-4252.

Kingdome Tour - 2-for-1 admission on the 11 a.m., 1 p.m., and 3 p.m. tours (this discount does not apply to children and senior citizen prices; proof of membership required). 201 King Street, 206-296-3128.

The Language School - 10% discount on tuition for foreign language classes - 909 Fourth Avenue, 206-682-6985.

Metsker Maps of Seattle - 10% discount on all purchases - 702 First Avenue, 206-623-8747.

Museum of Flight - $3 per person admission with a valid IYHF membership card - 9404 East Marginal Way South, 206-764-5720.

Museum of History and Industry - 1/3 off admission. Must show membership card. 2700 24th Avenue East, 206-324-1126.

Nordic Heritage Museum - 50% discount on admission with valid IYHF membership card - 3014 Northwest Market Street, 206-789-5707.

Pacific Science Center - $1.00 off admission to all exhibits and an IMAX film. Offer good Jan 4, 1993 through Dec 25, 1993. $1.00 off evening Laser Fantasy Shows. IYHF membership card must be shown. Near the Space Needle in Seattle Center, 206-443-2001.

R & E Cycles/Second Gear - 10% discount on bicycle rental rates and non-sale items, 5627 University Way Northeast, 206-527-4822.

Scenic Bound Tours - 10% discount on tours for all IYHF members. P.O. Box 58081, 206-443-6907.

Seattle Harbor Tours - Cruise the Seattle Harbor on either a one hour narrated tour (departs from Pier 55 on the waterfront) with 2-for-1 tickets or through the locks into Lake Union (departs from Pier 57) with 2-for-1 tickets. Must show IYHF membership. 206-623-1445 or 4252.

Shorey Book Store - 20% off any used books with valid IYHF membership card - 1411 First Avenue North, 206-624-0021.

Discounts

Seattle (continued)

Space Needle Corporation - $1 off Space Needle Observation Deck coupon available when a valid IYHF membership card is presented at the Seattle International AYH-Hostel. Coupon valid every day year-round before 11 a.m. in 1993. If You See Only One Thing In Seattle, See Everything: The Space Needle - Space Center, 206-443-2111.

Tillicum Village and Tours - Special discount (total cost $25.50) on tour from Seattle Harbor to Blake Island Marine State Park (includes salmon dinner and Indian cultural heritage program); reservations required October–May and recommended June–September (proof of IYHF membership required), 206-443-1244 for reservations and sailing times.

Unexpected Productions - 50% off any ticket for an Unexpected Productions performance with valid IYHF membership card - 1428 Post Alley, 206-781-9273.

Wide World Books and Maps - 10% discount on all "Let's Go" and "Lonely Planet" books. Must show valid IYHF membership. 1911 North 45th Street., 206-634-3453.

Tacoma

Metsker Maps of Tacoma - 10% discount on all purchases - 6249 Tacoma Mall Boulevard, 206-474-6277.

Washington

Bellingham

Fairhaven Rose Garden AYH-Hostel

The appropriately named Fairhaven Rose Garden AYH-Hostel is surrounded by dozens of rose bushes. The hostel borders Chuckanut Drive, which offers stunning views of Puget Sound, and is minutes from the historic Fairhaven District, where shops and cafes abound.

Just outside Bellingham harbor lie some of the 172 San Juan Islands created by glaciers. The islands, reachable by ferry, are big playgrounds for hikers, cyclists, swimmers, scuba divers, fishermen, and boaters. Orcas and San Juan Islands are two of the favorites. Western Washington University and the southern terminal of the popular Alaska State Ferry are located within walking distance of the hostel. Larrabee State Park, Mt. Baker, and the North Cascades National Park are close by.

Fairhaven Park
107 Chuckanut Drive,
Bellingham, WA 98225-8934.
Mail (✉): same.
Phone (☎): 206-671-1750.
Price (💲): $8.50 U.S.
Closed (X): December 19–January 8. November–February (except by reservation).
Office Hours: 7:30–9:30 a.m., 5–10 p.m.
Beds (🛏): 14. **Grade:** Hostel.
Facilities: kitchen, laundry facilities, linen rental, sleeping bags allowed, on-site parking, **MSA**.
Groups (🍴): reservations required.
Reservations essential (🔑): November–February. **Reservations advisable (🔑):** April–October. **By phone:** accepted.
Credit cards: MasterCard, Visa.
Managers: Daron Songer and Martha Tierney.

Directions: take exit #250 off Interstate 5, west on Old Fairhaven Parkway to set of lights, turn left (12th) over bridge, go left onto Chuckanut Drive to park. Or north on Chuckanut Drive to hostel north of Fairhaven Park entrance.
Greyhound Bus: walk one block south and one block west to terminal for local bus. Take bus 1B to Fairhaven Rose Garden.

Washington

Blaine

Birch Bay AYH-Hostel

The Birch Bay AYH-Hostel, located in Bay Horizon County Park, is six miles from the Canadian border and only 30 miles from Vancouver, B.C. The nearby Peace Arch State and Provincial Park is home to Peace Arch festivities.

First settled in the 1850s, Blaine is a fishing port and dairy farming region. Go hiking and skiing on the slopes of Mount Baker and spend sunny days swimming, fishing, boating, hiking, and picnicking in the million-plus acres of Mount Baker National Forest. Cycle on the flat terrain in the shadow of the Cascades, beachcomb for agates, watch for whales, swim, and windsurf on the beaches of Puget Sound.

4639 Alderson Road, #630, Blaine, WA 98230-9674.

Mail (✉): same.

Phone (☎): 206-371-2180.

Price (💰): $8.50 U.S.

Closed (X): November–March.

Office Hours: 7:30–9:30 a.m., 5–10 p.m.

Beds (🛏): 45. **Grade:** Hostel.

Facilities: equipment storage area, kitchen, laundry facilities, linen rental, on-site parking, **MSA**.

Family rooms (👪): available.

Groups (🏠): welcome.

Reservations: not essential. **By phone:** accepted.

Credit cards: MasterCard, Visa.

Directions: take Interstate 5 south to exit #270 (Birch Bay-Lynden Road), west (right) 3-1/2 miles on Birch Bay-Linden Road, south (left) approximately 1 mile on Blaine Road, west (right) 1/2 mile on Alderson Road to Bay Horizon Park; take Interstate 5 north to exit #266 (Grandview Road), west (left) 6 miles on Grandview, north (right) approximately 2 miles on Blaine Road, west (left) 1/2 mile on Alderson Road to entrance.

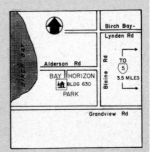

Washington

Chinook

Fort Columbia AYH-Hostel

The Fort Columbia AYH-Hostel sits atop a hill overlooking the Columbia River in Fort Columbia State Park. During the Spanish-American War the building was a military hospital. Relive those historic days by visiting the park's museum. Tour the officers' quarters, searchlight stations, and bunkers.

Go south through the woods and over the river to the Columbia River Maritime Museum and Victorian Captain Flavel House in Astoria, Oregon. Back in Washington, visit the Fort Canby State Park Lewis and Clark Museum and learn about the explorers' incredible 8,000-mile trek. A short bike ride or drive away is the Long Beach Peninsula, a great place to fish or bird and whale watch. The peninsula hosts summer festivals for kite flyers, garlic and cranberry lovers, and seafood connoisseurs.

Fort Columbia State Park.

Mail (✉): P.O. Box 224, Chinook, WA 98614-0224.

Phone (☎): 206-777-8755.

Price (●): $8.50 U.S.

Closed (X): December–February. October–November and March–April (except by reservation).

Office Hours: 7:30–9:30 a.m., 5–10 p.m.

Beds (🛏): 21 **Grade:** Hostel.

Facilities: equipment storage area, kitchen, laundry facilities, linen rental (sleeping bags allowed), on-site parking, **MSA.**

Family rooms (👪): 1 available.

Groups (🏠): welcome.

Reservations essential (☎): October–November and March–April. **By phone:** accepted.

Credit cards: MasterCard, Visa.

Managers: Tim Tierney and Tracy Rattelman.

Directions: 1 mile southeast of Chinook on U.S. Highway 101 in Fort Columbia State Park, 3 miles from Columbia River Bridge. Hostel on Pacific County Bus route.

Washington

Fort Flagler State Park (Nordland)

Fort Flagler AYH-Hostel

The Fort Flagler AYH-Hostel is located on the tip of Marrowstone Island in Fort Flagler State Park, near Port Townsend. This hostel is ideal for those who wish to get off the beaten track. With 800 acres of forest and seven miles of pristine beaches, the park is a wonderful place to enjoy hiking, biking, clamming, sea kayaking, and fishing. For history buffs, there are century-old gun emplacements, fort buildings, and a 19th-century lighthouse.

Enjoy a fantastic view of the Cascade Range from Mount Baker to Mount Rainier and the shipping lanes of Admiralty Inlet in Puget Sound. Olympic National Park is only an hour's drive away.

Fort Flagler State Park,
7850 Flager Rd., #17.
Nordland, WA 98358-9699.
Mail (✉): same.
Phone (☎): 206-385-1288.
Price (💲): $8.50 U.S.
Closed (X): December–February. October–November and March–April (except by reservation).
Office Hours: 7:30–9:30 a.m., 5–10 p.m.
Beds (🛏): 15. **Grade:** Hostel.
Facilities: large common room with Franklin wood stove, equipment storage area, information desk, kitchen, linen rental (sleeping bags allowed), on-site parking, **MSA.**
Family rooms (👪): limited availability; reservations required.
Groups (🛏🛏): reservations required.
Reservations essential (☎e): October–November and March–April.
Reservations advisable (☎a): May–September. **By phone:** accepted.
Credit cards: MasterCard, Visa.
Manager: Debbie Irwin.

Directions: from Seattle, take Winslow, Bremerton or Kingston ferry, follow signs to Hood Canal Bridge. Take highway 104W 5 miles, turn right on highway 19N, then right at light on Chimicum Rd. Next light turn right on Oak Bay Rd., follow 116E into park. From Olympia, take U.S. 101N to Quilcene, go right on Center Rd. toward Indian Island, turn right on Oak Bay Rd., follow 116E into park. From Port Angeles/Port Townsend, take highway 20 to highway 19S, go 3 miles, turn left on 116E, follow into park.

Washington

Port Townsend

Port Townsend AYH-Hostel

Enjoy a small, friendly hostel that is open all day on the famous Olympic Peninsula. Nestled into a hillside overlooking the Strait of Juan de Fuca, the Port Townsend AYH-Hostel offers the best of two worlds. In Fort Worden State Park (the setting for the movie "An Officer and a Gentleman"), hostellers enjoy hiking or biking the scenic trails, strolling the beaches, or marvelling at the creatures in the Marine Science Center. Whether kayaking, kite flying, or just relaxing under a tree, this 400-acre state park is a wonderful recreation destination.

In Port Townsend, guests enjoy the many beautiful Victorian homes, the bustling and picturesque main street, and the inviting eateries. Visit the county museum, take a guided tour of the historic homes, or try a guided kayak tour of the waterfront. Whatever your taste, this culturally hopping small town is sure to please.

Fort Worden State Park,
Port Townsend, WA 98368-3699.
Mail (✉): 272 Battery Way.
Phone (☎) 206-385-0655
Price (●): $8.50 U.S.
Closed (X): December 13–January 2.
November–February (except by reservation).
Office Hours: 7:30–9:30 a.m., 5–10 p.m.
Beds (🛏): 30. **Grade:** Hostel.
Facilities: information desk, kitchen, linen rental (sleeping bags allowed), **MSA**.
Family rooms (👪): available.
Groups (🏠): welcome.
Reservations essential (📞●): November–February.
Reservations advisable (📞a): May–September. **By phone:** accepted.
Credit cards: MasterCard, Visa.

Managers: Jennifer Whitney and Brent Vadopalas.
Directions: 2 miles northwest of downtown, follow signs to state park.

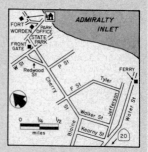

Washington

Seattle (International)

Seattle International AYH-Hostel

A former U.S. immigration station, the Seattle International AYH-Hostel still welcomes visitors from around the world. The new Seattle Art Museum and the Pike Place Market—full of farmers' stalls, eateries and shops—are both only a block away.

Walk down the waterfront and take a scenic ride on a Washington State Ferry, or stroll into Myrtle Edwards Park for a panoramic view of the Olympic Mountains across Puget Sound. The Space Needle, historic Pioneer Square, and the Pacific Science Center are all within easy walking distance.

84 Union St., Seattle, WA 98101.
Mail (✉): same.
Phone (☎): 206-622-5443.
Price (⊖): $14 U.S. + tax; full membership required, June–September.
Closed (X): never.
Office Hours: 7 a.m.–2 a.m.
Grade: Hostel.
Beds (🛏): 125.
Facilities: equipment storage area, information desk, kitchen, laundry facilities, linen rental, lockers/baggage storage, wheelchair accessible (♿), **MSA**.
Family rooms (👪): available (additional charge).
Groups (🏨): welcome; reservations required.
Reservations advisable (📅): June–September. **By phone:** accepted with credit card confirmation and 24-hour notice. IBN global reservation system available.
Credit cards: MasterCard, Visa, JCB.
Managers: Louise Kipping, Sean Woods, Buzz Schwall.

Directions: downtown at Union Street and Western Avenue. **Airport (✈):** take bus #194 or #174 marked "Downtown Seattle." If bus runs in tunnel, get off at University Station, turn right on Second Avenue, walk 1/2 block to Union Street, turn left and walk to First Avenue. (If bus runs on Third or Fourth Avenue, get off at Union Street.) Walk to First Avenue and look for steps at far corner of First Avenue and Union Street; hostel is at the bottom of the steps.

Washington

Seattle (Vashon Island)

Vashon Island AYH-Hostel

The Vashon Island AYH-Hostel offers a quick getaway from the city in a one-of-a-kind setting. Just a short ferry ride from Pier 50 at the Seattle waterfront will take visitors to this bicycling paradise. The hostel's hand-hewn log cabin is made from Douglas firs that grew on the 10-acre property surrounding the facility. The five Indian Sioux tipis offer couple and family rooms. Otherwise, sleep in the cozy covered wagons which surround a campfire. Be sure to get up early for free mouth-watering pancakes made from an old family recipe, then enjoy beautiful, rural Vashon by bicycles provided free at the hostel.

12119 SW Cove Road,
Vashon Island, WA 98070.
Mail (✉): same.
Phone (☎): 206-463-2592.
Price (⬤): $8 U.S.
Closed (X): November–April.
Office Hours: noon–10 p.m.
Beds (⊨): 36. **Grade:** Hostel.
Facilities: equipment storage, kitchen, linen rental, lockers/baggage storage, free bicycles, on-site parking, **MSA**.
Meals (🍴): free breakfast.
Family rooms (👪): available.
Groups (🏠): welcome; reservations required.
Reservations advisable (✍): always. **By phone:** accepted.
Credit cards: MasterCard, Visa.
Managers: Gwen Duckworth, Judy Mulhair.
Directions: from Interstate 5 (Seattle) take exit 163 A to West Seattle and follow signs to Fauntleroy Ferry. From Interstate 5 (Tacoma) take exit 132 and follow signs to Point Defiance. **Bus:** take city bus #118, #119 or #54 from Seattle. **Ferry:** (Monday–Saturday) passengers-only ferry from Seattle leaves from Pier 50, take bus to Thriftway grocery in Vashon, call hostel for free pick-up.

Washington

Spokane

The Brown Squirrel AYH-Hostel

The Brown Squirrel AYH-Hostel is located in a beautiful residential neighborhood on South Hill. Be sure to ask managers Tom Baker or Ron Devonport where to hike, cycle, and ski in the area. The hub of eastern Washington, Spokane offers big-city attractions close to untouched wilderness. The city's Riverfront Park, a legacy of the Expo '74 World's Fair, features an opera house, a convention center, and Eastern Washington Science Center. Enjoy a movie at the park's IMAX theater or a summer concert at the amphitheater. Don't miss Manito Park and the Japanese Gardens. Come in time for the Bloomsday Run, held the first week of May during the Lilac Festival.

930 South Lincoln,
Spokane, WA 99204.
Mail (✉): same.
Phone (☎): 509-838-5968.
Price (◉): $10 U.S.
Closed (X): never.
Office Hours: 7–10 a.m., 4–10 p.m.
Beds (🛏): 22. **Grade:** Hostel.
Facilities: pay phone, kitchen, laundry facilities, linen rental, on-site parking, **MSA**.
Groups (🎪): welcome.
Reservations advisable (📞): always. **By phone:** accepted.
Credit cards: not accepted.
Managers: Tom Baker and Ron Devonport.

Directions: 1/2 mile south of Interstate 90, take Lincoln exit north, west on Second Avenue, south on Monroe, east on Ninth Avenue to Lincoln.

Wisconsin

Helpful Organizations

AYH Council Office

Wisconsin Council
2224 West Wisconsin Avenue
Milwaukee, WI 53233
Phone (☎): 414-933-1170

State Tourism Office

Wisconsin Division of Tourist Information
123 West Washington Avenue
Madison, WI 53702
Phone (☎): 800-432-8747,
608-266-2161

Discounts

Present a valid hostel membership card at the time of purchase to receive the following discounts:

Laona

Lumberjack Special - $.50 discount on fare.
Nicolet Scenic Rail - $1.50 off 18-mile trip, $3 off 45- and 60-mile trips. P.O. Box 310, 715-674-6309.

Wisconsin

Cable

Ches Perry AYH-Hostel

Ches Perry AYH-Hostel is adjacent to the famous Telemark Ski Area and Resort. Telemark provides slopes for beginners and experts and offers NASTAR racing and ski lessons. Five other major downhill ski areas are within an hour's drive of the hostel.

Located amid forests and along the protected Namakagon River, the town of Cable is in an area rich in scenic beauty and recreational opportunities. There are excellent trails and low-traffic scenic roads for cycling and numerous nature trails for hikers. The Cable Community Center offers a Nature Lecture Series July–August.

Mount Telemark Road.
Mail (✉): P.O. Box 164
Cable, WI 54821.
Phone (☎): 715-798-3367.
Price: $8.75 U.S.
Closed (X): never.
Office Hours: 7–10 a.m., 5–9 p.m.
Grade: Hostel.
Beds: 58.
Facilities: kitchen, **MSA**.
Groups: welcome; reservations required for groups of 10 or more.
Reservations essential (e): April–November. **Reservations advisable (a):** always. **By phone:** accepted.
Credit cards: not accepted.

Directions: 2 miles east of Cable on County Road M, 2 miles south on Mount Telemark Road.

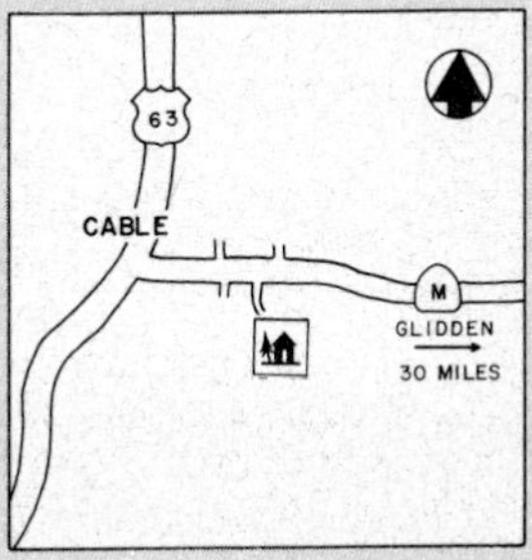

Wisconsin

Dodgeville

Folklore Village Farm AYH-Hostel

The greatest attraction at Folklore Village AYH-Hostel is its folk music and dance program. Activities include folk dancing, concerts, craft workshops, and regular festivals. Programs occur in their new Activity Center or in their historic one-room school-house. On Saturdays enjoy a potluck supper, followed by an old-time community dance.

Folklore Village is located at the heart of Wisconsin's scenic Uplands, a geographic crazy quilt combining rolling farmlands, rugged sandstone bluffs, and graceful wooded valleys, all embroidered with lakes and streams. A perfect area for exploring by bike or on foot. Nearby Governer Dodge State Park encompasses more than 5,000 acres. Visit the Pendarvis State Historic Site at Mineral Point, just eight miles south, an 1830s community established by Cornish lead miners. The Wisconsin Folk Museum is just 17 miles east in Mt. Horeb—the "Troll Capital of the World."

County Road BB.
Mail (✉): Route 3, Dodgeville, WI 53533.
Phone (☎): 608-924-4000.
Price (💲): $8 U.S.
Office Hours: 9 a.m.–noon, 4–8 p.m.
Closed (X): December 25–January 1.
Beds (🛏): 26. **Grade:** Hostel.
Facilities: equipment storage, kitchen, linen rental, on-site parking, showers, **MSA**.
Groups (卌): welcome; reservations required.
Reservations advisable (📞a): always. **By phone:** accepted.
Credit cards: accepted (4% service charge).

Manager: Doug Miller.
Directions: 6 miles east of downtown, south of U.S. Highway 18/151 on County Road BB.

Wisconsin

Laona

Laona AYH-Hostel

The Laona AYH-Hostel is located in the heart of the Nicolet National Forest in Wisconsin's Forest County, which has more than 800 lakes, miles of hiking and cross-country ski trails, and five rivers for canoeing. The Wild Wolf River and Peshtigo River feature some of the most difficult white water in the Midwest.

Send for our brochure for details on organized events. Enjoy bike/camping tours throughout the spring, summer, and fall. Cross-country ski tour groups are available in the snow season. Pick wild raspberries, blueberries, and blackberries in season. Collect wild rice in the fall, and enjoy some of the best fishing in the Midwest year-round.

5397 Beech Street.
Mail (✉): P.O. Box 325, Laona, WI 54541.
Phone (☎): 715-674-2615.
Price (💰): $9 U.S. + tax.
Office Hours: 8–10 a.m., 6–11 p.m.
Closed (X): never.
Grade: Hostel.
Beds (🛏): 12.
Facilities: boat rental, kitchen, linen rental, on-site parking, canoe, tube, cross-country ski rental, **MSA**.
Family rooms (👶): available.
Groups (🏠): welcome.
Reservations essential (📞): November–April. **By phone:** accepted.

Credit cards: not accepted.
Manager: Robert Foley.
Directions: on U.S. Highway 8, in Nicolet National Forest.

Wisconsin

Milwaukee (Greendale)

Red Barn AYH-Hostel

The Red Barn AYH-Hostel is "low-key and easy going—a great place to catch your breath after being on the road a long time," say managers, Tracy and Luis Vega. Located in Milwaukee's suburb of Greendale, the hostel is housed in a historic barn and sits right on the Milwaukee 76 Bike Trail. Hiking trails are also nearby. Canoe rentals are available.

Milwaukee, the "city of festivals," offers something different nearly every weekend of the summer. Visit several excellent museums, visit the Harley Davidson Factory, and take one of three free brewery tours, or enjoy a performance of the Milwaukee Symphony Orchestra, ranked among the top ten orchestras in the country.

6750 West Loomis Road, Greendale, WI 53129.

Mail (✉): same.
Phone (☎): 414-529-3299.
Price (☻): $8 U.S.
Closed (X): November–April.
Office Hours: 8–10:30 a.m., 5–10 p.m.
Grade: Hostel
Beds (⊨): 36.
Facilities: kitchen, linen rental, lockers/baggage storage, on-site parking, **MSA**.
Groups (⌂): welcome.
Reservations advisable (⊞): May–October. **By phone:** accepted.
Credit cards: not accepted.

Managers: Tracy and Luis Vega.
Directions: 11 miles south of downtown at intersection of Root River Parkway and Loomis Road. In addition, you can take #35 bus to the end of line.

Wisconsin

Milwaukee (North)
Halter Home Hostel

Mary and Hal Halter's "home away from home" provides a base for exploring Milwaukee. There's something different going on every month. Museums, sporting events, art, theater, and music are all plentiful. Take a tour of one of the three breweries here. Stroll the grounds of the famous Boerner Botanical Gardens. Attend one of the more than 3,000 performances at the Performing Arts Center.

Call for reservations.
Phone (☎): 414-258-7692.
Price (◔): $10 U.S.
Closed (X): never.
Grade: home hostel (🏠).
Beds (🛏): 4.
Facilities: piano, computer games, equipment storage area, kitchen, laundry facilities, on-site parking, **MSA**.

Family rooms (🏠): available.
Reservations essential (☎): always. **By phone:** accepted with 24-hour notice.
Credit cards: not accepted.
Managers: Hal and Mary Halter.
Directions: available upon reservation confirmation.

Newburg
Wellspring

Approximately a 35-minute drive from Milwaukee, Wellspring is a conference center along the Milwaukee River. There's good canoeing in the spring, and Lake Michigan is just 10 miles away. Hike the trails in Kettle Moraine State Forest-Northern Unit through kettles (bowl-shaped depressions), eskers (snake-like ridges), drumlins (elongated rounded hills), and other unique glacier landforms.

4382 Hickory Road,
Newburg, WI 53060.
Mail (✉): P.O Box 72
Phone (☎): 414-675-6755.
Price (◔): $10 U.S., $2 day use charge.
Office Hours: 8 a.m.–8 p.m.
Closed (X): never.
Grade: (SA).
Beds (🛏): 25.
Facilities (mixed use): kitchen, linen rental, on-site parking, **MSA**.
Meals (🍴): breakfast, lunch, dinner.
Family rooms (🏠): available.

Groups (🎫): welcome; make reservations 30 days before arrival.
Reservations essential (☎): always. **By phone:** accepted with 24-hour advance notice.
Credit cards: not accepted.
Manager: Mary Ann Ihm.
Directions: take Interstate 43 north from Milwaukee to Wisconsin Highway 33, west through Saukville to Newburg, right on Main Street, cross bridge, turn right on Hickory Road, hostel's gravel lane is on the right, 1/2 mile from the bridge.

Wyoming

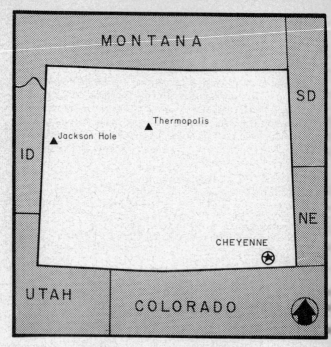

Helpful Organizations

AYH Council Office

Rocky Mountain Council
P.O. Box 2370
Boulder, CO 80306
Phone (☎): 303-442-1166

State Tourism Board

Wyoming Division of Tourism
Frank Norris, Jr. Travel Center
I-25 at College Dr.
Cheyenne, WY 82002
Phone (☎): 800-225-5996,
307-777-7777

Wyoming

Jackson Hole
The Hostel X

The Hostel X in Teton Village, just eight miles from Grand Teton National Park, features a game room, TV room, and nightly movies. The rugged Snake River is great for rafting. The Hostel X is also located on a Bikecentennial route.

3600 McCollister Drive.
Mail (✉): Box 546, Teton Village, WY 83025.
Phone (☎): 307-733-3415.
Price (💲): $15 U.S. + tax.
Closed (X): October–May.
Office Hours: 8–10 a.m., 4 p.m.–midnight.
Beds (🛏): 240. **Grade: (SA)**.
Facilities (mixed use): equipment storage, information desk, laundry facilities, on-site parking; operates as ski lodge with discount rates for hostellers during summer period.

Family rooms (🧑): available.
Reservations essential (📞): always. **By phone:** accepted. **By FAX:** 307-739-1142.
Credit cards: MasterCard, Visa.
Managers: Colby and Mike Wilson.
Directions: 12 miles northwest of Jackson, head west on Wyoming Highway 22 to Wyoming Highway 390, follow signs to Teton Village and Jackson Hole Ski Area, hostel is on the left as you drive into the village.

Wyoming

Thermopolis

Plaza Inn the Park AYH-Hostel

Plaza Inn the Park AYH-Hostel is located in a lovely resort facility in Hot Springs State Park, home of the world's largest mineral hot springs which gush over 18 million gallons of 135-degree water daily. Mineral water baths, steam rooms, and traditional tubs are available at the hostel to soak away those aches and pains after a day of hiking or cycling.

The hostel is within walking distance of downtown Thermopolis, tennis courts, skating rinks, and rodeo grounds. The Big Horn National Forest Recreation Area, Shoshone National Forest, and the Owl Creek Mountains are all an easy drive away. The hostel is also just three miles from Wind River Canyon, a geological museum. Go hiking or mountain biking in the spectacular Wyoming wilderness, or enjoy world-class trout fishing in the nearby Big Horn River.

Hot Springs State Park.
Mail (✉): P.O. Box 671, Thermopolis, WY 82443.
Phone (☎): 307-864-2251.
Price (☻): $10 U.S.
Closed (X): November–December.
Office Hours: 8–10 a.m., after 2 p.m.
Grade: Hostel.
Beds (⊨): 20.
Facilities: mineral baths, steam room, kitchen, linen rental, on-site parking, wheelchair accessible (&), **MSA**.
Family rooms (⚥): available.
Groups (⫶⫶⫶): welcome.
Reservations essential (⚓e): May–September.
Reservations advisable (⚓a): families, groups, holidays. **By phone:** accepted.

Credit cards: Discover, MasterCard, Visa.
Managers: Marvin and Nancy Lynn Jacobs.
Directions: East of U.S. Highway 20 in Hot Springs State Park.

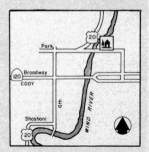

YOU HAVE TO SEE THE WORLD TO *UNDERSTAND* IT

As a member of HOSTELLING INTERNATIONAL, you'll be welcome at 6,000 hostels in 70 countries around the world. For information on hostelling in other countries, contact these hostelling associations:

Algeria
Fédération Algérienne des Auberges de Jeunesse, 213 Rue Hassiba Ben Bouali, B.P. 15, 16015 Alger El-Annasser. **Phone (☎):** 675430

Argentina
Asociación Argentina de Albergues de la Juventud, Talcahuano 214-200"6", 1013 - Capital Federal, Buenos Aires. **Phone (☎):** 45-1001, 2537

Australia
Australian Youth Hostels Association. P.O. Box 61, Strawberry Hills, Sydney 2012, New South Wales. **Phone (☎):** (02) 212-1266

Austria (ÖJHV)
Österreichischer Jugendherbergsverband Hauptverband, 1010 Wien, Schottenring 28 **Phone (☎):** 0222/533 53 53

Bahrain
Bahrain Youth Hostels Society, P.O. Box 2455, Manama. **Phone (☎):** 973/727170

Belgium
Centrale Wallonne des Auberges de la Jeunesse, Rue van Oost 52, B-1030 Bruxelles. **Phone (☎):** 322-215.31.00

Vlaamse Jeugdherbergcentrale, Van Stralenstraat 40, B-2060 Antwerp **Phone (☎):** 03/231 81 26

Brazil
Federação Brasileira dos Albergues de Juventude, Rua Gen. Dionisio 63, CEP 22271, Botafogo, Rio de Janeiro. **Phone (☎):** 286-0303, 246-5553

Bulgaria
Bulgarian Tourist Union, Zentralrat, Boul Tolbuchin 18, Sofia. **Phone (☎):** Sofia 879405

Canada
Canadian Hostelling Association, 1600 James Naismith Drive #608, Gloucester, Ontario K1B SN4. **Phone (☎):** (613) 748-5638

Chile
Asociación Chilena de Albergues Turísticos Juveniles, Av Providencia 2594, OF 420-421 Providencia, Santiago, Chile. **Phone (☎):** 231-5649

Colombia
IDEL-Albergues de Colombia para el Mundo "ALCOM", P.O. Box 3220, Carrera 7, No. 6-10, Bogotá. D.E. Colombia. **Phone (☎):** (91) 2803041

Cyprus
Cyprus Youth Hostel Association, 34Th. Theodotou Street, P.O. Box 1328, Nicosia, **Phone (☎):** 442027

Czechoslovakia
KMC Club of Young Travellers, Zitná 12, 12105 Prague 2. **Phone (☎):** 299941

Denmark
Landsforeningen Danmarks Vandrerhjem Vesterbrogade 39, DK-1620 Copenhagen V. **Phone (☎):** 45/31/313612

Egypt
Egyptian Youth Hostels Association, 7 Dr Abdel Hamid Saiid St., Maarouf, Cairo. **Phone (☎):** (2) 758099, 769673

England & Wales
Youth Hostels Association (England & Wales), Adventure Shop and Information Office, 14 Southampton Street, Covent Garden, London WC2E 7HY. **Phone (☎):** (71) 836 8541

Finland
Suomen Retkeilymajajärjestö-SRM ry, Yrjönkatu 38 B 15, 00100 Helsinki. **Phone (☎):** 90-6940377

France
Fédération Unie des Auberges de Jeunesse 27 rue Pajol, 75018 Paris. **Phone (☎):** 1/46070001

Germany
Deutsches Jugendherbergswerk, Hauptverband, Bismarckstr.8, Postfach 1455, D-4930 Detmold. **Phone (☎):** 05231/7401-0

Greece
Greek Youth Hostels Association, 4 Dragatsaniou Street, Athens 105-59. **Phone (☎):** 3234107

Hong Kong
Hong Kong Youth Hostels Association, Room 225-226, Block 19, Shek Kip Mei Estate, Shamshuipo, Kowloon. **Phone (☎):** 852-7881638

Hungary
Magyar Ifjúsági Házak-EXPRESS, 1395 Budapest V, Szabadság tér 16. **Phone (☎):** (1) 1129/887, 1530/660

Iceland
Bandalag Íslenskra Farfugla, Sundlaugavegur 34, P.O. Box 1045, 121 Reykjavik. **Phone (☎):** 91/38110

India
Youth Hostel Association of India, 5 Nyaya

Marg, Chanakyapuri, New Delhi 110 021.
Phone (☎): 3011969, 3016250

Ireland (Republic of)

An Óige, 39 Mountjoy Square, Dublin 1.
Phone (☎): Dublin 1/363111

Ireland (Northern)

Youth Hostel Association of Northern Ireland,
56 Bradbury Place, Belfast BT7 1RU.
Phone (☎): 232/324733

Israel

Israel Youth Hostels Association, P.O. Box
1075, 3 Dorot Rishonim Street, Jerusalem
91009. **Phone (☎):** 02/252706

Italy

Associazione Italiana Alberghi per la Gioventù,
Via Cavour 44, (terzo piano), 00184 Rome.
Phone (☎): 06/4746755

Japan

Japan Youth Hostels, Hoken Kaikan, 1-2
Sadohara-cho, Ichigaya, Shinjuku-ku,
Tokyo 162. **Phone (☎):** 03-269-5831

Kenya

Kenya Youth Hostels Association, P.O. Box
48661, Nairobi. **Phone (☎):** 723012

Korea (South)

Korea Youth Hostels Association, #604 Seoul
Youth Center, 27 Soopyo-Dong, Joong-Ku,
Seoul. **Phone (☎):** (02) 266-2896; 275-4203

Libya

Libyan Youth Hostel Association, 69 Amr
Ben Al-Aas Street, P.O. Box 8886, Tripoli,
Al-Jamahiriya, Libya. **Phone (☎):** Tripoli 45171

Luxembourg

*Centrale des Auberges de Jeunesse Luxem-
bourgeoises*, 18 Place d'Armes, BP 374,
L-2013, Luxembourg.

Malaysia

Malaysian Youth Hostels Association, 21, Jalan
Kampung Attap, 50460 Kuala, Lumpur.
Phone (☎): 03-2306870/71

Mexico

Comisión Nacional del Deporte (CONADE),
Dirección de Villas Deportivas Juveniles,
Glorieta Del Metro Insurgentes,
Local C-11 Y 12 Col. Cuauhtemoc, CP 06600
Mexico, D.F. **Phone (☎):** 5252548, 2153, 2699

Morocco

*Fédération Royale Marocaine des Auberges de
Jeunes*, Boulvard Okba Ben Nafii, Meknès.
Phone (☎): (05) 52-46-98

Netherlands

*Stichting Nederlandse Jeugdherberg Centrale,
(NJHC)*, Professor Tulpplein 4, 1018 GX
Amsterdam. **Phone (☎):** 020/5513155

New Zealand

Youth Hostels Association of New Zealand,
P.O. Box 436, Christchurch 1. **Phone (☎):** 799-
970

Norway

Norske Vandrerhjem, Dronningensgate 26,
N-0154 Oslo 1. **Phone (☎):** 02/421410

Pakistan

Pakistan Youth Hostels Association, 110-B-3,
Gulberg 111, Lahore 11. **Phone (☎):** 878201

Peru

Asociación Peruana de Albergues Juveniles,
Casimiro Ulloa 328, San Antonio, Miraflores,
Lima 18. **Phone (☎):** 46 5488

Philippines

*Youth & Student Hostel Foundation of the
Philippines (YSHFP)*, 4227 Tomas Claudio St.,
Parañaque, Metro Manila, Philippines.
Phone (☎): 832 0680/832 2112/832 2263

Poland

*Polskie Towarzystwo Schronisk Mlod-
ziezowych*, 00-791 Warsaw, ul Chocimska 28.
Phone (☎): 498354, 498128

Portugal

*Associação de Utentes das Pousadas de
Juventude*, Rua Andrade Corvo 46, 1000
Lisbon. **Phone (☎):** 3511/571054

Qatar

Qatar Youth Hostels Association, P.O. Box
2511, Doha. **Phone (☎):** 867180/863968

Saudi Arabia

Saudi Arabian Youth Hostels Association, P.O.
Box 2359, Riyadh 11451, Kingdom of Saudi
Arabia. **Phone (☎):** (01) 4055552, 4051478

Scotland

Scottish Youth Hostels Association, 7 Glebe
Crescent, Stirling FK8 2JA. **Phone (☎):**
0786/51181

Spain

Red Española de Albergues Juveniles, José Or-
tega y Gasset, 71, Madrid 28006. **Phone (☎):**
3477700

Sri Lanka

National Youth Hostel Association of Sri Lanka,
26 Charlemont Road, Colombo 6. **Phone (☎):**
584303

Sudan

Sudanese Youth Hostels Association, P.O. Box
1705, Khartoum. **Phone (☎):** 81464, 222087

Sweden

Swedish Touring Club, Box 25, 101 20 Stock-
holm. **Phone (☎):** 08/7903100

Switzerland

Schweizerischer Bund für Jugendherbergen,
Postfach, 3001 Bern. **Phone (☎):** 031/245503

Syria

Syrian Youth Hostels, Saleh al Ali Street 66
Damascus, Syria

Thailand

Thai Youth Hostels Association, 25/2 Phit-
sanulok Road, Sisao Theves, Dusit, Bangkok
10300. **Phone (☎):** 281-6834, 281-0361

Tunisia

*Association Tunisienne des Auberges de Jeu-
nesse*, 10 rue Ali Bach Hamba, B.P. 320-1015
Tunis RP. **Phone (☎):** 353277

United Arab Emirates

United Arab Emirates Youth Hostel Association,
P.O. Box 9536, Dubai. **Phone (☎):** 665078

United States of America

American Youth Hostels, 733 15th Street NW,
#840, Washington, D.C. 20005. **Phone (☎):**
(202-783-6161).

Uruguay

Asociación de Alberguistas del Uruguay, Pablo
de María 1583/008, 11200 Montevideo.
Phone (☎): 404245

Yugoslavia

Ferijalni savez Jugoslavije, 11000 Beograd,
Moše Pijade 12/V. **Phone (☎):** 011 339-802

EXPLORE

The World

Only a HOSTELLING INTERNATIONAL®
membership card gives you access to 6,000
hostels around the globe. As a cardholder
you'll meet exciting new people while enjoying some of the most dynamic and fun places
to stay. You'll keep travel costs low and
enjoy special member-only discounts on tours,
cruises, admission fees, and a whole lot more!

Benefits

* Automatic membership in HOSTELLING
  INTERNATIONAL®.
* Access to 6,000 hostels in 70 countries
  around the world.
* Free directory of hostels in Canada and the
  USA.
* Membership in the council nearest you
  with weekend trips, volleyball tournaments,
  bike rides, and other fun-filled activities.
* Participate in any and all activities, pro-
  grams, and events wherever you travel.

Eligibility and Validity

Membership in American Youth Hostels or Canadian Hostelling Association/Association canadienne de l'ajisme is open to anyone from age 5 (no upper limit) who has lived in the USA or Canada for at least a year. All memberships are valid for 12 months from date of issue and include automatic membership in HOSTELLING INTERNATIONAL.

What it costs to join

	AYH/US$	CHA/CDN$
Youth/Junior (under 18)	$10	$12
Adult/Senior (18-54)	$25	$25
Adult/Senior (24 months)	---	$35
Family	$35	---
Senior Citizen (over 54)	$15	---
Organization	FREE	$40
Life	$250	$175

Where the cards are issued

The HOSTELLING INTERNATIONAL® card is available from any regional office (see province or state listings), from any full-service hostel (see the hostel listings), or from hundreds of authorized membership selling agents. Call for the MSA nearest you.

To order by mail, send the application with credit card number, check or money order made payable to American Youth Hostels or Canadian Hostelling Association to the regional office nearest you (see province/state listings).

Discounts

Nationwide discounts in the United States are listed below. Be sure to check the province or state listings for local discounts.

Alamo Rent A Car - savings of 5% to 30% on daily and weekly rentals. Unlimited mileage and complimentary airport pick-up. Call 1-800-732-3232 and request Plan BY 19998 American Youth Hostels.

Lenscrafters - 20% discount on glasses and repairs; 10% discount on contact lenses. Numerous locations nationwide. Call toll free 1-800-522-LENS.

National Car Rental - 25% discount on daily rates; 5% discount on weekend, weekly, and holiday promotions. Call toll free 1-800-CAR-RENT and use recap number 5130368.

Membership Application

HOSTELLING INTERNATIONAL®

YES! I want to become a member of HOSTELLING INTERNATIONAL. I understand I'll receive a full 12-month membership with access to 6,000 hostels worldwide...HOSTELLING NORTH AMERICA, a directory of hostels in Canada and the United States...free membership in the AYH council nearest me...plus global discounts on car rentals, admissions, sightseeing tours, sports equipment, and other services. Please sign me on as a new member in the category I've checked below:

☐   Youth (under 18) $10

☐   Adult (18-54) $25

☐   Family (parent(s) or guardian(s) with children under 16) . . $35

☐   Senior Citizen (over 54) $15

☐   Life (all ages) $250

Please type or print in clear block letters.

Name   Departure Date (month/year)

Date of birth (month/day/year)   Sex

Permanent Address

Street

City   State   Zip   Phone

Shipping Address (if different from above)

Street

City   State   Zip   Phone

Method of Payment

☐   Check for $_____ made payable to American Youth Hostels

☐   Credit Card ___ MasterCard ___ Visa

Card number   Expiration Date

Signature

I'd also like to receive

☐ AYH Discovery Tours

This FREE 24-page catalog describes special hostelling adventures and learning experiences for all ages. All AYH Discovery Tours feature small, friendly groups plus an AYH-trained leader. AYH Discovery Tours emphasize low-impact travel techniques and the general hostelling principle of treading lightly on our environment. You'll find yourself face to face with new people, cultures, and environments.

☐ Free Organization Membership

AYH offers a FREE membership to scout troops, school groups, and other qualified nonprofit organizations (minimum 10 members). Valid internationally, the organization membership allows group members to travel together and to stay at 6,000 hostels around the world. Check the box above for a FREE application.

Return to:

Send completed application and payment to any AYH council (see state listings for addresses and phone numbers). Allow 2-3 weeks for delivery.

American Youth Hostels

Membership Application

HOSTELLING INTERNATIONAL®

YES! I want to become a member of HOSTELLING INTERNA-TIONAL. I understand I'll receive a full 12-month membership with access to 6,000 hostels worldwide...HOSTELLING NORTH AMERICA, a directory of hostels in Canada and the United States...free membership in the AYH council nearest me...plus global discounts on car rentals, admissions, sightseeing tours, sports equipment, and other services. Please sign me on as a new member in the category I've checked below:

- ☐ Youth (under 18) $10
- ☐ Adult (18-54) $25
- ☐ Family (parent(s) or guardian(s) with children under 16) . . $35
- ☐ Senior Citizen (over 54) $15
- ☐ Life (all ages) $250

Please type or print in clear block letters.

Name

Departure Date (month/year)

Date of birth (month/day/year)

Sex

Permanent Address

Street

City　　　　　State　　Zip　　Phone

Shipping Address (if different from above)

Street

City　　　　　State　　Zip　　Phone

Method of Payment

- ☐ Check for $_____ made payable to American Youth Hostels
- ☐ Credit Card ___ MasterCard ___ Visa

Card number

Expiration Date

Signature

I'd also like to receive

☐ AYH Discovery Tours

This FREE 24-page catalog describes special hostelling adventures and learning experiences for all ages. All AYH Discovery
Tours feature small, friendly groups plus an AYH-trained
leader. AYH Discovery Tours emphasize low-impact travel
techniques and the general hostelling principle of treading lightly on our environment. You'll find yourself face to face with
new people, cultures, and environments.

☐ Free Organization Membership

AYH offers a FREE membership to scout troops, school
groups, and other qualified nonprofit organizations (minimum
10 members). Valid internationally, the organization membership allows group members to travel together and to stay at
6,000 hostels around the world. Check the box above for a
FREE application.

Return to:

Send completed application and payment to any AYH council (see
state listings for addresses and phone numbers). Allow 2-3 weeks
for delivery.

American Youth Hostels

Yes, I would like to join Hostelling International–Canada.

To apply for a membership with Hostelling International–Canada, just fill in the application form on the back of this page and send it to:

Hostelling International–Canada
1600 James Naismith Drive, Suite 608
Gloucester, Ontario K1B 5N4

For more information,
call us toll free in Canada: 1-800-663-5777

To receive a free information package, please fill in your name and address on the back of this page and check off "information only".

HOSTELLING
INTERNATIONAL

Membership Application

To stay in one of the Hostelling International locations around the world, you must have a membership card from your own country–but getting one couldn't be easier.

Simply fill out the form below and drop it in the mail–or visit the Hostelling International–Canada office nearest you. You can even call us toll free at 1-800-663-5777 and process your membership over the phone!

Name _____

Address _____

City _____

Province _____ Postal Code _____

Telephone _____

Date of Birth _____

Membership

❒ **Information only**   **No charge**

❒ One year $ 25 (plus GST)
❒ Two year $ 35 (plus GST)

7% GST $ _____
Total Enclosed $ _____

Payment
❒ Cheque / Money Order
❒ Visa ❒ MasterCard
    Card Number _____
    Expiry Date _____
    Signature _____

Yes, I would like to join Hostelling International– Canada.

To apply for a membership with Hostelling International–Canada, just fill in the application form on the back of this page and send it to:

Hostelling International–Canada
1600 James Naismith Drive, Suite 608
Gloucester, Ontario K1B 5N4

For more information,
call us toll free in Canada: 1-800-663-5777

To receive a free information package, please fill in your name and address on the back of this page and check off "information only".

HOSTELLING INTERNATIONAL

Membership Application

To stay in one of the Hostelling International locations around the world, you must have a membership card from your own country–but getting one couldn't be easier.

Simply fill out the form below and drop it in the mail–or visit the Hostelling International–Canada office nearest you. You can even call us toll free at 1-800-663-5777 and process your membership over the phone!

Name _____

Address _____

City _____

Province _____ Postal Code _____

Telephone _____

Date of Birth _____

Membership

❒ **Information only**   **No charge**

❒ One year $ 25 (plus GST)
❒ Two year $ 35 (plus GST)

7% GST $ _____
Total Enclosed $ _____

Payment
❒ Cheque / Money Order
❒ Visa ❒ MasterCard
  Card Number _____
  Expiry Date _____
  Signature _____

CALL AHEAD TO BOOK A BED

Do-it-yourself phone reservations make booking a hostel bed as easy as 1-2-3

1. Call the hostel 1 day in advance about availability.
2. Give the hostel manager your name and date of arrival.
3. Have your MasterCard or Visa card ready. Giving your credit card number and expiration date will hold the bed until 10 p.m. If you do not arrive for your bed, the hostel will charge your credit card a cancellation fee equal to 1 night's stay.

Reservations are accepted on a space-available basis and may not be available at all hostels (check individual listings in this book). Restrictions may apply to groups of five or more.

Spend the day as you please without worrying about where to spend the night!

HOSTELLING
INTERNATIONAL
Canada • USA

Classified Advertisements

Maps/Guidebooks

Products/Services

Classified Advertisements

Products/Services (continued)

Tours

Transportation

Index of Hostels

Index of Hostels

Index of Hostels

Index of Hostels

Index of Hostels

Index of Hostels

Index of Hostels

Index of Advertisers

Drive our cars

Choose the city closest to your destination and enjoy an economical trip anywhere in North America.

AZ	Phoenix (602) 952-0339	IL	Chicago (312) 939-3600
	Tucson (602) 323-7659		
		IN	Indianapolis (317) 259-7060
CA	Anaheim (714) 956-9471		
	Fresno (209) 297-1441	KS	Kansas City (913) 381-2125
	Long Beach (310) 421-0583		Wichita (316) 945-2882
	Los Angeles (213) 661-6100		
	Sacramento (916) 967-1488	KY	Louisville (502) 456-4990
	San Diego (619) 295-8006		
	San Francisco (415) 777-3740	LA	New Orleans (504) 885-9292
	San Jose (408) 984-4999		
		MD	Baltimore (410) 366-8863
CO	Denver (303) 757-1211		
		MA	Boston (617) 731-1261
DC	Washington (703) 524-7300		
		MI	Detroit (313) 442-2335
FL	Ft. Lauderdale (305) 771-4059		Grand Rapids (616) 530-018
	Ft. Myers (813) 489-1262		
	Jacksonville (904) 398-4400	MN	St. Paul (314) 698-6929
	Miami (305) 456-228		Minneapolis (612) 926-0262
	(305) 931-8330		
	Orlando (407) 678-7000	MO	St. Louis (314) 726-2886
	Palm Beach (407) 439-7060		
	Tampa (813) 254-8411	NE	Omaha (402) 571-5010
GA	Atlanta (404) 364-0464	NJ	Elizabeth (908) 352-3800

For general information call (800) 346-2277

AUTO DRIVEAWAY CO.
310 S. MICHIGAN AVENUE, CHICAGO, IL 60604